"This rich book is an act of guardianship. Filled wit
essays, it probes the recrudescence of anti-liberal anc
often claim to be excellent democracies, better thai
those of us wishing to secure the rule of law and ind
political liberalism's hallmarks, there is no more vexir

Ira I. Katznelson, *Ruggles .* ....
and History, Columbia University

"In presenting a multiplicity of perspectives on the broad and timely issue of
illiberal democracy, *The Emergence of Illiberalism* fills a major gap in current
scholarly literature. Examining the rise of illiberal politics from numerous an-
gles, this volume will provide an excellent foundation for readers seeking to
understand contemporary political conditions."

Phillip W. Gray, *Assistant Professor of Political Science,*
Texas A&M University at Qatar

THE EMERGENCE OF ILLIBERALISM

As illiberal and authoritarian trends are on the rise—both in fragile and in seemingly robust democracies—there is growing concern about the longevity of liberalism and democracy. The purpose of this volume is to draw on the analytical resources of various disciplines and public policy approaches to reflect on the current standing of liberal democracy. Leading social scientists from different disciplinary backgrounds aim to examine the ideological and structural roots of the current crisis of liberal democracies, in the West and beyond, conceptually and empirically.

The volume is divided into two main parts:

- Part I explores tensions between liberalism and democracy in a longer-term, historical perspective to explain immanent vulnerabilities of liberal democracy. Authors examine the conceptual foundations of Western liberal democracy that have shaped its standing in the contemporary world. What lies at the core of illiberal tendencies?
- Part II explores case studies from the North Atlantic, Eastern Europe, Turkey, India, Japan, and Brazil, raising questions whether democratic crises, manifested in the rise of populist movements in and beyond the Western context, differ in kind or only in degree. How can we explain the current popular appeal of authoritarian governments and illiberal ideas?

The Emergence of Illiberalism will be of great interest to teachers and students of politics, sociology, political theory, and comparative government.

Boris Vormann is Professor of Politics and Director of the Politics Section at Bard College Berlin. His research focuses on the role of the state in globalization and urbanization processes; nations and nationalism; and the crisis of democracy. His most recent books are *Democracy in Crisis: The Neoliberal Roots of Popular Unrest* (with Christian Lammert, 2019) and *Contours of the Illiberal State* (2019).

Michael D. Weinman is Professor of Philosophy at Bard College Berlin. He is the author of three books, most recently, *The Parthenon and Liberal Education* (2018, co-authored with Geoff Lehman), and the editor (with Shai Biderman) of *Plato and the Moving Image* (2019). His research focuses on Greek philosophy, political philosophy, and their intersection.

THE EMERGENCE OF ILLIBERALISM

Understanding a Global Phenomenon

Edited by Boris Vormann and Michael D. Weinman

Routledge
Taylor & Francis Group

NEW YORK AND LONDON

First published 2021
by Routledge
52 Vanderbilt Avenue, New York, NY 10017

and by Routledge
2 Park Square, Milton Park, Abingdon, Oxon, OX14 4RN

Routledge is an imprint of the Taylor & Francis Group, an informa business

© 2021 Taylor & Francis

Library of Congress Cataloging-in-Publication Data
Names: Vormann, Boris, editor. | Weinman, Michael, editor.
Title: The emergence of illiberalism: understanding a global phenomenon /
edited by Boris Vormann & Michael Weinman.
Description: New York, NY: Routledge, 2020. |
Includes bibliographical references and index. |
Identifiers: LCCN 2020009409 (print) | LCCN 2020009410 (ebook) |
ISBN 9780367366261 (hardback) | ISBN 9780367366247 (paperback) |
ISBN 9780429347368 (ebook) | ISBN 9781000079081 (adobe pdf) |
ISBN 9781000079135 (mobi) | ISBN 9781000079180 (epub)
Subjects: LCSH: Populism. | Right and left (Political science) | Democracy. |
Populism—Case studies. | Right and left (Political science)—Case studies. |
Democracy—Case studies.
Classification: LCC JC423 .E48 2020 (print) |
LCC JC423 (ebook) | DDC 320.56/62—dc23
LC record available at https://lccn.loc.gov/2020009409
LC ebook record available at https://lccn.loc.gov/2020009410

ISBN: 978-0-367-36626-1 (hbk)
ISBN: 978-0-367-36624-7 (pbk)
ISBN: 978-0-429-34736-8 (ebk)

Typeset in Bembo
by codeMantra

CONTENTS

FIGURES

PREFACE

Political memory seems surprisingly short, given that the current crisis of neoliberalism has predecessors. In the West, market rule has run rampant before—at least twice in the 19th century (before the busts of the 1830s and 1840s, and again leading up to 1872) as well as, once more, in the "Roaring 20s" of the 20th century. In fact, the imbalance between economics and politics that we deem to be an important cause of today's crisis is a motif that keeps coming back.

It almost seems like, for several decades, belief in the market as an *ersatz* for politics dominates; then, politics seems to become important again as a way to rein in the markets. Despite this historical experience and these "open secrets," many (economic) liberals went on arguing time and again that a free market would, of necessity, lead to free societies. And they keep on doing so today. The only difference is that the crisis of conviction, limited at earlier moments to national and continental levels, now has more immediately global cascading effects.

The insight that liberal democracy, both as an idea and as a set of practices, is rooted in striking a balance between economic and political forces was already very much clear to a classical liberal like Adam Smith. Smith has been read, since his death, in a carelessly one-sided way as simply concerned with prosperity and the "invisible hand" of the market. This, despite the fact that the metaphor of an invisible hand was hardly of central importance to Smith and in any case was surely not meant to undermine the moral duty of states to ensure liberty and equality, values of at least as much importance to Smith as prosperity.

His concerns about the destabilizing and demoralizing potential in an unchecked economic liberalism were underscored by reformist liberals such as John Stuart Mill and Alexis de Tocqueville, who, despite their political and ideological differences, both articulated a vision of liberalism grounded in values other than those that can be commodified. In short: *homo economicus* is not enough; for liberalism to thrive, the ideal subject would also have to be *homo politicus*! For this political tradition within liberalism, freedom of opinion, religious freedom, and plurality mattered. Social progress, its enthusiasts thought, depended on the openness of societies. Yes, markets were important, but they were not sufficient, by themselves, for democracy to succeed.

This volume seeks to make sense of today's global crisis of liberal democracy in light of the recurrent amnesia concerning the insufficiency of economic liberalism alone among many liberals in power since World War II. Sometimes more, sometimes less directly, the myopic vision of market rule as an equivalent of democracy seems to underlie many of the critiques made in the theoretical and empirical chapters. Exposing the internal contradictions and shortcomings of liberalism, and how they interact with other causes, the chapters in this book seek to develop a clearer understanding of the parameters and dynamics that define an evolving set of crisis tendencies.

This book is the long-term result of a colloquium on "illiberal democracy" that the editors (and contributor Ewa Atanassow) organized at Bard College Berlin and the Hertie School of Governance in April 2018. We gratefully acknowledge our debt to both institutions and their leadership for making the colloquium possible. We would also like to express our gratitude to our colleagues at Bard College Berlin, Irina Stelea and Bendetta Roux, for their work in organizing and publicizing the Illiberal Democracy colloquium, and our student Simon Kastberg for editorial assistance.

We thank the authors who agreed to rework their colloquium presentations into book chapters. In the meantime, we had the good fortune to meet further scholars willing to contribute to the project. Their chapters were written specifically for this volume and have provided a compelling complement to the presentations that constituted the 2018 meeting. Moreover, three essays in this book are updated versions of texts that have recently appeared in journals. We thank *Foreign Affairs*, the *Journal of Democracy*, and *The New Statesman* for permission to reprint and slightly rework articles by Ivan Krastev, Marc Plattner, and Kristin Surak—and these scholars for their willingness to contribute to this volume.

We are very grateful to all the authors for their trust and enthusiastic work. We are particularly humbled for the opportunity to work with Roger Scruton, who kindly and carefully corresponded with us during months in which his health was failing, and to be able to share his contribution posthumously. Finally, we would like to thank the anonymous reviewers for their very careful reading of the entire manuscript and for many helpful comments and suggestions.

The editors
Berlin, February 2020

PART I
Democracy, Contested
Causes of Illiberalism

1

FROM A POLITICS OF NO ALTERNATIVE TO A POLITICS OF FEAR

Illiberalism and Its Variants

Michael D. Weinman and Boris Vormann

Introduction[1]

Liberal democracy is in crisis. This much seems undisputed in the literature and media comments that have proliferated since 2016, when the Brexit referendum and the election of Donald Trump ignited new debates about the meaning and limitations of liberal democracy. If anything, this verdict has been consolidated by subsequent electoral successes of populist parties in other European states, such as France, Austria, Italy, and Germany, as well as similar tendencies in Australia and Ontario, Canada's most populous and globally connected province. The dissatisfaction with the status quo was equally expressed in the initial shift toward the left in Southern European countries such as Greece, Spain, and Portugal—and the rise of right-wing parties that followed. Beyond the West, the election of Jair Bolsonaro as the President of Brazil, turmoil in former Soviet states in Eastern Europe, and an autocratic reinterpretation of democracy under Abe, Erdogan, Modi, and Putin only reinforce the sense that the triumphant era of liberalism is over.

The engines of neoliberal, market-led globalization, which appeared unparalleled in power after the fall of the Berlin Wall, seem to have come to a screeching halt. So, too, has the confidence or at least the hope that democracy, in tandem with markets, was on an inevitable course to expand happily ever after. In the West, what is common across otherwise wildly different cases is a distrust for existing parties, deep inequalities coupled with extreme polarization of the political spectrum, and the desire for anti-establishment politicians to clean up corruption and restore responsiveness to their constituencies. On both sides of the Atlantic, opponents of free trade and critics of globalization are organizing; so are ethnic nationalists, who see an opening for more authoritarian politics. More often than not, elections turn into tribunals on the establishment, with the judgment turning against the elites and the status quo.

On a global level, liberalism and theories of democratic peace seem to have lost explanatory power and normative appeal. Hopes for global convergence and integration are thwarted as the divide between the global north and the global south deepens further. Humanitarian interventions are being refuted as thinly veiled geostrategic maneuvers and the West seems to have lost its lure—a process accelerating as its core countries seem to be themselves turning away from the liberal creed. National interests are again dominating international relations (IR), while more normative approaches seeking cooperation and integration tend to be rejected as naïve do-goodism. Supranational institutions of the post-World War II era—the United Nations, NATO, the World Bank, and the World Trade Organization—are eroding under the pressures of protectionism and neo-mercantilist trade conflicts. In short, *Realpolitik* is back. And so are great power politics, weapons races, and zero-sum politics.

Illiberal forces quickly seek to fill the ideological vacuum left by a hollowed out liberal idealism. Once in office, however, demagogues not only fail to deliver most of their promises, but also and perhaps more importantly, alter the structures of the state and civil society in ways that are likely to inflict long-term damage. Undoing checks and balances, in particular through intervention in the judiciary, public officials' conflicts of interest, and the defamation of the media, they put essential pillars of democracy and core ideals of the enlightenment under attack. In the absence of meaningful reform, strongman leaders distract attention from their bankrupt political vision with xenophobic appeals and a politics of indignation, further unraveling prior commitments to liberal democracy. Meanwhile, they revise institutional and procedural pillars of democracy, indicating that illiberal politics—a fear-driven, authoritarian reorganization of the state around exclusive and patriarchal notions of an ethnic demos that seeks to undo the norms and institutions of political liberalism—will not be effaced easily with the next election, impeachment, or vote of no confidence.

We contend that the variegated forms of illiberalism—much like variegated neoliberalization patterns (Brenner et al. 2010)—materialize in otherwise very different contexts at the same historical moment because they have a set of common denominators. Illiberal tendencies seek to partially reshape neoliberal practices and ideas of the past half-century—the *politics of no alternative* that posited the inevitability of globalization and the superiority of market solutions—at a moment where these practices and ideas no longer seem legitimate in the core countries of the North Atlantic. While progressives have been criticizing neoliberalism for a long time, it is the right-wing critique of neoliberalism that is much more successfully redoing neoliberalism, and, potentially, undoing liberal democracy in the West and beyond.

Unlike the left, which argues for reform through redistribution and decommodification to address the consequences of welfare state retrenchment and deep inequalities, right-wing critiques operate from the understanding that the demos—defined in exclusive, ethno-nationalist terms—is under attack by overwhelming outside forces, while the state, corrupted by naïve or deluded elites—the much-scolded establishment—is unwilling or unable to protect its citizens. Calls for law and order, stricter security, and a reassertion of popular sovereignty are at the heart of this *politics of fear*.[2] From that perspective, reform won't do and the institutional safeguards of democracy, above all the separation of powers and the protection of minority rights, become viewed as hindrances to the defense of the "true" demos. Liberal democracy seems to stand in the way of "true" democracy.

How does this challenge to liberal democracy compare across contexts? How does the perceived failure of liberal policies and institutions in one region impact the global standing of liberal democracy in others? How far has the politics of fear progressed? And has a liberal vision of democracy been unseated? The chapters that follow explore the current crisis of liberal democracies conceptually and empirically, putting into perspective a wide range of country examples in the Western and Non-Western context, to seek answers to these questions and develop a vocabulary to better fathom illiberal tendencies. As they show, democracies around the world are facing a two-pronged crisis. One part of the crisis brought figures such as Trump, Johnson, and Orban into office in the first place. This is very much a crisis emerging from within the neoliberal paradigm. The second part of the crisis is currently unfolding as such political figures capture state power.

Comparing Global Variants of Illiberalism

Integral to the new illiberal international, understood as an internal outgrowth and not simply as an emulation of anti-Western autocrats such as Vladimir Putin, are the antipluralist, often demagogic, politicians who come to wield almost unchecked state power in both longstanding and emerging democracies (see also Galston 2018). Responding to recent electoral successes by non-establishment parties in very different contexts—from Brazil to the US, the UK to Israel—recent literature in the burgeoning field on "populism" is often written for a broad audience and, given the focus on one or another national readership, can lack the comparative scope and empirical depth for which this volume aims. To be sure, political context matters both for outcomes and potential ways of addressing crisis tendencies. Political cultures, institutional path dependencies, the role of a state in the international order as a hegemonic or peripheral power, are crucial for how the crisis dynamics play out in different settings. But because it tends to ignore important parallels that transcend, for instance, the specificities of a given party system—e.g. polarization in the US two-party system—or national context—e.g. Germany's divided past—existing work undertheorizes commonalities.[3]

There is, of course, a risk of treating all these cases—Brazil and the US, Germany, and India—the same. They are not. And we are not aiming to do that. The danger of such an endeavor would be to misunderstand common developments as though they naturally evolved in tandem developing such internal propulsion as to become almost inevitable—a wave of autocratization. What is the added value of bringing all these developments into one perspective, then? Above all, it enables us to explore the global scope of related phenomena and to stress parallels and potential pathways. This, in turn, helps us to theorize certain patterns that we otherwise would not see because they might appear conjunctural or coincidental in an individual context where they are not. Trump, for instance, is not simply chaotic even though he is often portrayed as such. Viewing him in comparison helps to outline what is actually a rather coherent pattern of policy visions.

While too much of the work on populism focuses only on state-by-state unit-level idiosyncrasies, we also hope to identify a broader context in which all this happens, common preconditions that facilitate the rise of autocrats, and certain strategies that they use to mobilize their voter base, seize state capacities, and act while in office. Although the empirical cases examined in this volume reflect a wide range of political systems, different democratic traditions, and economic contexts, the paths toward autocracy are contiguous. As such, we can sketch out something like an ideal-typical trajectory of de-democratization that we can witness in otherwise very different places—even if the starting point and (therefore) the end results differ in important ways.

The Problem with the Term Populism

Before we sketch these broader global patterns, an important terminological caveat is in order. Notwithstanding Chantal Mouffe's (2018) recent explicit call for a "left populism," it is difficult to find voices that self-identify as populist within the circle of those hoping to sustain liberal democracy through its current moment of crisis. The term is usually used in a pejorative manner to discredit different movements. This creates a series of problems. Populist critiques might well voice true grievances that should be taken seriously and surely not be rejected out of hand. Worse, knee-jerk reactions against populist movements ignore the democratic potentials of binding recently politicized populations back into actual politics (Eichengreen 2018; see Calhoun in this volume).

As such, the common deployment of the term "populism," both within social science and by political actors associated with liberalisms of the left, right, and center, only aggravates the well-known crisis of legitimacy. As Jan-Werner Müller crucially points out, "[n]ot everyone who criticizes elites is a populist" (Müller 2016, 101). But oftentimes, in practice, this distinction is blurred so that many public discussions do fall into a by-now familiar dichotomy: either you are with the status quo or a populist. The simple derogatory use of the term populist equates all such movements regardless of political ideology and direction, playing down actual fascist groups and aggrandizing fringe movements, placing anyone skeptical of liberalism into a single category: enemies of democracy. This is hampering an already fraught political discourse. We use different terms to refer to critics of liberalism, (civic or ethnic) nationalists, and fascists, and there are reasons for that.

From an analytical perspective, another crucial problem with the term populism is that, if used uncritically, it ignores the more structural and discursive factors that have given rise to widespread discontent in the first place. This, of course, has far-reaching implications. If one interprets the rise of illiberalism simply as the outbreak of a contagious craze at the populist fringes, the *status quo ante*, that is, a return to neoliberalism, might suddenly appear quite appealing. But "global Trumpism" (see Hopkin and Blyth in this volume) has its roots precisely in neoliberalization processes. It is not simply the result of an irrational aberrance. This is why simply returning to the politics that paved the way for illiberalism would do little to resolve the more fundamental problems at stake that emanate from an internal crisis of neoliberalism.

Neoliberalism's Implosion

Deep are the roots of those thinkers who advocate for free market capitalism. But Adam Smith (particularly in his *Theory of Moral Sentiments*), John Stuart Mill, and Alexis de Tocqueville would all have agreed that *homo economicus*—as someone who only strives for the maximization of their self-interest in a competitive struggle for survival of all against all—is not enough; for liberalism to thrive, the ideal subject would also have to be someone who can take informed choices and sometimes prioritize the common good: *homo politicus*! For this political tradition within liberalism, freedom of opinion, minority rights, and plurality mattered. Social progress, its enthusiasts thought, depended on the openness of societies. Yes, markets were important, but they were not sufficient, by themselves, for democracy to succeed. There needed to be associations, free media, and a *sensus communis* (not just "common sense" but also a sense of community) for democracy to be actually possible (see Atanassow and Scruton in this volume).

Liberalism consists of a set of practices and ideas that since the beginning of the enlightenment era have foregrounded the importance of individual liberty, private property, and the market in organizing societies. Importantly, however, liberalism is a deeply ambivalent term. Two hearts beat in its chest. Whereas *economic liberalism* emerged as a critique of the absolutist state and an attempt to strengthen the emerging bourgeois classes in 18th-century Europe, what we (along with others; e.g. Brown 2015) call *political liberalism* of the 19th century foregrounds the need for a minimal, but nonetheless interventionist, state and a strong civil society to hem in the outgrowths of the market and allow certain civic and political rights for the citizenry.

In short, *economic* liberalism is mostly concerned with market freedoms and assumes that there is an automatic expansion of political rights once markets grow. By contrast, it is *political* liberalism that develops a more profound understanding of democracy and that asks for certain institutional arrangements (such as elections, the separation of powers, political parties), for individual rights and certain substantive public goods (political freedoms, education, information, etc.) to ensure its existence. In the first half of the 20th century, it was ultimately this *political* tradition that fostered the rise of modern welfare states, in and beyond the West, to add certain social rights to protect citizens from social risks (such as unemployment, sickness, old age, etc.) and make possible deeper and wider participation in democratic institutions.

Since the late 1970s, however, neoliberalization processes—economic liberalism in practice, not theory—have reversed these achievements of political liberalism, under the pretense that if markets rule, the rest will follow (Brenner et al. 2010; Peck 2010). As we contend, it is this long-term crisis of political liberalism—hollowed out by a notion that economic liberalism would equally sustain and extend democracy—that has prepared the ground for illiberal tendencies. Thus, Smith, Tocqueville, and Mill would probably agree with our view.

At the risk of belaboring the point, it is important to emphasize that this is not an external crisis that has suddenly overcome all liberal democracies. Put differently, this is not simply a wave of autocratization analogous to Samuel Huntington's notion of waves of democratization (Huntington 1991). At the heart of this immanent crisis is a confusion. Or rather: a slippage. In Western democracies, economic liberalism has hijacked the political project of the enlightenment. It has inverted emancipatory social projects into social division, political apathy, and full-out anger. In economic and social policy, an impoverished understanding of liberal democracy, equaling democratization with the expansion of markets and the protection of individual property rights, has eclipsed the principles of political liberalism. As such, market fundamentalism has left us bereft of a language to think and act politically outside the terms set by economic thinking (Brown 2015).

Karl Polanyi, a central thinker to describe this predicament of market society, has been proven right in many things, but wrong on one key point: laissez-faire was by no means as dead as he thought, even if it might have seemed so in 1944, when he published his seminal book *The Great Transformation*. To be certain, he did write at a moment where it could easily have seemed that way: this moment saw the birth of a Bretton Woods order, through which social policies gradually expanded to ever larger sections of societies in the North Atlantic. In many contexts, the welfare state thus did take off the edges of economic liberalism (while the West became a role model for others to imitate). However, the 1970s resuscitated old beliefs. A bundle of crises—the OPEC oil crisis, stagflation, and fiscal crises at the local government level (as, most prominently, in New York City)—delivered a death blow to the Keynesian-Fordist compromise and the post–World War II order. The conservative revolution of the early 1980s was successful in developing a narrative that held government interventionism responsible for the crisis, and government leaders (with Ronald Reagan and Margaret Thatcher being just the most often-cited) proceeded to dismantle regulations and privatize public goods in the name of efficiency and under the banner of individual freedom. In most Western democracies, these processes included a period of rolling back Keynesian institutions in the 1980s, and rolling out and deepening neoliberal policy agendas through welfare state retrenchment, labor market deregulation, and free trade agreements in the 1990s and 2000s (see Brenner et al. 2010).

Again, markets took precedence over politics. In the process, Hayek's "road to serfdom" led instead to a radicalization of the concept of the market. Not only, now, were social progress and the growth of markets supposed to go together, as they did in the works of the classical economists. No, the argument went: without freely competitive markets, democracy would be utterly impossible. The more that social order was left to the market mechanism, the greater the degree of democracy, while the more active the state, the greater the degree of oppression. While market failure might well occur, the risks of government failure would always be worse still. This fanatical orientation of economic liberalism's market philosophy in the West was amplified after the fall of the Soviet Union, given that the failure of actually existing socialism seemed to spell out the lack of any viable alternative to liberal capitalism. The global expansion of neoliberalism under these preconditions also explains the impact of the crisis today as markets have expanded in every social sphere in and between nation-states.

The blind faith in market rule ignored the risks at stake. The promise of personal fulfillment that it incited in individuals worked so long as there was upward mobility because the belief in one's own opportunities for success could compensate for some of the retrenchment of the welfare state. In the wake of the financial crisis of 2008, however, this belief in individual success no longer seemed appropriate (Hopkin 2020). In the global north, the path of fulfillment through consumption could no longer be maintained with the help of cheap credit and affordable goods from abroad. Meanwhile, given the emphasis on individual responsibility in the unbundling of social systems since the Reagan-Thatcher revolution, the middle class had lost many of its rights to participate in decision-making both in the workplace and, increasingly, in politics. Just as public goods had been disappearing, individuals found themselves increasingly left alone (Honig 2017; Vormann and Lammert 2019), while the fragmentation of the public sphere made it more and more difficult, if not impossible, to articulate and pursue emancipatory political projects (see Milstein in this volume). The promise of prosperity, freedom, and peace, however, as supposedly enabled by market globalization proved to be only unevenly fulfilled, at best. Inequalities had grown by leaps and bounds within and between countries, and health care and social security systems are today massively underfinanced (see Lammert in this volume).

Not only did the blessings of the market, unanimously heralded after the Cold War, fail to materialize; the market also did harm. Instead of the salutary promise of "trickle-down" and the blooming fields of economic integration, there followed stagnating salaries, exploding living costs, and an ever-widening gap between rich and poor (see Hopkin and Blyth in this volume). In addition, the privatization of public goods made the logic of the highest bidder spread to many areas of life pushing the fragmentation of society to new extremes. As wealth became concentrated in the hands of a smaller and smaller number of individuals, the economization of society and politics began to threaten social cohesion. In numerous countries, the fissure today runs along the divide between urban and rural areas, highly qualified specialists and individuals with less education, self-designated elites and those who have been economically left behind.

As globalization seemed inexorable (and ultimately beneficial to all), increasingly technocratic politics did little to halt the hollowing out of market protections (see Berkowitz in this volume). In the West, the so-called Third Way of the immediate post-Cold War era instead promised many things to many people: the center-right was appeased through cuts in social spending in the name of competitiveness, while the center-left emphasized the cosmopolitan potentials of globalization. Interestingly, the "bloated state" that had been held responsible for the crises of the 1970s ultimately did not become any smaller. Its priorities simply shifted: from redistribution to militarization, from investments in public goods through federal and local governments to the so-called public-private partnerships that mimicked private competition by shifting costs and blame to the public actors—ultimately making these solutions across policy fields neither less expensive nor less exclusive or more democratic, for that matter. As flexible, precarious working conditions grew in number, however, as systems to buffer social risk were left unfunded, and politicians no longer seemed to listen to the citizenry (and sometimes were found to be corrupted), the dissatisfaction with the status quo grew and these politics of no alternative divided society along existing default lines.

Liberal democracy increasingly appeared as an empty shell. Even in those presumably stable democracies of the West, whole segments of the population no longer felt heard by politicians. Influence on the political process—a core element of functioning representative democracies—appeared as a privilege reserved for the lobbyists and water-carriers of business and the super-rich (Gilens 2012). A deep rift therefore opened up between privileged populations and those who feared losing their social status, an unsavory combination that, as Jill Frank (2005, 74–75) notes, Aristotle already identified in *Politics* (Book 3, Chapters 1–4) as anathema for rule by constitution, i.e. for a *politeia*, the "healthy regime type" where many share in rule that is aligned with and can degenerate into *demokratia*, the "popular" regime. As Robert A. Dahl (1989, 18) foregrounds with view to the Athenian city-state, "no state could hope to be a good polis if its citizens were greatly unequal." If citizens no longer act for the common good, if there is a disconnect between those who govern and the governed, questions of legitimacy arise quickly. The same still holds true for modern, large-scale democracy.

Cascading Effects: The Global Crisis of Liberalism

The crisis of liberal democracy is truly global mainly because the politics of no alternatives pursued by economic liberals in the name of market globalization had its origins in a similar premise in Europe and the US (Vormann and Lammert 2019), and by implication through extended networks of market exchange and finance, as well as Bretton Woods institutions and other entities of global governance, it extended beyond these countries of the core. A neo-classical vision of market rule has therefore dominated the politics of the last decades, not only in the settled democracies of the NATO alliance and in the EU but also in the so-called emerging democracies of Latin America and Asia. Within nation-states, it has meant shrinking governments through budget cuts and fiscal conservatism; privatizing public goods; and deregulating labor, financial, and health-care markets, while simultaneously transferring to individuals the responsibility for their social reproduction and employment. In international affairs, it has meant forcibly expanding free trade through the policies of the Washington Consensus, which was then—in a wish that quickly soured—also expected to ensure a democratic peace among rational state actors, thanks to the interdependence and mutual agreements between states that were supposed to accompany such policies.

While around the most recent turn of the century even autocratic leaders felt the need to aspire at least in rhetoric to the ideal of democratic governance— think of Putin's "sovereign democracy" or, for that matter, Orban's "illiberal democracy"—the enthusiasm of an American-led expansion of liberal democracy has lost all its momentum. The implosion of neoliberalism as an ideal and a set of practices are central to this. Not only were many cosmopolitan hopes thwarted, liberal democracy has increasingly been seen as a fig leaf for welfare state retrenchment in the West, and structural adjustment in the semi-periphery and the global south. Economic liberalism has failed, but political liberalism is being held responsible. The blame for underfunded social goods was shifted to the open society in an odd but by no means accidental reversal and distortion of causalities.

At the same time that the Washington Consensus hollowed out the hopes for integration and political emancipation, US hegemony entered a crisis which, since the turn of the century, has often been described, particularly with the wars in Afghanistan and Iraq, and the expansion of NATO (and EU) into

Eastern Europe, as the fallout from an imperial overstretch. In that context, the self-ascribed moral leadership of the US was fundamentally weakened by the use of torture under George W. Bush, the failure to close Guantanamo under Barack Obama, not to speak of Donald Trump's pivot from the idealist tradition to neo-realist zero-sum logics and full-on confrontation. Trump's decision to give up the ideal of American moral leadership altogether hence almost seems consequent. It is certainly consequential for the viability of a liberal vision of inter-state relations.

Unsurprisingly, this reorientation away from the post-Cold War liberal consensus is currently a hot topic in scholarly debates in the political science subfield of IR. The "realist" perspective welcomes it, pointing out how the liberal project had always been a set of high-flying ideals that were bound to fail from the outset and should be given up altogether. Stephen Walt's book with the telling title *The Hell of Good Intentions* paradigmatically argues that

> America's pursuit of liberal hegemony poisoned relations with Russia, led to costly quagmires in Afghanistan, Iraq, and several other countries [...] and encouraged both states and non-state actors to resist U.S. efforts or to exploit them for their own benefit.
>
> *(Walt 2018, 14)*

Like Walt, John J. Mearsheimer highlights the impossibility of the "liberal dream" (Mearsheimer 2018) which had dragged the US into unnecessary and dangerous engagements abroad, and urges policy-makers to balance offshore rivals through tactics of divide and conquer while redirecting military investments into the rebuilding of public goods at home—interestingly, a traditional claim of the left (for instance, Williams 1959). Even liberal theorists, while they don't share the prescriptive conclusions, agree that the liberal order is in peril (Ikenberry 2018; Rose 2019). The years of confidence and notions of an inevitable liberal expansion under the moral leadership of the US seem long gone. Against this backdrop of a compromised ideological consensus and the loss of a common compass, in the global south and in the semi-periphery, the hopes of the post-Cold War have abated (Krastev in this volume). The 1990s enthusiasm for marketization, very much at the center of cosmopolitan hopes of global emancipation and integration, now rings hollow.

Less discussed in the IR literature, but nonetheless crucial is the fact that, much in line with Karl Polanyi's observation, illiberalism springs spontaneously from a legitimate set of concerns and grievances within a multitude of different societies. It is not, at its origins, an "anti-liberal conspiracy" (Polanyi [1944] 2001, 151) concocted and premeditated by a new type of political consciousness. The nearly simultaneous parallels in re-nationalization not only in the US and the UK but clear across the world and encompassing established and new democracies from Brazil to India indicate something deeper. Namely, that and how the hopes of political emancipation, which still prevailed in the late 20th century, have disappeared precisely alongside the expansion and integration of the market within all spheres of politics.

Progressive Critiques: Liberalism Is Not Rule by Markets

It is not that the left didn't see it coming. A body of work emerged much before the first so-called populists came to power that voiced a very strong critique of the neoliberal politics of no alternative. Political scientists and economic sociologists, among others, explained the central themes at stake in today's debates about the crisis of democracy in great breadth and depth (Mouffe 2005; Crouch 2011; Wallerstein et al. 2013; Vogl 2015; Streeck 2017). As such, the downsides of globalization and the dangers that result from inequalities and threaten social stability have been identified, analyzed, and denounced in recent decades by many authors in Europe, North America, and beyond (Stiglitz 2003; Wilkinson 2005; Bartels 2008). Nor was it only academics and readers with specialized interests who began to think more deeply about inequalities and their dangers. The topic veritably exploded following the global financial crisis, and authors like Blyth (2013) and Piketty (2014) became very well-known far beyond the ivory tower.

The critique of neoliberalism included, as one of its elements, a critique of the market that essentially took aim at the negative consequences of the economization of societies—a tendency that, according to these authors, endangered democracy. Not everything, they argued, can be simply treated as a commodity (in other words, not all things can be commodified). Markets have technical, moral, and political limits.[4] Subsumed within the market, societies lose their ability to think and act politically. In that way, technocracy, as it has come to dominate education, the legal system, and political discourse, renders true politics impossible (Crouch 2015). Adding to this, market society's growing inequalities translate into unequal influence on politics. As such, responsiveness, the extent to which political representatives still attend to the interests of the people, is extremely unequally distributed.[5]

In sum, this progressive critique highlighted, democracy is sometimes at odds with (economic) liberalism, because even though the latter might aim to protect certain individual rights and thereby the constituents of the demos from the tyranny of the majority, its emphasis on individual liberty can contradict the need for public virtue. Put differently, liberalism—even more so in its economic version—gives only a partial vision of democracy that foregrounds individualism at the detriment of other potential understandings and practices of democracy (see Plattner in this volume). However, as innumerable authors have insisted since at least the 18th century—Smith, Tocqueville, and Mill again come to mind—democracy is more than market rule.

This progressive critique did not end with calling into question the current state of affairs. Many critics on the left even pointed to possible ways out of the crisis. Particularly since the 2008 global financial crisis, some authors stressed the role of the state as an important actor, despite globalization, and that, as in the past, government should be called to account on matters that concern the public. Since the government is responsible for constructing infrastructure and investing in science and education, for instance, and since it exerts an often-invisible influence on the distribution of resources, it bears a significant share of responsibility for social welfare (Peck 2010; Mettler 2011; Mazzucato 2015). Especially where there is upward redistribution, the government must act in accordance with the common good, not wealthy special interests—or so went the normative argument. In other words, the state needs to be foregrounded and held accountable.

This could indeed be a starting point for rebuilding the (center) left from its ashes, because recognizing such responsibility means that the state does have room for maneuver and therefore could engage in a politics of redistribution and decommodification—politics, in other words, are not without alternative. But, be that as it may, in practice, after every crisis, exactly the opposite seems to transpire: the costs and indebtedness of private interests have been foisted upon the public many times over, while the state has been regarded either as helpless, wasteful, or inefficient. The global financial crisis is the best example. In many countries, it was renamed a sovereign debt crisis (which it never was) to shift both burden and blame from the private to the public. Mark Blyth, on this subject, talks about the "greatest bait-and-switch operation in modern history" (Blyth 2013, 73). All this was happening before the backdrop of historical economic inequalities and, in many countries, long-term real wage stagnation for the majority of workers (Runciman 2018). Is it surprising that there would be anger against economic and political elites?

Under these conditions of frustration and disillusionment, of deep inequalities and precarious labor, little events can spark turmoil. Think of the fuel hikes in France that unleashed the yellow-vest movement and of the increase in public transportation prices in Santiago that triggered some of the largest protests of Chilean history. Add to this a series of external shocks, such as natural disasters (as in Turkey), terrorist attacks (as in France), foreign interference (as in the US), and an already frail system seems much more vulnerable than the immediate post-Cold War era would have made seem possible. The 20th century's hopes of equality and freedom, and of global peace and progress have been called off.

However, responses to the global crisis of neoliberalism are not preordained. What progressive voices offered as an alternative was to reject the dangers of market-led economic liberalism and embrace more political visions of society. They reasserted political liberalism to point out the divisiveness of market rule and the responsibility of the state. However, the left, despite movements such as Occupy Wall Street or Blockupy, was much less successful in articulating that political vision and translating it into electoral victories than the right.

The Critique from the Right: Who Belongs?

For the right, the solution to the long-term crisis of neoliberalism was not a salvaging of political liberalism, but its rejection in favor of a narrowly defined reassertion of popular sovereignty. As such, economic liberalism's (very) myopic vision of market-led democracy has been in the process of being replaced by another, equally partial understanding of the idea of democracy. For all the differences between regimes and actors (self-)identified as illiberal, today they each share a key conviction: popular sovereignty, not the rule of law or protection of minorities, is the *sine qua non* of democracy.

Despite their differences, contributors to this volume—who explore the crisis phenomena at hand from conservative and progressive points of view—share the sense that illiberalism is a symptom rather than a root cause of the crisis of liberal democracy. Both left and right critique an overexposure to globalization and break with the dominant post-Cold War discourse of liberalism. In practice, as we shall argue, illiberalism is mainly a phenomenon of the right and it has given rise to a strange hybrid—in essence, an authoritarian turn and reinvention of neoliberalism (see Peck and Theodore 2019), that holds on to some selected neoliberal traditions and democratic rituals, but rejects liberal democracy as a normative social goal and a guiding principle to govern global economic exchange and political relations.

Such right-wing illiberalism misconstrues the body politic as *Volkskörper*, that is as "an organicist and essentialist entity" in which 'the people' comes to be regarded as "a somehow unified organism" (Paul 2019, 128). Globalization in its different forms—financialization, trade, migration—by contrast, is regarded as a threat to that demos which needs to be diverted. Even from a very general point of view, the concept of democracy is always ambivalent because the root of the term—'rule by the many' or 'people's rule'—neither tells us which people (*demos* in Greek, whence "democracy" derives) it applies to nor by which means such people should rule and be ruled. As such, modern democracies are constantly disputed: who is in and who is not matter. Moreover, the methods of rule are contested. Under which conditions is a representative government legitimate? How and for whom to ensure democracy? (Dahl 1989) Illiberalism is concerned, quite precisely, with the rejection of the political and social claims of political liberalism as they extend to a widely defined demos. Such rights and privileges should only be extended to the "true" citizen (determined by rather arbitrary ethnic approximations defined by the illiberal politician).

This commitment to popular sovereignty around a narrowly defined demos, in short, constitutes the core characterization of illiberalism, traversing the conceptual and terminological fields discussed in different ways and with different assumptions in this book. Interestingly, at the same time, illiberalism, while it rejects tenets of inclusive political liberalism, does not necessarily refute all the precepts of economic liberalism. Domestically, illiberal politicians indeed tend to even strengthen market rule, while bracketing all democratic protection of individual and minority rights. It remains an open question, then, whether the commitment to popular and/or national sovereignty asserted by those who take up the mantle of "illiberal democracy" only pays lip service to those frustrated with the effects of globalization or whether it ought to be considered worthy of the name "democracy" at all. Even more so since in actual illiberal politics, more often than not, the closing of borders and erecting of (trade) barriers are matched by domestic hyper-deregulation and privatization. This will do little, of course, to address the problems of inequality and irresponsiveness at home— that we claim to be causal for the crisis of liberal democracy.

As discussed in detail in Marc Plattner's contribution to this volume, Fareed Zakaria's term *illiberal democracy* (Zakaria 1997), rendered famous in a 2014 speech by Hungarian Prime Minister Victor Orbán, is a misnomer in that sense. Rather, *undemocratic (purely economic) liberalism* would more aptly describe what we see in many contexts where a further rollout of privatization and liberalization of the economy—economic liberalism in its truncated and amplified form—dovetails with a retrenchment of civil liberties, voting rights, and other political freedoms and social rights.

Not Just Reaction: Illiberalism's Productive Capacities

So far, we have argued that, at this specific historical juncture, illiberalism rises as a promise to return to a vague pre-neoliberal era. Right-wing anti-globalization forces are seeking to protect nationals from the outside in a hostile world. But unlike the Keynesian-Fordist welfare state, there is hardly an articulation of an emancipatory political counter-vision—and if there is, it targets only an imagined ethnic core and seeks to restore traditional patriarchal values. Instead, we witness an extreme form of clientelism and the radical slashing of education budgets, a repealing of environmental protections—think of the environmental protection agency in the US, the burning down of rainforests in Brazil, or even the weak climate pact in Germany—and a massive deregulation of the financial sector. This is no longer quite neoliberalism *tout court*, given, for instance, the turn away from free trade or from the lip service to democracy and cosmopolitanism; nor quite fascism, because some democratic institutions persist, even if in an often very truncated way. This in-between phenomenon, described by some as a period of transition, or "interregnum" (Berman 2019), is what we see as the inflection point from which illiberalism emerges.

The illiberal alternative gestures toward a set of ways out of the neoliberal politics of no alternative. In its most extreme variants, essentially, what arises from the ruins of neoliberalism (Brown 2019), from the vacant ideological room left by undemocratic liberalism (Mounk 2018), in the absence of a strong center-left (or center-right) alternative, is a politics of fear. This politics of fear operates on prerational terms. It seeks to drive a wedge between the 'true demos' and the outsider. It works from the premise that the state is no longer performing its basic tasks. That it no longer holds the monopoly of violence and can no longer protect citizens from foreign invasion and inner disintegration, and that the citizen has to take self-defense in their own hands.

No longer, obviously, is this the left critique of inequality and the injustices of globalization that could be faced by addressing the shortcomings of the state in terms of redistribution or decommodification. It is a critique that shifts the blame from the economic inequalities between the haves and the have-nots, between the nation as a group of citizens and workers below—the 99%—against the 1% at the top (see OWS) to a critique of inside and outside: the ethnic nation that defends its traditional values and is under threat by overwhelming external forces that the state seems unwilling (because of its multicultural politics and openness to trade) or unable (see the critique of reduced state capacities that is shared with the mainstream discourse) to mitigate.

Under these circumstances of perceived emergency and threat to the very core of the populace, the institutions and procedures of liberal democracy no longer seem to hold. Everyone who opposes the 'will of the people' is an enemy: the media that spread fakenews to distract us from what is really going on, the foreigner who is taking away resources, the parliament that is dysfunctional and has been doing nothing but talking ("all talk, no action"). And so the essential pillars of the rational enlightenment, necessary to make democracy possible, are toppled. The checks and balances are unfit to tackle the challenges and are set aside. Government operates by decree and by state of emergency. The politics of fear, such as those we see in the wake of the still-unfolding global pandemic, make pluralistic debate impossible. They pose political problems as life or death questions. Once this threshold is passed, there is simply no place for reason and reasoned argument.

As such, illiberalism is *not only* a reaction to the inner tensions and contradictions of neoliberalism. It has productive capacities. To attain power, would-be autocrats reinforce the climate of anxiety—by creating fears of an ethnic exchange (a conspiracy theory of the extreme right), instrumentalizing dissatisfaction with migration inflows (such as European political mobilizations against refugees since 2015 and candidate Trump's call to "Build That Wall!"), and creating an impression of constant threats to physical safety from terrorists and other criminals (as in Duterte's war on drug dealers). By demonizing others, demagogues can demand a partial reversal of globalization processes, insisting on popular sovereignty, while at the same time reinventing the demos as an ethnic, rather than civic group, united by birth and territory rather than common values and interests.

What is at stake, then, is not just a conservative attempt to address the true grievances (that the political left would accept do exist) by shifting the focus from economic inequalities to outside threats and the blame to political rivals. Rather, it is to impose a different form of society. Illiberal actors seek to replace the multicultural and emancipated vision that was used under neoliberalism to paint economization in humanistic and cosmopolitan colors, by a more nationalistic vision of a new (but really very old) social project.

This restoration of a deeply conservative, imaginary primordial state of affairs (that, of course, never really existed) seeks to also enforce pre-modern patriarchal gender relations. As such, it rejects claims by the LGBTQ community, perceived as postmodern aberrations and extravagances. Feminism and gender studies departments become key targets of attack precisely because they undermine the legitimacy of such unquestioned traditions of patriarchy that autocrats seek to restore. This does not mean that critique of gender studies shouldn't be allowed or that all arguments in feminist work (as if this were one coherent set of arguments in the first place!) should be blindly accepted. Nor does it mean that concerns about ideological uniformity in academic contexts are inherently illiberal or empirically false.[6] Nevertheless, it is striking that across contexts where illiberal tendencies gain political force, such work is under direct attack and often has to suffer deep budget cuts. Beyond the academe, and immediately relevant to the life worlds of millions of women, illiberal actors push for antiquated, patriarchal gender roles, undermining women's reproductive rights (as, for instance, in Poland where the Law and Justice party, PiS, seeks to render abortions illegal). In that sense, the productive capacities of illiberalism have a lot to do with the reassertion of paternalistic notions of white masculinity.

Revising the Demos

Unsurprisingly, as illiberal and authoritarian trends are on the rise—both in fragile and seemingly robust democracies—there is growing concern about the longevity of both liberalism and democracy. One source of the growing popularity of illiberal policies, then, is an expression of a crisis of conviction owing to economic, cultural, and institutional distortions of citizens' self-interest as they understand it. Alongside this, there is a second source that cannot merely be written off as "populist." Namely, anti-system movements and political parties have been able to exploit the discrepancy between supranational institutions (the EU, the WTO, the UN) and respective national interests, conceived narrowly as those of an ethnic community in need of protection from outside forces. Different actors have used such outside threats to mobilize opponents of globalization and to raise claims for (often rural, majority ethnic) core constituencies. From this vantage point, (supranational) democracy has been viewed as a floodgate for foreign interests willing to exploit an already vulnerable national population whose national public goods (infrastructures, health-care systems, pension and retirement systems) have been destroyed by forces of globalization. These distortions of the constitutional protection of minorities in the service of authoritarian (or authoritarian-like) policies expose real tensions within the practice of constitutionalism and self-understanding of constitutionally elected representatives of "the whole people" who also explicitly identify with ethnically or ideologically defined partisans within that people.

In Western democracies, it is telling that upon closer examination, it is not actually those who have suffered most from globalization who are in uproar: for instance, the minorities exploited in highly precarious jobs along the supply chain, from resource extraction to consumption. Rather, it is a specific type of citizen (often white males in former manufacturing regions) who had previously benefited from the post-War compromise—an irony of history, yes that compromise struck by the forces of political liberalism to build the welfare state!—but now feels and more often than not *is* "left behind." If not exclusively—because fear mongering and hate speech do matter—this is a story of relative status decline, accompanied by a number of very real and harsh consequences, such as the opioid drug crisis and the surge in suicides in the US that many link (we think convincingly) to such economic hardship. It has a strong racial and gender component: the breadwinner that no longer can earn a sufficient household and loses a position of relative privilege (Fraser 2016). This motive recurs in the US after the welfare reforms of the 1990s and in Europe in the early 2000s as much as it does, in a curious, reversed scenario in Brazil, where existing middle classes have felt increasingly threatened by the rise of ethnically different working classes (Solano in this volume).

It is important to emphasize that the neoliberal compromise was not just imposed by conservatives, more often criticized for their proximity to the private sector. Rather, in a phenomenon labeled progressive neoliberalism by Nancy Fraser (2017), parties of the (center-) left grew increasingly fond of the so-called New Economy and Silicon Valley during the 1990s, becoming complicit in a market fundamentalism that is now creating a global backlash. This is now being leveraged against the left. In short, depending on context and political culture, tropes of ethno-nationalist nostalgia, fears of ethnic extinction, traditional Christian values, and/or critiques of political correctness are being mobilized to redefine the body politic and exclude minorities, feminists, intellectuals, social democrats, and the broader left. The strategic use of conservative narratives and the remaking of leftist markers has been a successful political tool and has also served as a smokescreen for those parties that actually made it to power: for instance, in Eastern and Central Europe (Krastev in this volume).

Remaking the State

Once in power, autocratic populists seek to weaken established democratic mechanisms that limit their power. The illiberal party undermines the separation of powers, particularly with attacks upon the independence of the judiciary; it assaults the fourth estate and sows doubts about its credibility and curtails the freedom of speech. All forms of contradiction to the strongman leader are rejected. What the leader says (not the 'corrupted' media) is supposed to become the truth. Truth, put differently, is not something arrived at through deliberation in the public sphere but through authority and tradition. Journalists and the free press constantly challenge this authority and therefore become themselves enemies of the people. The same holds, of course, for ivory tower intellectuals; spoilt middle-class students; and children environmentalists, à la Greta Thunberg, who are seen as part of the privileged elites who want to take the last shirt off the hard-working people's back.

Illiberal politicians seek to stabilize their power by surrounding themselves with loyal nepotists and family in public offices, intimidating and seeking political dirt on their opponents at home and abroad, and changing the rules of the electoral system. Gerrymandering and other political tools are used to reduce the competitiveness of political opponents, and electoral defeats are generally viewed as the result of irregularities—how could the demos not vote their true leader who is clearly the only one defending their interests? Only rarely, so far (as recently in the case of Poland), do illiberals advance (limited) social policy programs for the lower middle classes. What this indicates, nonetheless, is that they cannot act only by submission. This need to sustain their legitimacy leads such decision-makers to also accelerate economic growth through hyper-deregulation and privatization and the sell-off of remaining public goods, while at the same time pacifying economic elites (tending to be part of the majority population and not fearing resentments against minorities) through tax breaks and pro-business legislation. Securing the benevolence of the upper (middle) classes through major tax cuts contradicts earlier critiques of wasteful spending by old elites, but that does not seem to be important any more. Concerns with clientelism and conflicts of interest are equally brushed aside, claiming that everybody would rationally act this way, and that what was more important than focusing on these marginal details were the injuries inflicted on the true demos by others.

We are by no means saying that illiberalism automatically leads to fascism. But illiberal actors create a political climate in which lies, corruption, and violence become acceptable everyday phenomena and where democracy disintegrates to a point where these forces can gain power. In some cases, this process is incremental—Steven Levitsky and Daniel Ziblatt warn us that often "[d]emocracy's erosion is, for many, almost imperceptible" (2018, 6)—in others, it is accelerated by external shocks and systematically used states of emergency, i.e. attempted coups (see Coşkun and Kölemen in this volume), terrorist attacks or when these are absent, the potential for such (see Surak in this volume), and interethnic violence (see Sundar in this volume), *inter alia*. The suppression of opposition and the creation of a *de facto* one-party state through changes in the electoral system can be and are being legitimized along the same lines, as much as is the curtailing of political rights and the militarization of society. From that point onward, the distinction between this sort of democracy and a dictatorship, resting on little more than the fact of holding elections, but inciting political violence against political opponents and intimidating oppositional voices, becomes blurred.

Conclusion: Illiberalism Is Not Only Anti-Liberalism

Liberal democracy is at a crossroads. Four decades of market fundamentalism, put into political practice by elites from both the center-left and center-right, have hollowed out the promises of political liberalism, not just in the US or in the European Union and its individual member states (Blyth 2013; Offe 2015), but equally so in other nation-states with different commitments to democratization across the world. The promise of market efficiency has been used to reform labor markets, slash social budgets, and shift all social risks to individuals. All this happened under the pretext that no alternative was possible, simply because globalization—this seemingly overwhelming, external set of dynamics—had forced the hand of politicians on all levels of government in every region of the world, however advanced its economic development and whatever the status of its regime type. Meanwhile, elected officials, often unresponsive to their own constituencies, did in fact legislate in a way very much responsive to the desires of expanding transnational companies. This pattern of revolving doors and lucrative partnerships has led to a serious erosion of trust and a pervasive sense of injustice. As the West loses its faith not just in economic liberalism, but in what has been used as a justification to remake society in its image—liberal democracy—so do nation-states in the global south that are increasingly disappointed by the failed promises of liberalism and even come to see the liberal order as a ruse to extend colonial rule with the means of the market.

The critique of liberalism, and by implication of liberal democracy, is no longer only a progressive critique as it had been in the years immediately after the global financial crisis. Instead, more often than not, it has been rearticulated by reactionary movements into a critique of an aloof elitism. All boils down to a stylized face-off between the cosmopolitan globalists, jetting from global city to global city, and those who truly care for the real, hard-working people. But illiberalism is not just a reaction. Its agents actively seek to remake politics and follow specific interests—illiberalism is not just an irrational change of mood in parts of the population. It is characterized, from an economic perspective, by hyper-liberalization and clientelism at home as well as a neo-mercantilist recalibration on the inter-state level. Illiberal politicians tend to reject and hollow out some of the central institutions and procedures of liberal democracy (court-packing in the judicial branch, undermining the separation of powers, limiting the franchise, attacking free speech and opponents), and recast democracy in partial ways as a protection of sovereignty based on a clearly ethnically demarcated demos.

But this is not simply an autocratic wave: in fact, rather than a sudden surge at the right, we note a crisis of conviction in the center. If our analysis is right, ways out of an illiberal world therefore need to address two crises at once. The first is the protracted crisis of political liberalism itself. That is the root cause that led to the implosion of neoliberalism, particularly in the core group of Western democracies. Markets alone simply cannot bring social peace and stability domestically; consult Smith, Tocqueville, and Mill on this. Neither can they assure more legitimate and harmonious inter-state relations, as practice shows. Citizens need to be equipped with a modicum of political and social rights if the moniker of liberal democracy is to hold any credibility and describe viable processes. That includes limits on the influence of particular interests on government, the provision of a range of public goods (including health care, education, affordable housing, and mobility), options for social mobility, and the re-regulation of labor markets. Moreover, there needs to be a notion of the common good—an important reason why an integrative civic (not ethnically exclusive) type of nationalism indeed fulfills an important political role that shouldn't simply be abandoned for the sake of an idealistic cosmopolitanism (Calhoun 2007).

Populists in power offer none of this, but neither or only rarely do establishment parties. In national contexts where autocrats are not yet in office, for center-left parties in particular, this means that a political vision would need to be articulated in opposition not just to would-be autocrats but to almost a half-century of policies that have enriched the few and harmed the many—an alternative to the politics of no alternatives that does not revert to fear. Cosmopolitanism will have to mean something different from a simplistic embrace of open markets. On the center-right, questions of identity and belonging as well as the tradeoff between security and civil liberties will have to be reassessed and renegotiated in earnest to offer alternatives to citizens so-inclined. But these debates will have to be pursued strictly within the space of democratic contestation.

The question of scale is a reasonable and important one that democracies must face squarely, on the basis of a debate grounded in rational deliberation. What would be the most emancipatory way to organize politics, given that the global economy is as yet unmatched by global political institutions? What is the role of the nation and the nation-state in creating true alternatives to neoliberal globalization? Such a debate is best predicated on the observation that democracy thrives on visions of abundance. Such imaginaries make sharing in the common good possible, and don't limit politics to zero-sum games.

But if the crisis of democracy is older than the Trump presidency, illiberal politicians like him do add a new layer of complexity to the challenges liberal democracy is facing. The second crisis requires a different set of approaches. No doubt, autocratic movements learn from one another across national boundaries. They also have a structural advantage, given the conjuncture of apocalyptic scenarios dominating politics and fueling fear: chronic unemployment, displacement by technology, terrorism, pandemics, and even human extinction. And yet, illiberalism is not self-fulfilling or inexorable. Examples of autocracy elsewhere can also serve as a warning sign to those who want to defend the potentials of democracy and who seek to rearticulate them, not as a return to the market fundamentalism of the past, but as a set of political ideas and practices in their own right (see Wiesner in this volume for the case of the European Union).

Can the specters of illiberalism and hatred be overcome? It certainly has been done before and we do also see hopeful signs for a democratic revitalization, such as the repoliticization of public discourses, marches against antipluralists and racists, and solidarity between democratic actors in civil society. Even though they have been instrumentalized for the wrong purposes, we believe that there are indeed political values worth salvaging in the liberal tradition (Katznelson 2013). Political liberalism articulates social ideals that help provide mechanisms for (an approximation of) self-rule in modern large-scale society while seeking to protect the rights of individuals and minorities in a pluralistic society. It can bring with it a culture of political liberty and social emancipation that no other regime can. Liberal democracy will need to be reinvented to find a way out of its self-made crisis of legitimacy and an important part of this will be to rethink liberalism as a project in political economy, rather than a merely political *or* economic policy program. Only thus will it be possible to address the rightful concerns and true economic and ecological grievances that untrammeled market rule has brought with it.

Notes

1 The authors would like to thank Astrid Zimmermann and Christian Lammert for comments on earlier versions of this piece.
2 More often than not, it is the right that emphasizes the importance of sovereignty, but exceptions do exist. Gianpaolo Baiocchi (2018) argues for popular sovereignty because, according to him, it "radicalizes the meaning of democracy, insisting on the idea of the people as an egalitarian collective and the people's rule as a broad mandate to bring about social transformation" (23). In contradistinction to a right-wing perspective, however, he defines the people not in exclusive, ethno-nationalist terms, but as an open and inclusive "bloc against oppression and for emancipation" (25).
3 Although notable exceptions do exist (such as Judis 2016; Mounk 2018; Snyder 2018), even if most of them limit their comparison to cases in the West.
4 For one thing, there are certain goods we don't want to be put at the disposal of markets. Child labor, for example, is no longer socially acceptable in many countries. Many societies also consider the sale of human organs morally problematic, and their governments have banned it. These ethical constraints on markets are accompanied by technical limits, which have also been described and explained in much detail. Markets should be regulated, critics argue, because they cannot provide certain goods in sufficient quantities. Even economists, of whatever stripe, talk about market failure when, for example, factories dump their waste products into public waterways, thus shifting their waste management problems to the public (externalization); or when markets don't function because things like fresh, clean air; national security; and other public goods cannot be vouchsafed by individual private actors (see Satz 2010 as well as Sandel 2012 and Cassidy 2010; for a critical discussion of the concept of market failure, see also Vormann 2018). If everyone in a society simply pursues their own self-interest as a market participant without any regard to others, not much of that society will soon be left. Private vice does not add up to public virtue. Perhaps more importantly for our immediate purpose,

the authors of this longer-standing critique highlighted that the market form can present a political problem of its own. Nancy Fraser (2016), Robert Kuttner (2018), Jamie Peck (2010), Fran Tonkiss, and Don Slater (2001) are only some among a whole list of authors who emphasize that the logic of the market is, after all, fundamentally not consistent with the logic of democracy, or even, to refer to Karl Polanyi's (2001 [1944]) seminal argument many of these authors build on, corrosive to the survival of society itself.

5 In the US, by and large, it is only the super-rich and/or the corporations that store and expand their wealth that are still heard in the political process, while the interests of the middle class and lower income groups have become background noise that is barely perceived at all (Gilens 2012). In such a context, elections degenerate into a public spectacle of democracy, while political decisions are made behind closed doors, with the support of influential lobbyists (Bartels 2008).

6 Indeed, the attempt in this volume to include commentary from across the ideological spectrum alongside analysis that aspires to impartiality evidences that we, as editors, have our own concerns about the insularity of academic discourse.

Bibliography

Baiocchi, Gianpaolo. 2018. *We, the Sovereign*. Cambridge: Polity Press.

Bartels, Larry. 2008. *Unequal Democracy: The Political Economy of the New Gilded Age*. Princeton, NJ: Princeton University Press.

Berman, Sheri. 2019. "Interregnum or Transformation?" *Social Europe*. December 9. www.socialeurope.eu/interregnum-or-transformation

Blyth, Mark. 2013. *Austerity: The History of a Dangerous Idea*. Oxford: Oxford University Press.

Brenner, Neil, Jamie Peck, and Nik Theodore. 2010. "Variegated Neoliberalization: Geographies, Modalities, Pathways." *Global Networks* 10(2): 182–222.

Brown, Wendy. 2015. *Undoing the Demos. Neoliberalism's Stealth Revolution*. Brooklyn, NY: ZONE Books.

Brown, Wendy. 2019. *In the Ruins of Neoliberalism. The Rise of Antidemocratic Politics in the West*. New York, NY: Columbia University Press.

Calhoun, Craig. 2007. *Nations Matter. Culture, History and the Cosmopolitan Dream*. New York, NY: Routledge.

Cassidy, John. 2010. *How Markets Fail: The Logic of Economic Calamities*. New York, NY: Penguin.

Crouch, Colin. 2011. *The Strange Non-Death of Neoliberalism*. Cambridge: Polity Press.

Crouch, Colin. 2015. *The Knowledge Corruptors. Hidden Consequences of the Financial Takeover of Public Life*. Cambridge, MA: Polity Press.

Dahl, Robert. A. 1989. *Democracy and Its Critics*. New Haven, CT: Yale University Press.

Eichengreen, Barry. 2018. *The Populist Temptation. Economic Grievance and Political Reaction in the Modern Era*. Oxford: Oxford University Press.

Frank, Jill. 2005. *A Democracy of Distinction: Aristotle and the Work of Politics*. Chicago, IL: University of Chicago Press.

Fraser, Nancy. 2016. "Contradictions of Capital and Care." *New Left Review* 100: 99–117.

Fraser, Nancy. 2017. "From Progressive Neoliberalism to Trump—and Beyond." *American Affairs* 1(4) https://americanaffairsjournal.org/2017/11/progressive-neoliberalism-trump-beyond/

Galston, William A. 2018. *Anti-Pluralism: The Populist Threat to Liberal Democracy.* New Haven, CT: Yale University Press.

Gilens, Martin. 2012. *Affluence and Influence. Economic Inequality and Political Power in America.* Princeton, NJ: Princeton University Press.

Honig, Bonnie. 2017. *Public Things. Democracy in Despair.* New York, NY: Fordham University Press.

Hopkin, Jonathan. 2020. *Anti-system Politics. The Crisis of Market Liberalism in Rich Democracies.* Oxford: Oxford University Press.

Huntington, Samuel P. 1991. "Democracy's Third Wave." *Journal of Democracy* 2(2): 12–34.

Ikenberry, G. John. 2018. "The End of Liberal International Order?" *International Affairs* 94(1): 7–23.

Judis, John B. 2016. *The Populist Explosion: How the Great Recession Transformed American and European Politics.* New York, NY: Columbia Global Reports.

Katznelson, Ira. 2013. *Fear Itself. The New Deal and the Origins of Our Time.* New York, NY: W.W. Norton & Company.

Kuttner, Robert. 2018. *Can Democracy Survive Global Capitalism?* New York, NY: W.W. Norton & Company.

Levitsky, Steven, and Daniel Ziblatt. 2018. *How Democracies Die.* New York, NY: Viking.

Mazzucato, Mariana. 2015. *The Entrepreneurial State: Debunking Public vs. Private Sector Myths.* New York, NY: Anthem Press.

Mearsheimer, John J. 2018. *The Great Delusion: Liberal Dreams and International Realities.* New Haven, CT: Yale University Press.

Mettler, Suzanne. 2011. *The Submerged State. How Invisible Government Policies Undermine American Democracy.* Chicago, IL: The University of Chicago Press.

Mouffe, Chantal. 2005. *On the Political.* London and New York, NY: Routledge.

Mouffe, Chantal. 2018. *For a Left Populism.* London: Verso Books.

Mounk, Yascha. 2018. *The People vs. Democracy. Why Our Freedom Is in Danger & How to Save it.* Cambridge, MA: Harvard University Press.

Müller, Jan-Werner. 2016. *What Is Populism?* Philadelphia: University of Pennsylvania Press.

Offe, Claus. 2015. *Europe Entrapped.* Cambridge: Polity.

Paul, Heike. 2019. "Authoritarian Populism, White Supremacy, and *Volkskörper-Sentimentalism.*" In *The Comeback of Populism: Transatlantic Perspectives*, edited by Heike Paul, Ursula Prutsch and Jürgen Gebhardt, 127–55. Heidelberg: Universitätsverlag Winter.

Peck, Jamie. 2010. *Constructions of Neoliberal Reason.* Oxford and New York, NY: Oxford University Press.

Peck, Jamie, and Nik Theodore. 2019. "Still Neoliberalism?" *The South Atlantic Quarterly* 118(2): 245–65.

Piketty, Thomas. 2014. *Capital in the Twenty-First Century.* Cambridge, MA: Harvard University Press.

Polanyi, Karl. 2001 [1944]. *The Great Transformation: The Political and Economic Origins of Our Time.* Boston, MA: Beacon.

Rose, Gideon. 2019. "The Fourth Founding: The United States and the Liberal International Order." *Foreign Affairs* 98 January/February: 10–21.

Runciman, David. 2018. *How Democracy Ends.* New York, NY: Basic Books.

Sandel, Michael J. 2012. *What Money Can't Buy: The Moral Limits of Markets*. New York, NY: Farrar, Strauss and Giroux.

Satz, Debra. 2010. *Why Some Things Should Not Be for Sale: The Limits of Markets*. Oxford: Oxford University Press.

Snyder, Timothy. 2018. *The Road to Unfreedom: Russia, Europe, America*. London: Penguin.

Stiglitz, Joseph. 2003. *Globalization and Its Discontents*. New York, NY: W.W. Norton & Company.

Streeck, Wolfgang. 2017. *Buying Time: The Delayed Crisis of Democratic Capitalism*. London: Verso.

Tonkiss, Fran, and Don Slater. 2001. *Market Society. Markets and Modern Social Theory*. Cambridge, MA: Polity Press.

Vogl, Joseph. 2015. *The Specter of Capital*. Stanford, CA: Stanford University Press.

Vormann, Boris. 2018. "When Private Vice Hurts Public Virtue: Of Blind Men, Elephants and the Politics of Market Failure." *Economy and Society* 47(4): 607–26.

Vormann, Boris, and Christian Lammert. 2019. *Democracy in Crisis. The Neoliberal Roots of Popular Unrest*. Philadelphia: University of Pennsylvania Press.

Wallerstein, Immanuel, Randell Collins, Michael Mann, Georgi Derluguian, and Craig Calhoun (eds.). 2013. *Does Capitalism Have a Future?* Oxford: Oxford University Press.

Walt, Stephen. 2018. *The Hell of Good Intentions: America's Foreign Policy Elite and the Decline of U.S. Primacy*. New York, NY: Farrar, Strauss and Giroux.

Wilkinson, Richard. 2005. *The Impact of Inequality. How to Make Sick Societies Healthier*. New York, NY: The New Press.

Williams, William Appleman. 1959. *The Tragedy of American Diplomacy*. New York, NY: W.W. Norton & Company.

Zakaria, Fareed. 1997. "The Rise of Illiberal Democracy." *Foreign Affairs* 76(6): 22–43.

2

WHAT DOES A LEGITIMATION CRISIS MEAN TODAY?

Financialized Capitalism and the Crisis of Crisis Consciousness

Brian Milstein

Introduction

When we hear the expression "crisis of liberal democracy" today, more likely than not what is being referenced is the rise of right-wing populist movements. But democracy has been caught on the shoals for some time. Some two decades ago, Colin Crouch coined the term "post-democracy" (2004) to describe a society that still possessed all the formal trappings of liberal democracy, but they ceased to be of any substance, as real authority had passed to a technocratic elite serving the interests of financialized capitalism. Crouch did not believe that we were already living in such a society, only that we may be moving in that direction. In this respect, German Finance Minister Wolfgang Schäuble may have become the first self-consciously post-democratic politician when he reputedly declared at a 2015 Eurogroup meeting, "Elections cannot be allowed to change the economic program of a member state" (Varoufakis 2016). Years before Donald Trump publicly mused about disregarding the results of the U.S. presidential election, the European leadership was already making a practice of overriding democratic procedures to enforce its austerity policies. To the adage that the answer to the problems of democracy is more democracy, we might add the corollary that the problems of democracy, left unaddressed, only bring more problems.

There were many on the left who hoped that the political aftermath of the 2008 financial crisis would spark a *legitimation crisis* in capitalist societies—one that would at last overturn neoliberal forms of economic thought, kick-starting a revitalization of social democracy and a much-needed renewal of utopian energies. Others noted the startling absence of such a legitimation crisis in the years following 2008, despite the evident strains being put on democratic autonomy and legitimacy by international financial institutions and encroaching technocratic forms of governance, especially in the EU (Crouch 2011; Fraser 2015). There was even speculation that late-capitalist societies may have reached a point where it is effectively immune to serious legitimation challenges (Azmanova 2014a, 2014b, 2015; Roitman 2014; Streeck 2016).

The 2016 Brexit referendum and Trump's election as U.S. President made it clear that the symptoms of legitimation crisis have finally arrived. But they arrived in a form very different from what many expected, much less desired. Moreover, if the hegemony of the neoliberal world order has been shaken, it is far from clear what (if anything) might fully unseat it, for the populist movements that have sprouted up seem hardly any more stable in the long run. Nancy Fraser writes that we find ourselves in what Gramsci once described as an "interregnum," in which "the old is dying and the new cannot be born," during which time "a great variety of morbid symptoms appear" (Gramsci 1971, 276; Fraser 2017).

The concept of a "legitimation crisis" is most closely associated with Jürgen Habermas, and recently, his 1970s book on legitimation crisis tendencies in postwar capitalism has provided a common reference point for discussion of the various forms of political turmoil that have ensued in Europe and the U.S. over the last decade (Cordero 2014; Streeck 2014; Fraser 2015; Habermas 2015; Milstein 2015; Gilbert 2019; Ibsen 2019; Lebow 2019). Originally published as *Legitimationsprobleme im Spätkapitalismus* in 1973, *Legitimation Crisis* examines the deep-seated tensions between capitalism and democracy and the ways in which crises can be "displaced" from the economic realm into the administrative and political realms of society.

Using Habermas's original thesis as a point of departure, the purpose of this chapter is to explore the meaning of legitimation crisis under the financialized capitalism of the 21st century. My argument is that legitimation crises can take on specific and pathological forms under financialized capitalism, which Habermas's model failed to fully capture. At the same time, Habermas's argument contains theoretical resources that are invaluable to understanding the present crisis, though he did not always develop them sufficiently. In addition to his analysis of crisis tendencies in state-managed capitalism, Habermas's book is notable for the way it questions and reformulates the *concept* of crisis in capitalist society. As Rodrigo Cordero recently noted, a central claim of the book is that "the analysis of the reality of crisis cannot proceed without a critique of the concept of crisis" (Cordero 2014, 500). Habermas realized that, though we frequently describe crises as objective events accessible to social-scientific description and analysis, the "reality" of crises in modern societies is a function of crisis *consciousness* on the part of society's participants: societal contradictions, pathologies, systemic deficits, and the like only rise to the level of crisis phenomena to the extent that actors *experience* them as such. Furthermore, he realized that crisis consciousness in modern societies is enacted *discursively*, in the way crisis-conscious citizens bring their experiences and understandings of crisis to bear on each other *as a public*. But he did not carry through on the implications of this discursive conception of crisis consciousness, and particularly the ways the discursive deployment of crisis consciousness can be impeded or distorted under certain social conditions.

As we will see, the contours of a legitimation crisis under financialized capitalism differ from those described by Habermas in the 1970s. The contradictions of financialized capitalism are such that securing legitimacy can only be achieved via the virtual desiccation of the political public sphere. This has a side effect, however, in that, when the hegemony of financialized capitalism falls into legitimation crisis, the absence of a sufficiently robust public sphere compromises the ability of citizens to fully develop their collective sense of crisis consciousness. This allows society to fragment. It does not "cause" people to embrace illiberal or authoritarian populism, but it fosters an atmosphere in which such populism can gain a foothold. In this respect, financialized capitalism exacerbates the legitimation crises it generates for itself, leading them to take on pathological forms, including several of those we now group under the heading of "crisis of liberal democracy."

Habermas Revisited

For all its influence, *Legitimation Crisis* was a product of its time. Aside from its heavy reliance on the systems-functionalism of Talcott Parsons, its core thesis is aimed directly at the politics of the late 1960s and early 1970s, which were marked by widespread counter-cultural and protest movements across Europe and the U.S. The question concerning Habermas was whether the Keynesian welfare state really had overcome capitalism's tendencies toward contradiction and crisis (Habermas 1975, 30–31). Orthodox Marxism, after all, is built on the idea that capitalism is at its core afflicted by an ineradicable contradiction between the forces and relations of production, which drives it into periodic economic crises of increasing intensity, which articulate themselves politically in class conflict. But postwar economic policy had brought to the West near-continuous growth uninterrupted by major economic crisis, while the "welfare state compromise" brought the forces of labor and capital to a truce. Had the Keynesian welfare state really "resolved" the core contradictions of capitalism? If so, why all the discontent?

Habermas's argument was that the Keynesian welfare state had not eliminated capitalism's crisis tendencies; it merely *displaced* them. Habermas accepted the view that, under state-managed capitalism, economic crises are no longer necessary sources on legitimation crisis in the way they had been under the laissez-faire capitalism of the 19th century. At the same time, the capacities of the political system to absorb the tensions internal to capitalism come at a cost, which could only be paid through the ever-increasing intrusion of the administrative realm into the sociocultural lifeworld of society. This had the effect of making the administrative state the focus of political conflict instead of class division: the more the state expands into everyday life, the more legitimacy it must command. In Habermas's assessment, the increasing need for legitimacy creates for the capitalist state a new kind of problem (Habermas 1975, 68–75). As the state penetrates further and further into society, it begins to alter the social and cultural bases of society. Growing bureaucratization of social life increases senses of alienation and disillusionment. Economic prosperity means that citizens are no longer as driven by basic material needs as they once were, loosening the hold of privatist ideology. Eventually, the welfare state becomes its own source of public discontent by destroying the cultural resources it requires for legitimation (Habermas 197, 92–94).

In short, instead of resolving capitalism's crisis tendencies, the postwar welfare state transposes them from the economic to the cultural domain. Habermas was far from alone in locating the source of mid-century alienation and discontent in some complex of the administrative state and consumerist culture. Much of the criticism of the postwar period, such as that can be found in the works of Hannah Arendt, Michel Foucault, and the Frankfurt School, coalesced around suspicions of "the social" and associated forms of "discipline," "governmentality," or an "administered world" (Arendt 1958; Foucault 1977, 1991; Marcuse 2002 [1964]; Adorno 2003 [1968]). This is not to mention the ways state-managed capitalism was seen to reinforce gender-based and (especially in the U.S.) racialized status hierarchies (Fraser 2016; Fraser and Jaeggi 2018, 87–90, 103–6). Indeed, by the 1980s, the fault lines of social conflict as articulated in the "new social movements" appeared to have shifted toward a decidedly "post-materialist" terrain (Inglehart 1977; Habermas 1987a, 392–6; Fraser 1997).

Needless to say, the 2008 crisis and its aftermath threw cold water on this aspect of Habermas's thesis. Late-capitalist society remains quite capable of tumbling into economic crisis, and in retrospect, there appear a number of fronts on which his argument may have fallen short. One is Habermas's understanding of political economy. After all, his thesis about crises taking on post-materialist forms presupposes a capacity on the part of the administrative system to effectively subsume the economy. According to Wolfgang Streeck, Habermas overestimated the extent to which the state could transform owners and firms from "advantage-seeking profit maximizers" into "functionaries obediently carrying out government economic policy" (Streeck 2014, 21). For Streeck, the postwar arrangement could better be characterized as an uneasy partnership between capitalism and democracy, and in fact it had already begun to unravel around the time *Legitimation Crisis* was published. Over the next three decades, successive governments attempted a series of monetary, fiscal, and financial policy strategies to preserve standards of prosperity well after the postwar economy ran out of steam, including reliance on sovereign debt and deregulation of private finance, before the game finally expired in 2008.

More to the point, Habermas's account of the legitimation crisis of state-managed capitalism failed to anticipate how it might pave the way for the neoliberal revolution to come. Building in part on Streeck's analysis, Nancy Fraser argues that because Habermas did not duly recognize the political agency of capital, he could not account for the ways capital exploited or maneuvered the crisis. In her view, capitalists were ultimately able to channel progressive discontent with the welfare state in such a way that made "post-materialist" politics compatible with a regressive economic politics. This ultimately would lead to what she calls "progressive neo-liberalism," an alliance of identity politics and free-market capitalism with which Fraser associates the "Third Way" agendas of Tony Blair, Bill Clinton, Gerhard Schröder, and others (Fraser 2017; Fraser and Jaeggi 2018, 79–81, 200–04). For Fraser, the overtaking of center-left parties by an agenda that largely forfeits resistance to marketization and financialization would leave them unprepared for the political crisis that followed 2008 (and ultimately allow populist movements to draw away voters in former labor strongholds). But there is a deeper issue at play as well.

Underlying this objection is a point concerning the character of legitimation crises as such. Habermas wanted to situate his account of crises in a theory of social evolution, and he lists among the drivers of emergent crisis consciousness the progression of scientism, post-auratic art, and universal morality (Habermas 1975, 84–89). But in Fraser's view, this "culturalist" account does not take into account the specifically *political* forces that need to be in motion for the legitimacy of a given order to fall into crisis. It is not sufficient to speak, as Habermas sometimes does, of a mere "withdrawal" of legitimacy; rather, a full account of crisis requires an account of *hegemonic politics*—that is, the way social and political forces come together to shape the parameters of "normal" political debate, as well as the counter-forces that might challenge or upset such normality (Fraser 2015, 172–3). Disturbances in the sociocultural realm are not sufficient to spark political change without effective political mobilization; nor can they by themselves determine the *direction* of political change.

Indeed, the evolutionary model on which Habermas relies, as well as the (still not fully developed) model of communicative rationality to which he ties it, expects largely progressive outcomes of such crises. In *Legitimation Crisis*, and later in *Between Facts and Norms*, his analysis of transformative possibilities in times of crisis does not extend further than the prospect of a galvanized citizenry "mobilizing counterknowledge" and challenging established power (Habermas 1975, 96; Habermas 1996, 372–3, 380–4). Consequently, the model has no means for distinguishing between crises that reignite the progressive-democratic energies of the citizenry, those which are recuperated by elites in a different guise (see Boltanski and Chiapello 2007), and those which lead down a path toward authoritarian populism and destructive ideologies. As a result, not only was Habermas unable to foresee how the 1970s crisis paved the way for the neoliberal revolution, but it also appears underequipped for discerning how the 2008 crisis paved the way for the present crisis of liberal democracy.

Despite the above-named problems, Habermas's model of late-capitalist legitimation crises remains pertinent. After all, the story Streeck tells about the "delayed crisis of democratic capitalism" has purchase precisely because states continue to assume responsibility for economic performance and crisis management (cf. Lebow 2019, 388). As much as states attempt to renounce their regulatory authority in favor of first public and then private modes of financialization, the history of late 20th-century capitalism is one tailored to the dilemma of a political system that, having openly acknowledged capitalism's crisis tendencies and staked its own legitimacy on its capacities to successfully mitigate them, has yet to convincingly extricate itself from these burdens in the way a genuine free-market ideology would demand. This suggests that Habermas's more fundamental diagnosis of the tensions between capitalism and democracy continues to be relevant. In what follows, I will argue that how these tensions are managed under financialized capitalism, and at what cost, remains problematic as they create specific legitimation demands that can only be met by compromising society's ability to successfully process crisis.

The Modern Concept of Crisis

But it could well be argued that the real legacy of Habermas's contribution lies not in the particulars of his sociological diagnosis but in how he engages our understanding of "crisis" as such. *Legitimation Crisis* also contains Habermas's first sustained engagement with his famous distinction between "lifeworld" and "system" aspects of society. Believing both the Marxist and cultural-conservative conceptions of crisis to suffer crucial limitations, his two-level approach avoided the pitfalls of a fully "system"-oriented view as well as an exclusively "culturalist" view by recasting crisis phenomena as disturbances felt by lifeworld-embedded participants grappling with intrusion by system imperatives (Habermas 1975, 3; Cordero 2014, 500–01). Consequently, "crisis" must be treated no longer as a diagnosis applied by an external observer but as—in Cordero's words—"an act of communication with critical intentions," whose validity claims reside in the end in the discursive activity of the participants themselves (Cordero 2014, 502). I would argue, however, that Habermas himself does not fully capitalize on the implications of this discursive reformulation of the crisis concept. A more in-depth exploration will afford us necessary tools for understanding the dynamics and—more importantly—the potential *deformations* of legitimation crises in late-capitalist societies.

Andrew Simon Gilbert recently noted how a postmetaphysical reconstruction of the crisis concept implies "a focus on 'crisis' rather than crisis" (Gilbert 2019, 177). Particularly in light of the linguistic turn in 20th-century philosophy and theory, the meaning and import of "crisis" must be understood above all in the discursive contexts within which it is put into play by social actors: "first as a conceptual vehicle for validity claims, only second as a candidate for social theory or history" (Gilbert 2019, 177). This account has the potential to answer criticisms that the crisis concept necessarily invokes a "philosophy of history" (cf. Koselleck 1988; Roitman 2014); more importantly, it allows us to account for abuses, exploitations, and distortions in social practice.

The word "crisis," of course, comes to us from Ancient Greece, and it possessed a variety of connotations in medicine, politics, law, and theology, which inform the ways we understand the concept today (Koselleck 2006 [1982], 358–61). Yet the concept of crisis, in the sense that we know it today as a moment of broad social or political urgency, is a distinctly *modern* concept. The idea of a political crisis did not take shape until the 17th and 18th centuries, and the idea of an economic crisis only entered into widespread circulation with the rise of liberal capitalism in the 19th century. This is not to say that there were no phenomena prior to modernity that could be described as crises. Crisis-like events certainly happened, but in the modern period, they became "routinized" in a specific way. One reason is the growing complexity and accelerated pace of social life: though Europe had seen some notable events that resembled the modern economic crisis, such as "Tulip Mania" in the 1630s and the South Sea Bubble of 1720, only in the 1800s was it possible to refer to "economic cycles" that alternated regularly between periods of boom and bust. But it is also the concept itself that standardizes these situations of unexpected urgency and uncertainty, and that makes them all of a type that is to be approached in a particular way with a particular consciousness.

Put another way, the crisis concept presupposes some distinctly modern assumptions about one's relation—that is, the relation of one who *makes use* of the crisis concept—to the social world. "Crisis" emerges as social participants cast off their reliance on traditional authority or divine order, taking on instead a reflexive attitude toward themselves and their societal context (Milstein 2015, 144–5). But it also emerges alongside a certain level of social complexity, whereby society appears to acquire the status of a "second nature" (Habermas 1987a: 173). Sociologists have long noted a paradoxically dual character to modern society, thematized through such distinctions as "labor" and "capital," "agency" and "structure," and "lifeworld" and "system." Society appears, on the one hand, as something that can be *acted upon by its members*, and that can be made transparent and shaped according to their own collective will and reason; yet it also appears, on the other hand, as something that *acts upon its members*, and that remains external and opaque to everyday life, carrying its own objective force, to which the self-understanding of participants must bend (Milstein 2015, 146). As a basic concept (*Grundbegriff*) of modernity, "crisis" functions as a conceptual tool for navigating this duality. We speak of the economy, the state, or the environment being "in crisis" only to the extent that we can point to a discrete entity called "the economy" or "the state" or "the environment" that behaves according to rules we can comprehend and manipulate if not make transparent. As unpredictable, wild, overpowering as a crisis may be, this is what distinguishes one from a plague, disaster, or scourge of the gods. To the latter, one may contain it, adapt to it, or repent for it. Crises, in contrast, emanate from a source we believe *can be mastered*, at least in principle.

It is not difficult to note the promethean element of modern crisis consciousness, which Koselleck once tied to modernity's entanglements with utopian arrogance and revolutionary excess (Koselleck 1988 [1959]). Once the crisis concept is understood *discursively*, however, the situation becomes more ambiguous. On the one hand, modern crisis consciousness implies a form of "positive freedom": in declaring the existence of a crisis, one is not only making a normative judgment about how things should or should not be and that action is urgently needed, one is also assuming for oneself a certain ownership or authority over the situation. "Crisis" is a public concept, which members of a public deploy to alert each other to a matter of public concern and to bind one another to a set of commitments for taking action (Milstein 2015, 148). To possess crisis consciousness is to assume ownership of one's social world, in the sense of being capable and assuming oneself authorized to make judgments and demand actions. On the other hand, the actualization of this positive freedom now depends on the ability of crisis-conscious citizens to *successfully* make discursive sense of their stakes in the crisis and claims to action. This raises the question of whether the means of the discursive realization of crisis consciousness can be somehow disturbed or distorted.

Among the early Frankfurt writers, Erich Fromm was especially sensitive to this dilemma. In *Escape from Freedom*, Fromm, too, locates the core of modern crisis consciousness in society's emergence from what he calls the "primary ties" of traditional authority. But this move only earns the modern individual "negative" freedom, a freedom *from* constraining bonds and dogmas. To fully make good on one's freedom, the participant must progress to "positive" freedom, which Fromm associates with the development of "an active, critical, responsible self" (Fromm 1969 [1941], 108). Otherwise, participants find themselves overwhelmed by the forces of a society that now appears alien and unremitting:

> The rationality of the system of production, in its technical aspects, is accompanied by the irrationality of our system of production in its social aspects. Economic crises, unemployment, war, govern man's fate. Man... has become estranged from the product of his own hands, he is not really the master any more of the world he has built; on the contrary, this man-made world has become his master, before whom he bows down, whom he tries to placate or to manipulate as best he can. ...He keeps up the illusion of being the center of the world, and yet he is pervaded by an intense sense of insignificance and powerlessness which his ancestors once consciously felt toward God.
>
> *(Fromm 1969 [1941], 117–18)*

Crisis consciousness is awareness of the conflict wherein it remains to be decided whether it is the participants who steer society or vice versa, whether we will make our own history or be made by it. Stripped of "primary ties" of traditional modes of life, a merely negative freedom unaccompanied by positive freedom can become too burdensome, leading people to seek *escape* from freedom altogether in search of ontological security. In Fromm's analysis, such tactics of retreat can take the form of authoritarianism, destructiveness, and conformism: deprived of power over themselves, they are driven to exert power over others; lacking in purpose, they submit themselves to the cause of a leader; overburdened by the tasks of critical thought, they embrace unthinking or "pseudo-thinking" conformism (Fromm 1969 [1941], 140–204). Fromm believed that the appeal of fascist doctrines such as National Socialism was in their—ultimately futile—promise to replace the "primary ties" lost to modernity.

Fromm's approach is psychoanalytic. Yet despite searching for frustrated crisis consciousness in individualized psychological experience, Fromm locates the inhibitions to positive freedom in prevailing *social* conditions. He blames the monopoly capitalism of the early 20th century for stifling prospects for self-actualization: as capital becomes increasingly concentrated in the hands of fewer and fewer, class domination and the commodification of social relations strip away the resources available to individuals to develop themselves.

We can reconstruct this pathological deprivation of positive freedom in communications-theoretic terms. Habermas does not theorize the ways a legitimation crisis can take on pathological forms, but we can do so using the above-discussed conception of crisis as "an act of communication with critical intentions" (Cordero 2014, 502). Understood thusly, the collective development of crisis consciousness hangs not on the successful psychic development of self-world relations but on the communicative exercise of public autonomy. Understood as a publicly articulated discursive process, crisis consciousness begins as a personal *intuition* of crisis, but its full development into a fruitful sense of crisis consciousness—one capable of generating a collective understanding of the crisis and ultimately reasserting agency over the causes and mechanisms of crisis—can only be achieved for the citizenry at large in public discourse. This requires, among other things, a sufficiently (even if imperfectly) open and active civil society and public sphere where citizens and their representatives can voice and reconcile their diverse experiences, action claims, and stakes in the crisis. This implies a conception of public freedom that is less demanding than Fromm's and easier to translate into institutional terms. Conversely, we can hypothesize about the forms of alienation that result from being denied voice and representation in the public realm, from being denied the resources with which to make sense of crisis intuitions.

Financialized Capitalism's Crisis of Crisis Consciousness

Recalling Streeck's analysis, financialized capitalism relies on a contradictory arrangement. *On the one hand*, it demands the deregulation of markets and the dramatic rolling back of social welfare protections. Not only do such moves exacerbate the iniquities of capitalism, allowing for extreme concentrations of wealth among owners of capital, the dismantling of protections for sellers of labor power leaves them exposed not only to stagnated standards of living generally but to the ravages of economic convulsions. *On the other hand*, because elites cannot openly rewrite the terms of democratic capitalism in so onerous a fashion, the political order must continue to stake its legitimacy on the postwar commitment to manage economic crises and sustain prosperity, even as it relinquishes its capacities for doing so. As we now know, the strategies of first public, then private financialization through which states sought to compensate their loss of regulatory capacity only increased the likelihood and magnitude of crisis, and, in so doing, it all but invited their metamorphosis into administrative and then legitimation crisis as the remnants of the postwar commitment finally prove themselves a façade (Thompson 2012; Ibsen 2019).

But there is more. Not only does the contradiction of financialized capitalism contain the seeds of its own legitimation crisis, it also distorts the discursive processing of crisis consciousness in pathological ways. This is due to the exorbitant and contradictory legitimation demands financialized capitalism must place on itself to sustain this already contradictory arrangement. Such demands could only be met through a ruthless depoliticization of the economy, which was achieved via the cartelization of the political party system and the post-democratic desiccation of the public sphere. This had the effect of keeping capitalism out of the political realm, but it also had the collateral cost of depriving society of the resources necessary to fully generate a collective sense of crisis consciousness.

Habermas notes that all capitalist societies must confront "the problem of distributing the surplus social product inequitably and yet legitimately" (Habermas 1975, 96). In postwar social democracy, this meant, first, that governments took responsibility for quelling the harshest iniquities and instability of market forces, and, second, that sellers of labor power would be granted the formal rights of citizenship. Hence, Gøsta Esping-Andersen described the postwar welfare state as a project of "decommodification": these measures shield individuals from the "sense of insignificance and powerlessness" Fromm attributes to a post-traditional state of "mere" negative freedom by facilitating a modicum of positive freedom (Esping-Andersen 1990). A fully empowered form of positive freedom, in contrast, is not a viable option, as Habermas explains: "Genuine participation of citizens in the processes of political will-formation [*politischen Willensbildungsprozessen*], that is, substantive democracy, would bring to consciousness the contradiction between administratively socialized production and the continued private appropriation and use of surplus value" (Habermas 1975, 36). In Habermas's assessment, legitimacy under capitalism requires a "structurally depoliticized public realm" that exhibits the trappings of formal democracy but largely encourages citizens to resign themselves to a limited role of granting and withholding electoral acclamation. This passive orientation is buttressed, in turn, by an ideology of "civic privatism": citizens remain motivated by personal, careerist, and consumerist pursuits, while trusting political matters to a qualified elite (Habermas 1975, 37).

Fraser, too, argues that democracy must perforce be limited in all capitalist societies, but the "hollowing out" of democracy takes an extreme form under financialized capitalism (Fraser 2019; see also Crouch 2004). Despite the "truce" declared between capital and labor during the postwar years, even politics under welfare-state capitalism retained traces of class partisanship, even as major political parties shifted from old cleavage structures to "catch-all" organizations (cf. Kirchheimer 1966; Lipset and Rokkan 1967). By the 1990s, the "economic cleavage" had become largely depoliticized as even center-left parties deprioritized social policy in favor of free-market agendas (Ibsen 2019, 808–9). Richard Katz and Peter Mair refer to a process of *cartelization* of Western party systems whereby major political parties begin to not only converge in their political platforms but, in certain ways, "cooperate" with one another (Katz and Mair 2009). Though partisan rivalry appears no less acrimonious in some cases, topics of debate become restricted to matters of culture and identity or personal scandal, while dissenting voices are marginalized.

This depoliticization process comes to be reflected in the public sphere as well. Katz and Mair note how domination of mass media in politics has greatly reduced the dependence of party elites on members and activists, while increasing their dependence on money in political campaigns (Katz and Mair 2009, 758). Commercial mass media and television have, in turn, altered the character of political discourse, forcing politicians and journalists alike to prioritize the scandalous and the sensational (Crouch 2004, 46–49). Moreover, ownership of mass media outlets are settling into fewer and fewer hands, which has the effect of exerting additional pressure on the part of capital on the constraint of political agendas. As Colin Crouch observed:

> Control over politically relevant news and information, a resource vital to democratic citizenship, is coming under the control of a very small number of extremely wealthy individuals. And wealthy individuals, however much they might compete with one another, tend to share certain political perspectives, and have a very strong interest in using the resources at their command to fight for these. This does not just mean that some parties will be favoured rather than others by the media; the leaders of all parties are aware of this power and feel constrained by it when they formulate their programmes.
>
> *(Crouch 2004, 50)*

Political systems under post-democratic conditions thus find themselves doubly gate-kept by capital: first, at the level of party politics and political campaigns, as political elites become more dependent on corporate funding and various lobbies; second, at the level of the public sphere, as political messaging must be both sufficiently attention-grabbing and inoffensive to pass the filters of media conglomerates. What was established, in short, was a rigid form of political hegemony whereby the legitimation demands posed by the contradiction of financialized capitalism were met by a full expulsion of capitalism from the political realm. In the years following 2008, this hegemony faltered as governments proved unable or unwilling to manage the fallout of the economic crisis.

In *Legitimation Crisis*, Habermas wrote that when the contradictions of the prevailing order are exposed, causing its legitimacy to evaporate, "the latent violence [*Gewalt* (translation amended)] embedded in the system of institutions is released," inviting an "expansion of the scope for participation" (Habermas 1975, 96). Conditions appear to (temporarily) resemble that of a "substantive democracy" able to "bring to consciousness the contradiction" contained in the existing social order, opening the horizon to societal progress (Habermas 1975, 36). Years later, in *Between Facts and Norms*, Habermas likewise describes crisis consciousness as periods of public "problematization" wherein "the attention span of the citizenry enlarges" in "an intensified search for solutions" (Habermas 1996, 357). Even in a "power-ridden" public sphere dominated by corporate mass media, it should remain possible *in principle* for a galvanized citizenry to successfully countermand a critically exposed order of hegemony.

But there is another possibility—namely, that the post-democratic public realm proves itself inhospitable to the collective processing of crisis consciousness. As Fraser observes, the conversion of a legitimation crisis into a successful overturning and replacement of prevailing hegemonic order with a more equitable and democratic order requires the successful organization and mobilization of "counter-hegemony," one that reflects a broad coalition of identity and class interests (Fraser 2015, 172–3; Fraser and Jaeggi 2018, 216–7). But such a movement requires crisis-conscious actors to be able to reconcile their various understandings and claims across identities and classes. They must be able to mobilize around collective understandings of the crisis; its causes, character, magnitude, and effects; the social norms, values, and capabilities it threatens; and what an adequate response looks like. A political public sphere beholden to corporate interests that largely echoes the issue-agendas of a cartelized political system may prove ill-equipped if not hostile to this task. Elites may not want to relinquish the ability to direct the public narrative, and they may even have interests of their own to pursue in the midst of the crisis. Meanwhile, mass media may indirectly or overtly marginalize efforts to propagate counterhegemonic understandings or alternative strategies. A media atmosphere constructed around sound-bites and "politainment" may inhibit efforts to gain broad support for new ideas and critiques, while political journalists may join elites in casting them as fringe, radical, or otherwise lacking in seriousness.

If welfare-state capitalism had a propensity to find itself faced with "crises of crisis management" (Offe 1984 [1973]), financialized capitalism finds itself exposed to *crises of crisis consciousness*. This need not mean that the public is left unaware of the "latent violence" behind the system; on the contrary, citizens may have strong intuitions that their representatives are acting in interests other than those of their constituencies. But while the hegemony of the establishment may be faltering, the citizenry is hampered in mobilizing an effective counter-hegemony. Deprived of the sense of positive freedom necessary to redeem their sense of crisis in the public realm, citizens may be led to reject the public realm altogether. In the face of elite corruption and hypocrisy, appeals to "unity" or "civility" sound increasingly self-serving; in the face of a closed-off and intransigent mass media, claims of "fake news" or *Lügenpresse* in this context carry a certain resonance. Lacking an effective public sphere within which to assess claims, justify knowledge, or synthesize judgments, citizens may be drawn to act on prejudice, seek alternative fora, or embrace conspiracy theories, while offensiveness to established pieties becomes the primary standard for evaluating authentic challenges to the status quo. The public realm fragments and the political atmosphere becomes fertile for exploitation by charismatic figures and demagogues. This scenario is not by itself sufficient to *cause* illiberal populism to take root, but it fosters an environment in which the appeal of indiscriminate anti-elitism, simplistic promises, or finding scapegoatable "others" can more easily take hold.

Conclusion

One of Habermas's core theses was that legitimation crises manifest themselves differently under different formations of capitalism. Under the liberal-competitive capitalism of the 19th century, economic crises remained the immediate source of legitimation crises in the form of class conflict, while postwar welfare-state capitalism pushed the contradictions of the capitalist system into the administrative and cultural realms (Habermas 1975, 29–30, 68–75, 92–94). The aforementioned reflections suggest that, under 21st-century financialized capitalism, the character of legitimation crisis transforms yet again, by pushing the contradictions into the political sphere. As we have seen, the contradiction of financialized capitalism consists in the fact that the demands of sustaining legitimacy for a political order, which claims ability to manage economic crises while dismantling the regulatory capacities to actually do so, are such that hegemony can only be maintained via an increasingly desiccated public realm that allows minimal scrutiny and the formulation of no alternatives. In the process, it deprives citizens of the capacity to discursively come to terms with the consequences of major crisis and participate in the formulation of solutions, leaving them with a Frommian "sense of insignificance and powerlessness" that invites exploitation by charismatic leaders with illiberal agendas. The present "crisis of liberal democracy" is then a consequence of a propensity in financialized capitalism to exacerbate the crises it generates for itself—a propensity which begins, ironically, with the hollowing out of liberal democracy by financialized capitalism.

Bibliography

Adorno, Theodor W. 2003 [1968]. "Late Capitalism or Industrial Society?" In *Can One Live after Auschwitz?*, edited by Rolf Tiedemann, 111–25. Stanford, CA: Stanford University Press.

Anderson, Elizabeth. 2017. *Private Government*. Princeton, NJ: Princeton University Press.Arendt, Hannah. 1958. *The Human Condition*. Chicago, IL: University of Chicago Press.

Azmanova, Albena. 2014a. "The 'Crisis of Capitalism' and the State—More Powerful, Less Responsible, Invariably Legitimate." In *Semantics of Statebuilding: Language, Meanings, and Sovereignty*, edited by Nicolas Lemay-Hébert, Nicholas Onuf Vojin Rakić, and Petar Bojanić, 150–62. London: Routledge.

Azmanova, Albena. 2014b. "Crisis? Capitalism is Doing Very Well. How Is Critical Theory?," *Constellations* 21(3): 351–65.

Azmanova, Albena. 2015. "The Crisis of the Crisis of Capitalism," unpublished manuscript. Accessed 4 August, 2017 at https://www.academia.edu/11034347/The_Crisis_of_the_Crisis_of_Capitalism.

Boltanski, Luc, and Ève Chiapello. 2007. *The New Spirit of Capitalism*. London: Verso.

Brandom, Robert B. 1994. *Making It Explicit*. Cambridge, MA: Harvard University Press.

Cordero, Rodrigo. 2014. "Crisis and Critique in Jürgen Habermas's Social Theory." *European Journal of Social Theory* 17(4): 497–515.

Crouch, Colin. 2004. *Post-Democracy*. Cambridge: Polity.

Crouch, Colin. 2011. *The Strange Non-Death of Neoliberalism*. Cambridge: Polity.

Esping-Andersen, Gøsta. 1990. *The Three Worlds of Welfare Capitalism*. Princeton, NJ: Princeton University Press.

Foucault, Michel. 1977. *Discipline and Punish*. New York, NY: Vintage Books.

Foucault, Michel. 1991. *The Foucault Effect: Studies in Governmentality*, edited by Graham Burchell, Colin Gordon, and Peter Miller. Chicago, IL: University of Chicago Press.

Fraser, Nancy. 1997. *Justice Interruptus: Critical Reflections on the "Postsocialist" Condition*. New York, NY: Routledge.

Fraser, Nancy. 2015. "Legitimation Crisis? On the Political Contradictions of Financialized Capitalism." *Critical Historical Studies* 2(2): 157–89.

Fraser, Nancy. 2016. "Contradictions of Capital and Care." *New Left Review* 100: 99–117.

Fraser, Nancy. 2017. "From Progressive Neoliberalism to Trump—and Beyond." *American Affairs* 1(4): 46–64.

Fraser, Nancy. 2019. "Die Krise der Demokratie: Über politische Widersprüche des Finanzmarktkapitalismus jenseits des Politizismus." In *Was stimmt nicht mit der Demokratie?*, edited by Hanna Ketterer and Karina Becker, 77–99. Berlin: Suhrkamp.

Fraser, Nancy, and Rahel Jaeggi. 2018. *Capitalism: A Conversation in Critical Theory*. Cambridge: Polity.

Fromm, Erich. 1969 [1941]. *Escape from Freedom*. New York, NY: Henry Holt.

Gilbert, Andrew Simon. 2019. *The Crisis Paradigm: Description and Prescription in Social and Political Theory*. Cham: Palgrave Macmillan.

Gramsci, Antonio. 1971. *Selections from the Prison Notebooks*. New York, NY: International Publishers.

Habermas, Jürgen. 1973. "What Does a Crisis Mean Today? Legitimation Problems in Late Capitalism." *Social Research* 40(4): 643–67.

Habermas, Jürgen. 1975. *Legitimation Crisis*. Boston, MA: Beacon Press.

Habermas, Jürgen. 1987a. *The Theory of Communicative Action, Volume II: Lifeworld and System*. Boston, MA: Beacon Press.

Habermas, Jürgen. 1987b. *The Philosophical Discourse of Modernity*. Cambridge, MA: MIT Press.

Habermas, Jürgen. 1996. *Between Facts and Norms*. Cambridge, MA: MIT Press.

Habermas, Jürgen. 2015. "Democracy or Capitalism? On the Abject Spectacle of a Capitalistic World Society Fragmented along National Lines." In *The Lure of Technocracy*, translated by Ciaran Cronin, 85–102. Cambridge: Polity.

Ibsen, Malte Frøslee. 2019. "The Populist Conjuncture: Legitimation Crisis in the Age of Globalized Capitalism." *Political Studies* 67(3): 795–811.

Inglehart, Roland. 1977. *The Silent Revolution: Changing Values and Political Styles among Western Publics*. Princeton, NJ: Princeton University Press.

Katz, Richard S., and Peter Mair. 2009. "The Cartel Party Thesis: A Restatement." *Perspectives on Politics* 7(4): 753–66.

Kirchheimer, Otto. 1966. "The Transformation of the Western European Party System." In *Political Parties and Political Development*, edited by Joseph LaPalombara and Myron Weiner, 177–200. Princeton, NJ: Princeton University Press.

Koselleck, Reinhart. 1988 [1959]. *Critique and Crisis: The Pathogenesis of Modern Society* Cambridge, MA: MIT Press.

Koselleck, Reinhart. 2006 [1982]. "Crisis." *Journal of the History of Ideas* 67(2): 357–400.

Lebow, David. 2019. "Trumpism and the Dialectic of Neoliberal Reason." *Perspectives on Politics* 17(2): 380–98.

Lipset, Seymour Martin and Stein Rokkan. 1967. "Cleavage Structures, Party Systems, and Voter Alignments: An Introduction." In *Party Alignments and Voter Systems: Cross-National Perspectives*, edited by Seymour M. Lipset and Stein Rokkan, 1–64. Glencoe: The Free Press.

Marcuse, Herbert. 2002 [1964]. *One-Dimensional Man*. London: Routledge.

Milstein, Brian. 2015. "Thinking Politically about Crisis: A Pragmatist Perspective." *European Journal of Political Theory* 14(2): 141–60.

Milstein, Brian. 2019. "Über das Ergänzungsverhältnis von Krisenbewusstsein und Demokratie: Eine Anmerkung zum politischen Widerspruch des Kapitalismus." In *Was stimmt nicht mit der Demokratie?*, edited by Hanna Ketterer and Karina Becker, 111–20. Berlin: Suhrkamp.

Neumann, Sigmund. 1956. *Modern Party Politics*. Chicago, IL: University of Chicago Press.

Offe, Claus. 1984 [1973]. "'Crises of Crisis Management': Elements of a Political Crisis Theory." In *Contradictions of the Welfare State*, edited by John Keane, 35–64. London: Hutchinson.

Peirce, C. S. 2006 [1878]. "How to Make Our Ideas Clear." In *Pragmatism, Old & New*, edited by Susan Haack and Robert Lane, 127–50. Amherst, NY: Prometheus Books.

Roitman, Janet. 2014. *Anti-Crisis*. Durham, NC: Duke University Press.

Rousseau, Jean-Jacques. 1987 [1762]. *On the Social Contract*. In *Basic Political Writings*, trans. and edited by Donald A. Cress, 139–227. Indianapolis, IN: Hackett.

Streeck, Wolfgang. 2014. *Buying Time: The Delayed Crisis of Democratic Capitalism*. London: Verso.

Streeck, Wolfgang. 2016. *How Will Capitalism End? Essays on a Failing System*. London: Verso.

Thompson, John B. 2012. "The Metamorphosis of a Crisis." In *Aftermath: The Cultures of the Economic Crisis*, edited by Manuel Castells, João Caraça, and Gustavo Cardoso, 59–81. Oxford: Oxford University Press.

Varoufakis, Yanis. 2016. "Why We Must Save the EU." *The Guardian*, April 5. www.theguardian.com/world/2016/apr/05/yanis-varoufakis-why-we-must-save-the-eu.

3

ILLIBERAL DEMOCRACY AND THE STRUGGLE ON THE RIGHT

Marc F. Plattner

Introduction[1]

One of the biggest challenges to democracy today is posed by the dramatic change in the political-party landscape, especially in Europe but in some other parts of the world as well. Attention understandably has focused on the rise of a variety of populist candidates and movements, but what has enabled their rise is the drastic decline in support for the parties that had long dominated the political scene. Without grossly exaggerating, one can say that for decades, the modal configuration of Western political systems has featured strong center-left and center-right parties or coalitions that support the basic principles and institutions of liberal democracy but compete with each other in regard to a variety of specific issues within this larger framework. The primary cleavage separating these parties has been economic, with center-left parties typically favoring more government spending and allying themselves with trade unions, and center-right parties leaning toward more friendliness to the private sector and market-oriented policies. These days, however, virtually every new round of elections indicates that this longstanding pattern of dominance by the center-left and center-right is losing its hold.

Although the United States and Britain, with their first-past-the-post electoral systems, have so far resisted this trend, it can be observed in numerous countries in Europe and Latin America. In France's 2017 elections, both the Socialists and the center-right Republicans failed to make the presidential runoff, and the recently formed centrist "En Marche" movement of newly elected president Emmanuel Macron won an absolute majority in the National Assembly. In Germany, both the Christian Democratic Union and the Social Democrats have been hemorrhaging support, a trend that accelerated in elections at the state level in Bavaria and elsewhere in 2018, and that has made the far-right Alternative for Germany the third-largest party in the Bundestag. In Italy's 2018 elections, the center-right and the center-left each received less than a fifth of the votes, leading to a coalition government between two populist formations, the Five Star Movement and the Northern League (running under the less regional-sounding label of just "Lega").

Similar results have been seen in Latin America. In Brazil, for example, the weakening of the Workers' Party and the implosion of the center-right led to the 2018 presidential victory of far-right candidate Jair Bolsonaro. In Costa Rica, meanwhile, neither of the two long-dominant parties (the National Liberation Party and the Social Christian Unity Party) made the 2018 presidential runoff, and for the first time, they account between them for fewer than half the seats in the Legislative Assembly.

Overall, it is the parties of the center-left (mostly socialist or social-democratic) that have been experiencing the steepest decline, and there are signs that the commitment to liberal democracy of some emerging forces on the left is questionable. But at the moment, I believe the graver threat to liberal democracy is that it will wind up being abandoned by substantial segments of the right. I am not referring here to small extremist groups such as the "alt-right" in the United States, which have always been present in one form or another, but have previously never been able to attain real electoral significance. Instead, I am concerned with the threat that mainstream center-right parties will be captured by tendencies that are indifferent or even hostile to liberal democracy. I believe that the struggle of these tendencies to win over the right will be the most consequential development affecting the future of democracy in the period ahead. And it increasingly appears that this battle will be fought out not only in the arena of party competition but also in the realm of political thought.

The Battle over Terminology

Since much of the coming contest on the right will be a battle over terminology, let me begin by offering brief and generally accepted definitions of the key terms at issue. "Liberal democracy" is the most common way of labeling the form of government that has long prevailed in the United States and Western Europe, and that, since the mid-1970s, many countries throughout the world have tried to establish. It combines two constituent elements that often go together and yet are sometimes in tension with each other—a democratic element and a liberal element.

Each of those words has a long and complex history, and each has taken on different meanings in different eras and places. "Democracy" is derived from a Greek word meaning rule by the people, while "liberal" and "liberalism" derive from a Latin word meaning free. Today, however, democracy is often used as shorthand for liberal democracy and thus is also thought to incorporate the protection of individual freedom. Consequently, features such as the rule of law and the freedoms of speech, assembly, religion, and the press, though more properly categorized as liberal, are often regarded as hallmarks of democracy.

Further confusion stems from the fact that the term liberalism, in addition to the broad sense conveyed by the expression liberal democracy (or liberal education, meaning literally the education befitting a free person), is also used in a more narrowly political sense: in the United States, "liberalism" denotes support for an activist government and is typically regarded as the opposite of conservatism. To compound the confusion, in Europe, the term liberal has been applied to parties that support the free market and a more limited role for government. Moreover, especially outside the United States, figures on the left pin the label of "neoliberalism" on those they regard as too friendly to market capitalism.

Democracy and liberalism may be understood as addressing two different questions: democracy is an answer to the question of who rules. It requires that the people be sovereign. If they do not rule directly, as they did in the ancient Greek polis, they must at least be able to choose their representatives in free and fair elections. Liberalism, by contrast, prescribes not how rulers are chosen but what the limits to their power are once they are in office. These limits, which are ultimately designed to protect the rights of the individual, demand the rule of law and are usually set forth in a written constitution (hence, "constitutional democracy" sometimes serves as an alternative term for liberal democracy).

Although democracy was typically conjoined with liberalism in the 20th-century West, the two are not inseparably linked. Premodern democracies were not liberal, and historically, there have been liberal societies (some European constitutional monarchies in the 19th century and Hong Kong under British rule in the 20th) that were not governed democratically. The fact that liberalism and democracy do not inevitably go together is reflected in the current debate about illiberal democracy.

The central figure in this debate is Hungary's Prime Minister Viktor Orbán, who is arguably the most influential figure today on the European right. By seeking to embrace democracy and at the same time to jettison liberalism, Orbán is blazing a trail that he hopes to lure others on the right to follow. It is useful to review the strange history of the term "illiberal democracy" in order to understand how Orbán has tried to wield it for his own purposes.

The Strange History of "Illiberal Democracy"

The distinction between the liberal and the democratic aspects of liberal democracy has long been a topic of scholarly discussion, but the term "illiberal democracy" is not so old. It was first introduced by Fareed Zakaria (1997), in an influential article that he wrote for *Foreign Affairs*. Zakaria argued that in the past virtually all modern democracies were liberal democracies. In fact, in most

Western democracies, a commitment to constitutionalism, the rule of law, and individual rights had preceded the broadening of the franchise to encompass universal suffrage. Thus, the world's leading democratic regimes had been liberal before they became democratic.

But, Zakaria argued, as a result of the "third wave" of democratization that began in the mid-1970s, democracy in the form of free elections spread to countries that wholly lacked a liberal tradition. The result was the emergence of many regimes that, although they had adopted the democratic mechanism of elections, were not liberal and hence could not be considered genuine liberal democracies. The policy implication that Zakaria drew from his analysis was that prematurely introducing elections in such countries would actually reduce the chances of their evolving into liberal democracies. The path through "liberal autocracy," he suggested, might be a surer route than the path through illiberal democracy for reaching the ultimate goal of liberal democracy.

Two key aspects of Zakaria's essay are worth emphasizing here. First, he agreed that liberal democracy was the most desirable political regime—the debate that his essay sought to ignite was over the most effective way of achieving this ultimate goal. Second, Zakaria made it clear that he regarded a liberal political order as an unmixed good; by contrast, democracy, the choosing of political leaders via free elections, was good only if it fostered and was accompanied by liberalism.

It is a sign of the time at which the essay was written that almost no critics objected to the privileged status that Zakaria assigned to liberalism. During the years preceding 1989, liberalism and free markets had already experienced a remarkable intellectual and political revival. The demise of European communism accelerated a growing global consensus that constitutionalism, the rule of law, the protection of individual and minority rights, and even market economies were universally desirable, even if they were not easily achievable in countries with long histories of authoritarian rule.

In two articles I wrote at the time in response to Zakaria (Plattner 1998, 1999), I sought to explain why liberalism is unlikely to survive in the contemporary world unless accompanied by democracy. I noted that the exaltation of liberalism had been accompanied by "a clear weakening of the view that popular majorities should play a more active role in deciding on governmental policies" (Plattner 1999, 131). This heightened suspicion of popular majorities was reflected in the global spread of judicial review and the rise of independent agencies (such as central banks) explicitly intended to be insulated from the branches of government most responsive to popular sentiment. As I concluded then, "the popularity of the attack on illiberal democracy may itself be regarded as a sign of the triumph of liberalism" (Plattner 1999, 132).

There was no question that Zakaria intended "illiberal democracy" to be a term of disparagement. The term designated countries that had initiated a transition away from authoritarian rule and had adopted free elections, but had failed to build the liberal institutions that could guarantee individual rights. To be no more than an "illiberal democracy" was a mark of failure. It was not a label that any regime sought, much less a banner that national leaders would proudly fly.

Viktor Orbán Transforms the Debate

By the 2010s, however, the global landscape had changed. Following the 2008 financial crisis, market economies were no longer in such high repute, and the travails of Western democracies, together with the rise of China, were attenuating the appeal of liberalism. The "liberal consensus" that had prevailed in Central Europe was visibly weakening already, as had been demonstrated by the 2005–07 first tour in power (as part of a coalition government) of the Law and Justice (PiS) party in Poland and then by the sweeping triumph of Orbán's Fidesz party in Hungary in 2010. A formerly center-left formation that had moved to the right, Fidesz won 53% of the vote, but that was enough to give it a two-thirds majority in parliament, enabling it to radically revise Hungary's constitution. Fidesz's numerous and far-reaching changes to the basic law had the effect of weakening checks on majority rule and entrenching Fidesz's control of the courts, other independent agencies, and the media.

In July 2012, the *Journal of Democracy* published a set of articles analyzing "Hungary's Illiberal Turn." Although Orbán's party was initially inclined to counter charges that it was governing in an illiberal fashion, at some point, Orbán decided to accept (and later even to embrace) the idea that Fidesz had turned against liberalism. In a speech he delivered in July 2014 at an annual summer program held at Bãile Tunad in a part of Romania that has long had a large ethnic-Hungarian population, Orbán offered the first positive endorsement of illiberal democracy of which I am aware.[2]

Although his remarks at the time seemed shocking coming from the leader of an EU member state, Orbán's language was somewhat cautious—according to the official English translation of his speech, he never actually used the precise phrase "illiberal democracy." Nonetheless, he surely implied that this was the concept he was endorsing. Citing the economic success of Singapore, China, India, Russia, and Turkey under "systems that are not Western, not liberal, not liberal democracies and perhaps not even democracies," he went on to state that "a democracy does not necessarily have to be liberal. Just because a state is not liberal, it can still be a democracy." And he added that "the new state that we are constructing in Hungary is an illiberal state, a non-liberal state." Despite his seeming reluctance to adopt the phrase "illiberal democracy," Orbán openly stated that his intent was to break with "dogmas and ideologies that have been adopted by the West," and there was little doubt about the antiliberal direction in which his thought was heading.

In the ensuing years, especially with the global surge of populism, the theme of illiberal democracy has received growing attention. Populism, after all, is an outlook that emphatically claims to be democratic and that relies for its legitimacy on elections as expressions of the popular will. Yet when populists come to power, they tend to infringe upon the rule of law, the independence of the courts and the media, and the rights of individuals and minorities, as has been the case in Hungary. Moreover, these illiberal aspects of populism had begun to surface not just in countries lacking a liberal tradition but even in longstanding Western democracies.

As a result, discussions of illiberal democracy flourished anew among political theorists. I will have more to say about this in the concluding section of this chapter, focusing on political thinkers on the right. Here, I note that the relationship between liberalism and democracy has also recently been addressed by theorists on the center-left (see, among others: Galston 2018a, 2018b; Mounk 2018a, 2018b). Jan-Werner Müller (2016, 56) offers a critique of the "thoughtless invocation of 'illiberal democracy'" by opponents of Orbán; Jeffrey C. Isaac (2017) offers a counterargument in his review of Muller's book. In my view, "illiberal democracy" is a reasonable term for political scientists to use to describe regimes whose rulers win genuine elections but then violate liberal freedoms. I doubt, however, that illiberal democracy is a stable regime form. Although it can move back toward liberal democracy (as appears to be happening in Ecuador), it often becomes a way-station for authoritarianism, as it clearly has been in Russia, Venezuela, and Turkey.

The next step in Orbán's embrace of "illiberal democracy" came on July 28, 2018, when, at the same venue where he gave his 2014 speech, Orbán emphatically and unequivocally expressed his support for illiberal democracy. He contended, first, that "there is an alternative to liberal democracy: it is called Christian democracy." But he underlined that Christian democracy as he understands it "is not about defending religious articles of faith." Instead, it seeks to protect "the ways of life springing from Christian culture." And this, he added, means defending "human dignity, the family and the nation."[3]

Orbán then went on to warn his listeners to avoid an "intellectual trap"—namely, "the claim that Christian democracy can also, in fact, be liberal." To accept this argument, he told his partisans, is tantamount to surrendering in the battle of ideas. Therefore, he urged his listeners, "Let us confidently declare that Christian democracy is not liberal. Liberal democracy is liberal, while Christian democracy is, by definition, not liberal: it is, if you like, illiberal."

Why does Orbán insist that his brand of "Christian democracy" cannot be liberal? He addresses this question by citing three key issues on which the two differ: (1) liberal democracy favors multiculturalism, while Christian democracy "gives priority to Christian culture"; (2) liberal democracy "is pro-immigration, while Christian democracy is anti-immigration"; and

(3) liberal democracy "sides with adaptable family models" rather than the Christian family model. With respect to each of these three issues, Orbán emphatically states that the Christian view can be categorized as an "illiberal concept."

What is Orbán's purpose in drawing such a sharp and unbridgeable distinction between liberal democracy and Christian democracy? And why is he so concerned with refuting the view that Christian democracy can also be liberal—a claim that would seem to be borne out by the crucial contribution that Christian Democratic parties have made to liberal democracy in Europe since the end of World War II?

Part of the answer is broadly ideological. Orbán wishes to make support for liberal democracy seem inseparable from support for multiculturalism, open immigration policies, and nontraditional family structures such as gay marriage. Historically, of course, this has not typically been the case. Until the last half-century, many liberal democracies tended to be fairly strict in terms of family law. Apart from settler countries such as the United States, Canada, and Australia, they were not very welcoming toward immigrants, and the countries that did accept large-scale immigration tended to favor assimilationist rather than multicultural approaches to integrating newcomers.

It is true that in most democratic countries today there is considerable support, especially on the left, for accepting multiculturalism, high rates of immigration, and gay marriage. In some places, such policies now are backed by popular national majorities and have been enacted into law. At the same time, sizeable portions of the voting public take a different view, even among those who remain firm adherents of liberal democracy.

In the past, it was generally accepted that citizens may take opposing views on these matters without ceasing to be good liberal democrats, and that policies regarding such controversial issues should be decided on the basis of a free and open political process. Orbán, however, is attempting to convince Europeans who find themselves on the conservative side of these social issues that they are being ill-treated and disrespected in contemporary liberal democracies. What is more, he warns them that they are in danger of losing out demographically and ideologically in the future. He seeks to equate the term liberal as it is used in the phrase "liberal democracy" with the term liberal as it is used to characterize the left side of the political spectrum in the United States—that is, to denote "progressives" as opposed to "conservatives." Orbán's effort to blur these two different meanings of liberalism gains some purchase from the fact that the "Brussels elites" he is so fond of attacking tend to hold views close to those of United States liberals on social and cultural issues.

The attempt to identify liberal democracy as such with United States-style progressivism also fits neatly with Orbán's efforts to demonize Hungarian-born United States billionaire George Soros. Soros is a strong supporter of liberal democracy but also of United States-style political liberalism. Thus, at the same time that his philanthropies make generous grants to organizations working on behalf of freedom and against authoritarianism around the world, they are also among the largest funders of the United States Democratic Party and of nongovernmental organizations on the left.

The Recent Electoral Battle in Europe

Orbán seeks to use the dissatisfaction of conservatives with "liberal" social and cultural policies to pry them away from their fundamental commitment to liberal democracy. But his motives are also more narrowly partisan, as he candidly revealed both in his July 28 speech and in an earlier speech delivered on June 16 at a conference honoring the memory of Helmut Kohl, the Christian Democrat who served as German chancellor from 1982 to 1998.[4] Orbán made it clear that his goal is to take over the mainstream European right and to shape its future direction.

In his memorial address for Kohl, who died in 2017, Orbán states that "it would be easy" to establish a new far-right grouping of European parties drawn from those opposing immigration. But he advocates resisting this "temptation" and opting instead to stick with and to renew the European People's Party (EPP). This is the center-right grouping that has long had the largest bloc in the European Parliament and that has been home to Fidesz since Kohl invited it to join in 2000. The EPP, a strongly pro-EU formation with deep Christian Democratic roots, has produced within its ranks some of the EU's top leaders.

Within the EPP, the continuing membership of Fidesz has been a source of great controversy, with some EPP members calling for its expulsion in light of the illiberal policies and rhetoric that it has adopted. Orbán so far has successfully defended Fidesz against these attempts, but the two speeches cited above suggested that he was preparing to go on the offensive and try to redirect the EPP's orientation.

In his Kohl memorial speech, Orbán characterized the EPP's current—and, in his view, failing—strategy as one of forming an "antipopulist front" that seeks to work together with all the traditional European parties (from Communists and Greens to social democrats, liberals, and Christian Democrats) to oppose the "emerging new parties" (that is, the populists). Instead, Orbán advocates the strategy that he says has been successfully followed by the parties in power in Austria and Hungary—in effect, borrowing from the playbook of their far-right competitors in addressing issues such as immigration.

Orbán characterizes Fidesz as occupying the right wing of the EPP, comparing its situation to that of the Bavarian Christian Social Union in relation to German chancellor Angela Merkel's Christian Democratic Union. Orbán's goal is for Fidesz to lead a right-wing takeover of the EPP and to steer it toward Fidesz-style policies at the European level. What is more, in his speech on July 28, 2018, he recommended a plan of action to his followers: to "concentrate all our efforts on the 2019 European Parliament elections."

Orbán acknowledges that elections for the European Parliament generally are not taken seriously by voters, who often cast their ballots, if they turn out to vote at all, on the basis of national political issues rather than Europe-wide concerns. The May 2019 contest, Orbán asserted, would be different for two reasons—the growing right-wing sentiment in Europe and the rise of immigration as an issue that can motivate voters across the EU. In short, Orbán's calculation was that the composition of the European Parliament could be significantly altered by mobilizing anti-immigration sentiment. He hoped that this would lead to a new balance of forces within and around the EPP, with rightist tendencies and parties such as Fidesz gaining greatly expanded influence, as well as to a new composition of the EU leadership, with European ruling elites (whom Orbán calls "liberal" but who prominently include moderate Christian Democrats) giving way to a new generation of populist leaders like himself.

Hungary on Trial

In September 2018, Orbán's project suffered an apparent setback when the European Parliament narrowly achieved the two-thirds majority needed to initiate so-called Article 7 proceedings against Hungary. These proceedings invoke a provision in the Treaty on European Union that provides for disciplinary action against a member state when it has been found to present a "clear risk of a serious breach" of EU values.

It is also noteworthy that Fidesz failed to win majority support within the EPP; those EPP members of parliament who were present (the EPP then controlled 219 seats in the 750-member body) approved the report charging Hungary with breaching EU values by a vote of 114 to 57 (with 28 abstentions). In an additional setback for Orbán, the vote against Hungary was backed by some of his previous key supporters, including Austrian chancellor Sebastian Kurz and Bavarian politician Manfred Weber, the leader of the EPP in the European Parliament.

The document that the parliamentarians approved was compiled by rapporteur Judith Sargentini, a Dutch MEP from the GreenLeft party. In her report, Sargentini (2018) alleges a very wide range of violations of EU values by the Fidesz government. Some of these strike at the most basic components of liberal democracy, including the independence of the judiciary and the freedoms of expression and religion. Others, however, stray into areas of social and cultural policy (for example, family law, immigration policy, the extent of welfare benefits) whose relationship to liberal-democratic principles is by no means obvious. As policy analyst Dalibor Rohac (2018) persuasively argues, the report mixes "two issues, social conservatism and authoritarianism," in a way that is likely to undermine the EU's credibility among conservatives and to divide the opposition to Hungary's genuinely illiberal policies.

The approval of Sargentini's report launched a process that is still ongoing. In principle, this process could result in Hungary having its EU voting rights suspended, but a later stage of the proceedings will require unanimity among the member states, and PiS-governed Poland has already indicated that it will not give its approval. In any case, the inquiry is not likely to produce results anytime soon.

At the EPP Congress held in Helsinki in early November 2018, the delegates approved some "emergency resolutions" intended to make Fidesz commit itself to supporting European values. The first of these resolutions, on "Protecting EU Values and Safeguarding Democracy," includes strong endorsements of democracy, the rule of law, and individual freedom, but the word liberal occurs only once (in the phrase "liberal democracy") in a historical reference in the preamble. The fourth resolution (on "A Prosperous and Secure Europe") states that "EU taxpayers' money should not be spent in countries where fundamental EU values and the rule of law are not respected."[5] As Gerardo Fortuna (2018) reported, this sentence initially contained the words "liberal democracy" instead of "the rule of law," and this change was made at the request of Fidesz. So while Orbán felt compelled to support these resolutions, he did manage to avoid openly endorsing liberal democracy.

In his July 28, 2018 speech, Orban boasted, "The opportunity is here. Next May we can wave goodbye … to liberal democracy and the liberal non-democratic system that has been built on its foundations." The May 2019 elections for the European Parliament, however, did not realize Orban's hopes. Although populist parties made gains and the traditional center-right lost some support, the latter remains dominant within the EU. In March 2019, Fidesz was suspended from the EPP, but it was not expelled. Since then, many EPP member parties have continued to push for the expulsion of Fidesz, but as of April 2020 they had not succeeded in reaching their goal. So the struggle for control of the center-right remains at the heart of European political competition, both within the EU and within national parliaments.

The Conflict in the Realm of Political Theory

Signs of the emerging partisan and ideological struggle over the future of the center-right are also evident in some recent writings by political theorists identified with the conservative side of the political spectrum. One prominent example is Ryszard Legutko. A professor of political theory at Jagiellonian University in Kraków and a onetime member of Solidarity, Legutko has also been active in current Polish politics, having served as minister of education and as an elected senator, both on behalf of PiS. Currently, he is a member of the European Parliament, where he is the vice-president of the European Conservatives and Reformists Group.

Legutko (2016) is, to say the least, deeply disappointed in Poland's transition to liberal democracy. The burden of his book is to show the many respects in which the reign of liberal democracy in Poland resembles the preceding reign of communism. (He does grudgingly acknowledge that there are also differences between the two, especially with respect to individual freedoms.) Chief among the similarities he cites is that both doctrines favor the ideas of "modernization" and progress. He also makes the dubious claim that liberal democracy is animated by the same totalizing spirit as communism, citing as evidence various instances of groupthink and political correctness. Although he suggests that these aspects of liberal democracy have worsened markedly since it became infected with the liberationist ethos of the 1960s, his attack is directed not against the recent decline or the present condition of liberal democracy but against both liberalism and democracy as such. And his withering criticism does not spare those "classical liberals" (such as F.A. Hayek) who are heroes to much of the right.

This has not prevented many conservatives from praising his book. Its favorable reception among United States conservatives may have been aided by the fact that it carries a Foreword by the distinguished British journalist John O'Sullivan, a former speechwriter and advisor to Margaret Thatcher who has also served as editor of *National Review* and other United States-based conservative publications. Yet it is doubtful whether O'Sullivan's interpretation of the book accurately reflects Legutko's own understanding. In O'Sullivan's view, Legutko is writing about the "transformation" of liberal democracy in recent decades: "The regime described here by Legutko," O'Sullivan remarks in his Foreword,

> is not liberal democracy as it was understood by, say, Winston Churchill or FDR or John F. Kennedy or Ronald Reagan. That was essentially majoritarian democracy resting on constitutional liberal guarantees of free speech, free association, free media, and other liberties.
>
> *(Legutko 2016, vi)*

Indeed, O'Sullivan goes on to say that Legutko "hyphenates liberal-democratic as an adjective in the book; maybe he should do the same with the noun 'liberal-democracy' to distinguish it from the liberal democracy of the nineteenth and twentieth centuries" (Legutko 2016, vi–vii). But I find no evidence in the book that Legutko himself sees his aim to be that of restoring liberal democracy to the healthier condition that it enjoyed in previous centuries. I think he wants it to be superseded by other kinds of governments and societies, presumably including those that PiS and its leader Jarosław Kaczyński are trying to build in Poland.

Patrick Deneen (2018) has recently published a book in the spirit of Legutko's work. Unlike Legutko's unmistakably European book, Deneen's is American through and through—he barely even mentions any other countries in the contemporary world. Indeed, in a mostly laudatory review of Deneen's book, Legutko (2018, 2) suggests that there is something distinctively American in Deneen's "misplaced hope" that democracy can offer a solution to the problem posed by liberalism. While Deneen's title and the conservative slant of his previous writings might lead readers to expect that his critique is primarily directed at the left in the United States, Deneen (2018, 18) makes it clear that he is going after a bigger target. He calls contemporary progressivism and conservatism ("classical liberalism") two sides of "the same counterfeit coin," united by the fact that both accept the fundamental principles of the broader liberal tradition. The failure that Deneen's book indicts is that of liberal democracy as such.

Since the liberal tradition is so deeply rooted in the history and politics of the United States, it has typically been revered by American conservatives. An American thinker with a conservative disposition is naturally drawn to honor the accomplishments of the country's Founding Fathers. Deneen, however, does not hesitate to attack the work and the thought of the Founders, including the United States Constitution and the Federalist. Deneen (2018, 46–50) is quite explicit in his opposition to the entire liberal tradition, and especially its seminal thinker, John Locke. Yet after all his efforts to demolish the foundations of liberalism, Deneen does not feel obliged to put forward an alternative theory. Instead, his occasionally eloquent jeremiad against liberalism weakly concludes with the following tepid and airy recommendations:

> What we need today are practices fostered in local settings, focused on the creation of new and viable cultures, economics grounded in virtuosity within households, and the creation of civic polis [sic] life. Not a better theory but better practices.

Nonetheless, his book not only has been given a sympathetic reception in many conservative quarters but also has been prominently and respectfully discussed in high-profile publications in the United States (Drochon 2018, Szalai 2018; for a critical review, see Plattner 2018).

Yoram Hazony (2018) is the author of *The Virtue of Nationalism,* a book that has attracted wide attention among conservative thinkers. As its title suggests, it offers a spirited defense of nationalism, which Hazony (2018, 3) characterizes as "a principled standpoint that regards the world as governed best when nations are able to chart their own independent course, cultivating their own traditions and pursuing their own interests without interference." Hazony (2018, 3) labels the opposing viewpoint as "imperialism, which seeks to bring peace and prosperity to the world by uniting mankind, as much as possible, under a single political regime." The contemporary examples he gives of such imperial projects are the European Union and the post-Cold War effort of the United States to create a "world order" based upon its own hegemony.

Hazony's philosophical-historical account claims to find a solid foundation for a nationalist order in what he calls the "Protestant construction" of the political world that was built in the 17th century and, he argues, was deeply influenced by the Hebrew Bible. Hazony (2018, 29–36) insists that this is something wholly different from the "liberal construction," whose principal architect is John Locke; he devotes an entire brief chapter to a simplistic analysis of Locke's political thought intended to show its "radical deficiency" (Hazony 2018, 34).

In a 2017 article coauthored with his fellow Israeli political theorist Ofir Haivry, Hazony criticizes those conservatives who have risen "in defense of liberal democracy" and who have seen preserving and strengthening liberal democracy as the "historic task of American conservatism"; Hazony regards this stance as confirmation that many conservative defenders of liberal democracy in the United States and Britain "see conservatism as a branch or species of liberalism—to their thinking, the 'classical' and most authentic form of liberalism," with its foundations "in the thought of the great liberal icon John Locke" (Haivry and Hazony 2017, 1). According to Hazony, this view overlooks an authentically conservative Anglo-American tradition that can be identified with older British thinkers such as Sir John Fortescue, Richard Hooker, Sir John Selden, and Edmund Burke, who allegedly rejected the universalism and rationalism embraced by Locke.

Hazony, who unlike Deneen presents himself as an admirer of the United States Constitution, contends (unpersuasively) that support for limited government and the defense of individual freedoms can find firmer roots in this earlier Anglo-American conservative tradition than in liberalism. His argument, however, does not seem to leave room for conservatives to embrace the Declaration of Independence, with its unquestionably Lockean elements. Moreover, Haivry and Hazony try to claim Alexander Hamilton for their antiliberal conservative lineage even though Hamilton cowrote the Federalist, with its strong defense of Lockean-style liberalism. In any case, they argue that the supposedly genuine conservative tradition they have recovered provides a superior theoretical basis on which to defend nationalism and state support for religion, both of which they strongly endorse with regard to contemporary politics.

The three thinkers discussed above are in many ways very different. Among other things, Hazony explicitly draws upon Jewish and Protestant teachings, while Legutko and Deneen are both Catholics (though neither of their books especially appeals to Catholic teachings). Would any of them accept the label of illiberal? I suspect Legutko would do so, but I am less confident that Deneen would. As for Hazony, he bemoans the "intensive use of the term illiberal as an epithet to describe those who have strayed from the path of Lockean liberalism" (Haivry and Hazony 2017, 24–25). Still, it seems fair to describe all three thinkers as engaged in a more theoretical version of the enterprise that Viktor Orbán is pursuing at the political level. The common goal is to conflate liberal democracy with contemporary progressivism and thus to suggest that conservatives should have no interest in supporting or defending liberal democracy.

Many other conservatives, of course, including most of the still dominant center-right parties in Europe, remain committed to liberal democracy. But today's intellectual and political currents do not appear to be trending their way. Although illiberal forces made only small gains in the May 2019 elections to the European Parliament, there are signs that their influence may still be on the ascent. The most interesting and consequential developments for the future of liberal democracy are likely to emerge from the continuing internal struggles on the right.

Notes

1 This chapter is a slightly updated and revised version of an article that originally appeared in the January 2019 issue of the *Journal of Democracy*.
2 For an English translation of Orbán's speech on illiberal democracy of July 26, 2014, see www.kormany.hu/en/the-prime-minister/the-prime-minister-s-speeches/prime-minister-viktor-orban-s-speech-at-the-25th-balvanyos-summer-free-university-and-student-camp.
3 For an English translation of Orbán's July 28, 2018 speech, see www.miniszterelnok.hu/prime-minister-viktor-orbans-speech-at-the-29th-balvanyos-summer-open-university-and-student-camp.
4 For Orbán's Kohl memorial speech in English, see www.miniszterelnok.hu/prime-minister-viktor-orbans-speech-at-a-conference-held-in-memory-of-helmut-kohl.
5 "Protecting EU Values and Safeguarding Democracy," Emergency Resolution Adopted at the EPP Congress, 7–8 November 2018, www.epp.eu/papers/protecting-eu-values-and-safeguarding-democracy; and "A Prosperous and Secure Europe: EPP Calls for a Timely Adoption of the EU Budget Post-2020," Emergency Resolution Adopted at the EPP Congress, 7–8 November 2018, www.epp.eu/papers/a-prosperous-and-secure-europe-epp-calls-for-a-timely-adoption-of-the-eu-budget-post-2020.

Bibliography

Deneen, Patrick. 2018. *Why Liberalism Failed*. New Haven, CT: Yale University Press.
Drochon, Hugo. 2018. "The Anti-Democratic Thinker Inspiring America's Conservative Elites," *Guardian*, April 21, 2018.
Fortuna, Gerardo. 2018. "EPP Warns Orbán, but Fidesz Still Influences the Line," EUROACTIV, November 8, 2018. www.euractiv.com/section/eu-elections-2019/news/epp-warned-orban-publicly-but-fidesz-still-influences-the-line
Galston, William A. 2018a. "The Populist Challenge to Liberal Democracy." *Journal of Democracy* 29: 5–19.
Galston, William A. 2018b. *Anti-Pluralism: The Populist Threat to Liberal Democracy*. New Haven, CT: Yale University Press.
Haivry, Ofir and Yoram Hazony. 2017. "What Is Conservativism?" *American Affairs* 1 https://americanaffairsjournal.org/2017/05/what-is-conservatism
Hazony, Yoram. 2018. *Virtue of Nationalism*. New York, NY: Basic Books.
Isaac, Jeffrey C. 2017. "What's in a Name?" *Journal of Democracy* 28: 170–74.
Legutko, Ryszard. 2016. *The Demon in Democracy: Totalitarian Temptations in Free Societies*. New York, NY: Encounter.

Legutko, Ryszard. 2018. "Can Democracy Save Us?" *American Affairs*, February 2018. https://americanaffairsjournal.org/2018/02/can-democracy-save-us

Mounk, Yascha. 2018a. "The Undemocratic Dilemma." *Journal of Democracy* 29: 98–112.

Mounk, Yascha. 2018b. *The People vs. Democracy: Why Our Freedom Is in Danger and How to Save It.* Cambridge, MA: Harvard University Press.

Müller, Jan-Werner. 2016. *What Is Populism?* Philadelphia, PA: University of Pennsylvania Press.

Plattner, Marc. F. 1998. "Liberalism and Democracy: Can't Have One Without the Other." *Foreign Affairs* 77: 171–80.

Plattner, Marc. F. 1999. "From Liberalism to Liberal Democracy," *Journal of Democracy* 10: 121–34.

Plattner, Marc F. 2018. "Liberal Democracy Is Not the Problem." *Washington Monthly*, April–May–June 2018.

Rohac, Dalibor. 2018. "In Hungary, Social Conservativism and Authoritarianism Aren't the Same." *Foreign Policy*, September 11, 2018. https://foreignpolicy.com/2018/09/11/in-hungary-social-conservatism-and-authoritarianism-arent-the-same

Sargentini, Judith. 2018. "Report on a Proposal Calling on the Council to Determine, Pursuant to Article 7(1) of the Treaty on European Union, the Existence of a Clear Risk of a Serious Breach by Hungary of the Values on Which the Union Is Founded." *European Parliament* A8–0250/2018, July 4, 2018. www.europarl.europa.eu/sides/getDoc.do?pubRef=-//EP//NONSGML+REPORT+A8-2018-0250+0+DOC+PDF+V0//EN

Szalai, Jennifer. 2018. "If Liberalism Is Dead, What Comes Next?" *New York Times*, January 17, 2018.

Zakaria, Fareed. 1997. "The Rise of Illiberal Democracy." *Foreign Affairs* 76: 22–43.

4

ILLIBERAL DEMOCRACY? A TOCQUEVILLEAN PERSPECTIVE

Ewa Atanassow

Introduction: Illiberal Democracy?

Around the world today, movements and political parties labeled "populist" and regimes calling themselves illiberal have claimed the mantle of democratic sovereignty. In the name of egalitarian values and of effecting the popular will, these movements contest the liberal status quo by calling into question not only concrete policy orientations but also embedded norms and institutional practices that have long been recognized as the bedrock of any constitutional system. The rising popularity of anti-liberal models even within established liberal democracies feeds on a growing skepticism—shared by the political right and left—concerning the capacity of liberal institutions to deliver political legitimacy, national security, and economic well-being (Haidt 2016; Sides and Varick 2016).

On the right, state sovereignty is being reclaimed both as the only viable response to democratic deficits, economic hardship, and high waves of migration and cultural dislocation especially since the refugee crisis of 2015, and as a brake on the perceived globalism of liberal policies. From this vantage, driven by their own class and partisan interests, liberal elites have severed ties with democratic publics, and failed to provide for their well-being. Liberalism, these critics aver, lacks a coherent vision of national and economic security, and of the moral substance that holds a democratic polity together (Deneen 2018; Hazony 2018). If the right considers the liberal status quo as inherently thin and recklessly universalist, the left sees it as all too thick and partial, pointing to its structural or normative underpinnings as evidence of inegalitarian biases. Decrying the failures of liberal institutions to guarantee democratic representation, critics on the left question the sincerity of liberal ideals (Brown 2015;

Moyn 2019). Charging that liberalism's universalistic assumptions about reason and humanity are little more than rhetorical flowers covering over real chains of political and economic exploitation, these critics unmask core liberal values, including the rule of law or human rights, as cynical instruments of neocolonial domination (Chatterjee 2007; Sassen 2015; Mishra 2017).

Alongside these theoretical and practical contestations of the liberal democratic order, a debate is taking place in academic and policy circles around the question how best to understand our populist moment, and whether "illiberal democracy" as a concept helps or hinders efforts to address present discontents, and chart a way forward. Most influentially, Jan-Werner Müller (2017) has questioned the term illiberal democracy and the claim that there can be a genuine democracy that is divorced from liberal constitutionalism. Warning against populist efforts to undermine liberal democratic values, Müller insists on conceptual clarity as indispensable to resisting these efforts. Such clarity requires that we reserve the term "democracy" only for polities committed to the rule of law, liberal rights, and a constitutional system of checks and balances. Conversely, to speak of "illiberal" democracy, "sovereign" democracy, etc., is to proliferate analytical and normative confusions. Analytically vexed, Müller claims, such notions are also strategically harmful, allowing populist and authoritarian forces to claim a democratic legitimacy they do not merit.

And yet, if driving a conceptual wedge between liberalism and democracy is the main weapon in the current attack on liberal democracy, insofar as it carries explanatory power, the term "illiberal democracy" could also be seen as critical to its defense. While some reject its analytical and practical utility in accounting for and addressing what seems like a rising wave of authoritarianism, a growing number of academic and policy publications, some included in this volume, adopt the concept as a historically grounded and resonant way of thinking about the crisis of democracy in the 21st century. In defense of this analytical and rhetorical practice, they point out that, in a broader sense, the global conflicts of the past two centuries have been contests about the meaning of democracy and its relationship to liberal norms and institutions, whose landmarks include the rule of law, separation of powers, individual rights, and political representation (Isaac 2017). If the fall of the Berlin Wall marked a moment of convergence and global confidence in a liberal future, three decades later, the relation between democracy and liberalism is again in question in the West and beyond (Krastev 2017).

Along with registering the question and its violent history, the concept of "illiberal democracy" also captures the most striking feature of recent developments: the rhetorical and in some contexts also practical dismantling of independent institutions by democratically elected governments that, in the name of popular sovereignty or egalitarian values, oppose key liberal tenets. The concept refers to the political ascent of parties, movements, and charismatic leaders that try to divorce democratic governance from constitutional principles, thus eroding structural limits on the exercise of power. Staying within formal electoral rules, these forces seek to consolidate authority by undermining substantive commitments to practices and norms such as minority rights, individual autonomy, or constraints on the government through law and independent institutions. Behind them stand democratic publics that seem to condone or welcome this state of affairs (Mounk 2018; Daly 2019). The concept thus points to the deeper tectonic shifts taking place in democratic societies and political systems worldwide that are bringing such governments to power—often in the face of poor performance and at the price of economic hardship. Attacking liberal institutions in the name of democratic values, they evince or explicitly embrace the possibility of a democratic order that is not liberal, or is expressly anti-liberal.

In short, "illiberal democracy" is at the center of a heated academic debate with real-life implications: how to describe what is going on in the world; and whether our way of thinking and talking about it aids or rather compromises both analytic and policy efforts to meet with what is referred to as a populist challenge. While diagnoses differ in focus and appreciation, they point to the clash between liberal principles and democratic aspirations as critical for the current political conjuncture and the very problem of our time. As Marc Plattner argues in this volume, rethinking the relationship between democracy and liberalism, and addressing the ideological and political tensions between them are indispensable for rehabilitating the political center in the eyes of both disillusioned elites and disabused voters, and for reinvigorating a broad-based commitment to liberal democracy.

While broadly diagnostic, Plattner's essay helps to clarify the overarching goal and also the particular means of resisting democratic erosion. If the goal should be to resuscitate inclusive, widely shared commitment to liberal democracy, Plattner points to a double strategy with which the anti-liberals of today must be met: first, by rethinking the relationship between liberalism and democracy; and second, by recovering a richer, less dogmatic liberalism that would offer liberal democratic alternatives to contested liberal policies.

This chapter takes up the challenge to rethink the compatibility of liberalism and democracy and the current flaring up of tensions between them by drawing on the work of Alexis de Tocqueville, one of liberal democracy's most esteemed champions and penetrating critics. It aims to show that, while newly urgent, the rise of illiberal and populist movements in the past two decades is not in itself new. Though conjured up by particular circumstances and political constellations, these movements reflect and respond to the dilemmas and conflicts that are constitutive of modern democratic society. Among the first to theorize these constitutive tensions, Tocqueville is well poised to illuminate the enduring dimensions of our illiberal moment.

In light of Tocqueville's analysis, the emerging illiberal impetus finds its source in the clash between two distinct, if interrelated, understandings of democracy: between the universal scope of the principle of equality, which pushes against all limits and borders, and popular sovereignty, i.e. the ideal and practices of political self-rule that require a particular collective self, a people, and a notion of rule or sovereignty. For Tocqueville, democracy cannot be liberal if either of those elements is missing. But their combination generates tensions and fault-lines that shape the stakes of modern politics.

Liberalism vs. Democracy in Tocqueville

As early as 1835, Tocqueville hailed democracy's global rise and proclaimed that there is no viable alternative to the principle of social equality and its political counterpart—popular sovereignty—in the modern world. In the wake of the American and the French Revolutions, the defeat of aristocracy as a social system relocated political struggle within the framework of democracy itself. Henceforth, Tocqueville insisted, the primary political question was no longer whether to have democracy but of what kind: how to embody democratic ideals in institutions and practices, and what precise shape these should take. Tocqueville expected the same questions to reach and revolutionize every corner of the world and reshape the global order.

If Tocqueville hailed democratization as "irresistible," he did not view it as following a fixed path. Inflected by historical traditions, and variety of other factors, the struggle for democracy is undetermined in crucial respects. Indeed, democracy's social base and the passion for equality that, Tocqueville claimed, define the modern age are compatible with two radically different political scenarios: one that postulates universal rights and protects equal freedoms, and another predicated on an omnipotent state that pursues equality by demanding the equal powerlessness of all. These alternative outcomes stand as two global models, which Tocqueville famously and perspicaciously identified with the US and Russia (Tocqueville 2009, 6, 89–90, 610, 655–6).

And so, against the hopes of 20th-century modernization theory, freedom, for Tocqueville, is not a necessary outcome of democratization. While pointing to democratic equality as the defining feature of the modern world, he also worried about the political order it may bring about. With the ascendance of the democratic principle of legitimacy, and the demise of traditional orders and alternative regime types, the fundamental modern political choice, Tocqueville claimed, is that between democratic self-rule and egalitarian despotism. Not only does democracy not necessitate a liberal outcome: the drive toward ever-greater equalization makes liberty's prospects ever less certain. For "equality produces, in fact, two tendencies: one leads men directly to independence [...]; the other leads them by a longer, more secret, but surer road toward servitude" (Tocqueville 2009, 1193).

Tocqueville, in short, saw the danger of illiberal democracy: the very specter haunting our times. Hailing the irresistible rise and global scope of democratization, his work highlights the tensions between democracy and liberalism as defining both the character and the main challenges of the modern world. If today's anti-liberals distinguish liberalism from democracy and purport to embrace the latter in order to reject the former, Tocqueville insisted on this distinction to enhance liberal self-understanding and protect democracy against modern threats to liberty (Atanassow 2017; see also Rahe 2010 and Richter 2006).

Yet unlike current and past attempts to draw a clear line between democracy and liberalism, hence between liberal and non-liberal forms of democracy, the distinction is both comprehensive and ambiguous in Tocqueville's telling (Schmitt 1988 [1923, 1926]; Schmitter and Karl 1991; Snyder 2018). It is not a matter of choosing between institutional forms (representative vs. direct), or of abstract principles (majoritarianism vs. minority rights), nor does it rest on a particular definition of freedom (individual vs. collective), as scholars have recently insisted (Müller 2017; Randeria et al. 2019; Urbinati 2019). A decent and free democratic order must include all these dimensions. More importantly, Tocqueville makes clear that a healthy liberal democracy depends on deeper things: intellectual and spiritual orientations, modes of relating to the past and to the political community as the product of a particular historical trajectory, or a view of religion's place in social and political life.

While Tocqueville's classic study of American democracy and his works as a whole are go-to sources for recovering the richer and deeper liberalism Plattner calls for, in the remaining, I focus on a foundational aspect and point of departure of that study, i.e. the tension between two distinct and potentially conflicting meanings of democracy: democracy understood as the principle of social equality vs. as political self-rule, and the illiberal potential each of these carries. Liberal democracy, seen through Tocqueville's eyes, depends on how the tensions between these distinct democratic imaginaries, and the policy dilemmas behind them, are understood and navigated. Revisiting Tocqueville's account of these dilemmas may help us put our troubled moment in perspective, and distill useful lessons.

Democracy's Dilemma: Social Equality vs. Popular Rule

Modern democracy, for Tocqueville, is premised on the notion of the moral equality of human beings. Not primarily a political concept, democracy is fundamentally a "social state." It defines a condition of society in which status is not fixed at birth but must be acquired. This egalitarian condition need not deny that at any given point, there may be extensive inequalities, say, between rich and poor, or between more or less educated, to mention Tocqueville's two key metrics. Indeed, the universal striving for social eminence and economic success is what democracy is all about. What social equality means above all is the promise that no one has by virtue of origin or inherited qualities a political precedence over any other person; or no person's social prospects are simply determined by the fortuitous circumstances of birth and heritage.

Equality, then, means social mobility: the possibility of rising—and falling— on the social ladder. It draws on a peculiar moral imaginary: a way of seeing the social world that glosses over existing inequalities to insist on fundamental human similarity. It also entails a peculiar mindset characterized by the "ardent, insatiable, eternal, invincible" love of equality itself (Tocqueville 2009, 878). This passionate commitment to equality ensures that the democratic social state is not a static regime but a dynamic, ever-changing condition that continuously questions social conventions and presses against social boundaries and institutional forms. The motor of this progressive dynamic is the individual desire for independence and flourishing, and claiming the right to shape one's own life.

Yet, Tocqueville warns, while a central feature of democratic freedom, this desire for individual independence is also its foremost danger. Encouraging fixation on private interests and goals, it tends to hide from view each person's reliance upon—and duty toward—fellow citizens and the social world. Focused on the here and now, and privileging self-interest, democracy's individualistic mindset works to shrink the citizens' understanding of interest and utility and militates against social cohesion. Left to itself, it narrows the scope of what is held in common and facilitates taking short-sighted and self-serving decisions, whose costs are externalized to invisible others: classes, countries, and generations. This, in turn, triggers solidarity deficits that undermine the ethical and psychological preconditions for liberty: civic allegiance and trust in the institutions, and the citizens' confidence in their capacity to effectively shape their personal and collective fate. As Steven Levitsky and Daniel Ziblatt (2018) have pointedly argued, the result is an alienation from the political culture and its norms, which suddenly appear to have lost their *raison d'être*.

Arguably, it is the deepening of just such alienation and the decline of social cohesion that facilitates the current rise of populist leaders and movements, and their successful bid on power. Various studies of Trump's ascent have shown that the 45th President has been much more popular in areas that have experienced community breakdown, and where feelings of resentment and powerlessness are rampant. As Timothy Carney's (2019) *Alienated America* shows, Trump numbers were high where social capital was low.

And so, the passion for equality, which has revolutionized and continues to transform the modern world by opening new avenues for individual self-assertion, can both support democratic freedom and undermine its preconditions. Though a check against abuse of social and political power, the drive to individual independence can erode the social fabric and undermine confidence in the institutional order. Abandoned to itself, it weakens attitudes that one may call *liberal* in both meanings of the word: i.e. disinterested and generous, on the one hand, and freedom-loving, on the other hand. It can lead to losing the ability to attain, in common, common ends, which is of the essence of a free democratic government. As Tocqueville warns, in times of hardship, in crises financial or other, the isolated individual would quickly learn the limits of his independence and power. Having lost the ties to his fellow citizens or the taste for seeking out their support, begrudging the status of those who seem to fare better, he would likely turn to the only agent that has retained uncontestable agency: the state. Paradoxically enough, the obsession with individual independence is only likely to augment the competences of the state, and tip public opinion in favor of what Robert Dahl (1991) once called "guardianship democracy." In a kind of dialectical reversal, it may result in forms of government least conducive to individual freedom (Zakaria 2003).

Popular Sovereignty

If equality is the social meaning of democracy, its political principle is popular sovereignty. In its broadest meaning, this principle postulates that political arrangements, in order to hold, must be validated by the people over whom they rule. If the moral equality of individuals grounds the principle of human rights, the claim that the people are sovereign underpins the fundamental liberal norm of government by consent, and of the accountability of government to the governed.

Although popular sovereignty, for Tocqueville, is an indispensable ingredient and integral element of democratic liberty, it is not simply a guarantor of freedom. Like the passion for equality, it too can support both liberal and illiberal arrangements. If democracy requires the consent and support of the governed, reflecting the nation's will and serving the people is, Tocqueville claims, what "schemers of all times and despots of all ages" have purported to do (Tocqueville 2009, 91). As an abstract principle or ideological slogan, popular sovereignty easily lends itself to populist manipulation, and to abusing rather than effecting the power of the people. And so, while a crucial element of a free democracy, popular sovereignty is not in itself liberal. Its liberal character depends on how this principle is institutionalized and how the popular support indispensable for the functioning of institutions is being generated and expressed. What distinguishes the American polity—Tocqueville's example of a free democracy—is not the popular principle itself, but the particular way this principle has been put into institutional and social practice.

Tocqueville celebrates the constitutional system and political culture of the US for the wide variety of institutional forms that enable broad-based popular participation: from the direct democracy in the township, to the representative state and federal governments. He views the full range of spontaneous and established associations, participatory and representative institutions as so many different instantiations of the popular principle. Despite the variety of ways in which they articulate this principle, all institutional arrangements have a single legitimating force: the people, and a single court: public opinion. This is how, as one of Tocqueville's chapter headings has it, "It Can Be Strictly Said That in the United States It Is the People Who Govern" (Tocqueville 2009, 271).

Tocqueville famously credits the participatory spirit of public life in America with the "real advantages" of America's democratic government, including political education, public spiritedness, commitment to rights, and respect for law (Tocqueville 2009, 375). As he claims, it is the people's widespread perception and, to a significant degree, the reality of being in charge that sustains popular allegiance to liberal democratic institutions and liberal values. And without this allegiance, the balanced government mandated by the Constitution would be a mere theory, as the Constitution itself would be reduced to a sheet of paper.

In other words, what makes the American polity liberal, for Tocqueville, is its being robustly republican. To be meaningful and viable, along with enshrining constitutional rights, democratic liberty must connote the active exercise of those rights: a capacity to participate, individually and collectively, in determining one's present and future. Freedom, in short, implies sovereignty, and the meaning of sovereignty is self-rule or, to use Lincoln's formula, a government not only *of* the people, *for* the people, but in decisive ways *by* the people as well.

Yet if Tocqueville comes close to equating democratic freedom with democratic sovereignty and republican self-rule, he does not fail to point out the dangers that threaten to turn popular self-rule into democratic tyranny. Precisely because all democratic institutions draw on the same social base, and are the applications of one and the same popular principle, there are no structural barriers that could prevent a self-aware democratic multitude, numerous enough, from embracing or exercising tyrannical power. Ironically, it is the majority's commitment to constitutional principles that alone can limit the power of the majority. Yet if the constitutional system of checks and balances works because the majority sees it not as inimical to but as enhancing popular rule, what happens if they come to see otherwise?

Democratic freedom, then, is endangered by both of democracy's core principles: by the radicalization of equality and individualistic erosion of the social solidarity that is needed to uphold the constitutional order; as well as by a reified and often reactive notion of "we, the people" that threatens, as Ivan Krastev writes in this volume, "to turn democracy from an instrument of inclusion to that of exclusion," and democratic sovereignty into the very meaning of oppression. While seemingly antithetical, these two dangers have a way of morphing into each other. If the anxiety and sense of disempowerment that may arise amidst the relentless dynamism of democratic life can render the pressures to conform and join a powerful majority all the more irresistible, what makes that majority oppressive if not the breakdown of broader solidarities and a narrow understanding of collective identity and self-interest, i.e. selfishness writ large?

The larger threat Tocqueville's work points to is not only the tyranny of this or that particular formation, or local outbreaks of illiberalism, but a global discrediting of sovereignty of the people, and of democratic politics as such (Bickerton et al. 2007; Rhodes 2018). Put differently, if one form of democratic despotism issues from an essentializing view of the people as a hard-edged, tyrannical whole, the other, depicted in *Democracy in America*'s final chapters, consists in losing sight of peoplehood altogether and, with it, of political agency and freedom. In the latter scenario further down the egalitarian road, the citizens are reduced to an indiscriminate "crowd of similar and equal men" (Tocqueville 2009, 1249). No longer bound by collective categories or civic membership, each becomes a stranger to the destiny of the others, and to the idea of directing one's own life. As discrete identities lose their meaning and legitimacy, so do political and existential alternatives. The space for choice and action radically shrinks, and self-government gives way to a top-down technocratic governance laboring for the happiness of all by relieving each from "the trouble of thinking and the care of living" (Tocqueville 2009, 1251).

Conclusion: What Is to Be Done?

Seen through the lens of Tocqueville, the current rise of illiberalism appears as a clash between two dimensions of democracy: equality and popular self-rule. While the egalitarian passion is the engine of social transformation with no visible end, the principle of popular sovereignty implies limits: those of membership in the people. If love of equality rests on the sentiment of universal similitude, the popular principle bespeaks a particular solidarity based on shared history, political experience, and a distinctive way of life, in a word: on difference. How modern democracies navigate these conflicting aspirations to similarity and difference, and the tensions between universal principles and the particular political order, is critical for the future of democratic freedom.

If Tocqueville's analysis of the inherent tensions between the social and political definitions of democracy is correct, our illiberal moment is an instance of a dynamic that is inscribed in democratic life. While liberal institutions were designed to harness this dynamic into a process that is both progressive and stable, as Julia Azari (2019) has argued for the American case, these centuries-old institutions now appear out of sync with social developments. A gap seems to have opened up between institutional frame and citizens' self-understanding. From facilitating democratization, representative institutions have come to be seen as an obstacle both to democratic progress, and to popular control.

Even if we agree that the root of our present discontent is the clash between institutions and mindsets, to insist that the problem is simply that the institutions don't deliver on the expectations of social mobility and prosperity is to take a narrow view on what they are to deliver, or on the preconditions for democratic success. While institutional innovation or repair may be one kind of response called for, addressing the citizens' self-understandings and their solidarity deficits—and so, civic repair—is another (Putnam 2016; Offe 2017).

To be liberal, in other words, a popular regime vitally depends on nurturing social trust and broad-based identification with the constitutional arrangement, and the unwritten norms that underpin the political and civic practices. As Tocqueville argues, this identification is partly achieved through civic participation and engagement in the task of ruling. But in our busy world of constantly changing social landscape and ever more dazzling technological environment, the key question is often how to trigger this participation in the first place. What motivates citizens to get involved, and make an effort on behalf of the public interest, rather than focus on their private lives or get absorbed in virtual reality?

Tocqueville's American study goes a long way to probe the psychology of civic engagement, and the mechanisms that propel naturally selfish and conventionally independent individuals to become dedicated democratic citizens. Crucial among those motives and mechanisms are the citizens' sense of moral distinctiveness and the pride they take in their collective identity. This involves their sharing a sense of belonging, and their self-understanding as a community of fate bound by a joint political project. While participatory practices are a vital generator of civic identities, because of their narrow scope, the affective ties stirred up on a local level, by civil groups and NGOs, or even by nation-wide associations such as political parties, may not translate to the polity as a whole. Indeed, the stronger those ties and the sense of distinctiveness they evince, the more polarizing and productive of political disaffection they can become. As Sheri Berman (1997) has shown in the example of Weimar Germany, under certain conditions, vigorous civil society can deepen rather than balance solidarity deficits, thus fatally compromise democratic stability. And so, along with reaffirming the civic ideals of equal participation and the people's right to self-rule, there is a need for comprehensive narratives that would weave the great variety of civic experiences into the larger, multicolor whole that is a democratic people. In other words, how individual citizens exercise their rights and duties, and whether they engage in civic life and reach out across social divides, critically depends on how the people, and membership in the people, are defined and understood.

In a recent paper, the political scientist Rogers Smith argues that populist success can be studied to devise strategies for liberal recovery.[1] The first elements of this success, he claims, are persuasive stories that invoke popular sovereignty and democratic ideals. What populists offer is not only an outlet for anger and frustration, or targeted proposals for addressing urgent policy issues, but also compelling stories of popular identity and rule: democratic stories affirming the dignity of the people against conniving elites or impersonal global forces, and explaining how sovereignty can be restored, and the political system revamped to serve those it is supposed to be serving: the people. Not simply rejecting such stories but telling better—truer, more complex, and more liberal ones—is, Smith contends, the way to combat the ascent of illiberal populism.

In a like spirit, Harvard historian Jill Lepore (2019) has issued a clarion call to fellow historians to make the nation central to their craft again. In her bid to restore the dignity and purpose to national history writing, Lepore points out that if academic historians may have graduated from painting national tableaus to crafting multi-layered canvases set in a global frame, democratic publics have not. These publics see and feel the world in terms of nations, and look for a historical narrative that reflects and instructs their self-perception. "They can get it from scholars or they can get it from demagogues, but get it they will" (Lepore 2019, 20). Democratic freedom, in Lepore's telling, crucially relies on the way popular identity is understood. A people, to be free, needs to have a vision of itself. Much depends on the quality and resonance of that vision; and on whether those most qualified to offer it are up for the job.

In sum, for liberal institutions to be stable, the confidence in the liberal democratic polity has to be built and rebuilt both from below and from above. Liberal democracy relies on the citizens' constant practice and experience, as well as on the elite's willingness to interpret that experience in a meaningful light and provide unifying narratives that can bridge the distance between individuals and institutions, majority and minority, people and elites. To be free, democracy requires broad-based civic participation as well as political and moral leadership: that is, ongoing efforts to sustain the sense of common membership and reimagine "we, the people."

Note

1 Rogers Smith, "Popular Sovereignty, Populism, and Stories of Peoplehood," paper presented at an SSRC Workshop on Popular Sovereignty, Swarthmore, October 2017. See also Smith (2015).

Bibliography

Atanassow, Ewa. 2017. "Tocqueville's New Liberalism." In *Liberal Moments: Reading Liberal Texts*, edited by Ewa Atanassow and Alan S. Kahan, 51–9. London: Bloomsbury Academic.

Azari, Julia. 2019. "It's the Institutions, Stupid: The Real Roots of America's Political Crisis." *Foreign Affairs*, June 11. www.foreignaffairs.com/articles/united-states/2019-06-11/its-institutions-stupid.

Berman, Sheri. 1997. "Civil Society and the Collapse of the Weimar Republic." *World Politics* 49(3): 401–29.

Bickerton, Cristopher et al. 2007. *Politics without Sovereignty*. London: Routledge.

Brown, Wendy. 2015. *Undoing the Demos*. Cambridge, MA: MIT Press.

Carney, Timothy P. 2019. *Alienated America*. New York, NY: Harper Collins.

Chatterjee, Partha. 2007. "Empire, Nations, Peoples: The Imperial Prerogative and Colonial Exceptions." *Thesis Eleven* 139(1): 84–96.

Dahl, Ronald A. 1991. *Democracy and Its Critics*. New Haven, CT: Yale University Press.

Daly, Tom G. 2019. "Democratic Decay: Conceptualising an Emerging Research Field." *Hague Journal on the Rule of Law*, 11(1): 9–36.

Deneen, Patrick. 2018. *Why Liberalism Failed*. New Haven, CT: Yale University Press.

Fukuyama, Francis. 2018. *The Demand for Dignity and the Politics of Resentment*. New York, NY: Farrar, Straus and Giroux.

Haidt, Jonathan. 2016. "When and Why Nationalism Beats Globalism," *American Interest* 12(1), July. www.the-american-interest.com/2016/07/10/when-and-why-nationalism-beats-globalism/

Hazony, Yoram. 2018. *The Virtue of Nationalism*. New York, NY: Basic Books.

Isaac, Jeffrey C. 2017. "Is There Illiberal Democracy? A Problem with No Semantic Solution," *Public Seminar*. www.publicseminar.org/wp-content/uploads/2017/07/Isaac-Jeffrey-Is-There-Illiberal-Democracy-Public-Seminar.pdf

Krastev, Ivan. 2017. *After Europe*. Philadelphia: University of Pennsylvania Press.

Lepore, Jill. 2019. *This America: The Case for the Nation*. New York, NY: Norton.

Levitsky, Steven, and Daniel Ziblatt. 2018. *How Democracies Die*. New York, NY: Penguin.

Mishra, Pankaj. 2017. *Age of Anger: A History of the Present*. New York, NY: Farrar Straus & Giroux.

Mounk, Yasha. 2018. *The People vs. Democracy*. Cambridge, MA: Harvard University Press.

Moyn, Samuel. 2019. *Not Enough: Human Rights in an Unequal World*. Cambridge, MA: Harvard University Press.

Müller, Jan-Werner. 2017. *What Is Populism?* London: Penguin.

Offe, Claus. 2017. "Referendum vs. Institutionalized Deliberation: What Democratic Theorists Can Learn from the 2016 Brexit Decision." *Daedalus* 146(3): 14–27.

Putnam, Robert. 2016. *Our Kids: The American Dream in Crisis*. New York, NY: Simon and Schuster.

Rahe, Paul. 2010. *Soft Despotism, Democracy's Drift: Montesquieu, Rousseau, Tocqueville, and the Modern Prospect*. New Haven, CT: Yale University Press.

Randeria, Sahlini et al. 2019. *Wenn Demokratien demokratisch untergehen*. Wien: Passagen Verlag.

Rhodes, Aaron. 2018. *The Debasement of Human Rights: How Politics Sabotage the Ideal of Freedom*. New York, NY: Encounter Books.

Richter, Melvin. 2006. "Tocqueville on Threats to Liberty in Democracy." In *Cambridge Companion to Tocqueville*, edited by Cheryl B. Welch, 245–75. Cambridge, MA: Cambridge University Press.

Sassen, Saskia. 2015 [1996]. *Losing Control? Sovereignty in the Age of Globalization*. New York, NY: Columbia University Press.

Schmitt, Carl. 1988 [1923, 1926]. *The Crisis of Parliamentary Democracy*. Cambridge, MA: MIT Press.

Schmitter, P.C., and Karl, T.L. 1991. "What Democracy Is… and Is Not." *Journal of Democracy* 2(3): 75–88.

Sides, John, Michael Tesler, and Lynn Vareck. 2018. *Identity Crisis: The 2016 Presidential Election Campaign and the Battle for the Meaning of America*. Princeton, NJ: Princeton University Press.

Smith, Rogers. 2015. *Political Peoplehood: The Roles of Values, Interests, and Identities*. Chicago, IL: The University of Chicago Press.

Snyder, Timothy. 2018. *The Road to Unfreedom: Russia, Europe, America*. New York, NY: Penguin.

Tocqueville, Alexis de. 2009 [1835]. *Democracy in America*. Indianapolis, IN: Liberty Fund.

Urbinati, Nadia. 2019. *Me, the People: How Populism Transforms Democracy*. Cambridge, MA: Harvard University Press.

Zakaria, Fareed. 2003. *The Future of Freedom: Illiberal Democracy at Home and Abroad*. New York, NY: Norton.

5

THE OPEN SOCIETY FROM A CONSERVATIVE PERSPECTIVE

Sir Roger Scruton

Introduction

Given the rise in popularity of openly illiberal politics, both in political systems and in theoretical discussions, it is of pressing importance to articulate a positive conservative view of the classical liberal idea of the open society. This chapter aims to offer just such an articulation, focusing on the need to balance freedom—especially individual freedom—and openness with the trust required for the preservation of social integrity. I shall argue that conservatism is not against openness and change; it is concerned with the social conditions—chiefly solidarity, continuity, and trust—that must be kept in place if those things are to be possible. The danger in liberal individualism, to which the current "illiberal" turn is a reaction, is that it sees any constraint of individual freedom as unjustified, until proven to be necessary. By shifting the onus of proof constantly in favor of the individual, liberalism jeopardizes the trust on which liberal policies and the very possibility of an "open" society ultimately depend.

First, a bit of context. The idea of the "open society" was introduced by the French philosopher Henri Bergson (Bergson 1932), with a view to contrasting two ways of creating social cohesion: the magical and the rational. Magical thinking involves the submission to mystical forces that must be appeased and obeyed, and societies founded on magic are closed to innovation and experiment, since these threaten the dark powers that govern human destiny. Rational thinking, by contrast, involves exploring the world with a view to discovering the real laws of nature, and exerting ourselves to find reasoned solutions to our social and political problems. Rational thinking leads to an open society, in which differences of opinion and lifestyle are accepted as contributions to the collective wellbeing.

The distinction was taken up by Sir Karl Popper who, writing in the wake of World War II, saw totalitarianism, whether of the fascist or the communist variety, as a return to magical ways of thinking and to a society based on fear and obedience rather than free rational choice (Popper 1962). For Popper following Bergson, magical thinking has persisted in new forms, and intellectuals—those who live by their reasoning powers—had been in part responsible for this. Thus, in his account, the real enemies of the open society were those thinkers, Plato, Hegel, and Marx in particular, who—at least on Popper's view of them—had advocated submission to the collective, rather than individual freedom, as the goal of politics. Such thinkers, Popper argued, failed to see that without individual freedom, reason has no purchase in human affairs. To Popper's mind, thinking through the cataclysm of the mid-20th century and at the dawn of the cold war, the worst of the gods that European intellectuals (following the lead of Hegel and Marx) had superstitiously imposed on us, in order to perpetuate our submission, has been history itself. Thus, Popper argues, historicism proselytized a fatalism just as inexorable and dogmatic as that of traditional and fundamentalist religion. The hecatombs of sacrificial victims went to their death, under the fascist and communist regimes, because 'history' required it.

Both the thesis Popper advanced concerning totalitarian tendencies in the history of Western thought and the vehemence with which he pursued that thesis can be and have been criticized by the political right (see, for instance, Bialas 2019). Nevertheless, we cannot deny that the issues to which Popper referred are still very much alive, even if they have taken on a new form. We are still besieged by the idea that history is a force to which we must submit, and that attempts to resist it—whether in the name of freedom, or in the name of tradition—will always be futile. But the superstitious submission to history is now more commonly associated with those who call themselves liberals than with Marxists or nationalists. In particular, many who advocate for the open society tell us that globalization is inevitable and that with it comes new forms of trans-national government, new attitudes to borders, migration and governance, and new ideas of civil society and legal order. The message coming down to us from many of those who propose themselves as our political leaders has been 'globalization is the future, it is inevitable, and we are in charge of it'—the same contradiction that was announced by the advocates of totalitarian political systems. (For if it is inevitable, nobody can really be in charge.) But is it inevitable? Is it really compatible with the open society?

In one sense, then, Popper's conception of the open society derives from Bergson and the quest to purify 20th-century European thought and society of lingering traces of magical thinking and their pernicious political consequences. But the Open Society is also a recent manifestation of a far older idea, namely that of liberal individualism as this took shape during the Enlightenment. Followers of John Locke saw legitimacy as arising from the sovereignty of the individual. Free individuals confer legitimacy on government through their consent to it, and the consent is registered in a contract in which no individual has an actually operative veto. The result is a reasonable and reasoning form of government since it draws on individual rational choice for its legitimacy. In such an arrangement, individual freedom is both the foundation and the goal of politics, and the resulting society is open in the sense that nobody is in a position to impose opinions or standards of conduct unless the people can be persuaded to accept them. There will be dissenters of course, but an open society shows itself by nothing so much as by its attitude to the dissenter, whose voice is allowed in the political process, and whose freedom to express dissenting opinions is protected by the state. This idea underlies Popper's vision, and it is an idea of perennial appeal. However, it is open to an objection, made vividly by Hegel, whose writings on political philosophy Popper seems willfully to have misunderstood.

The objection is this: freely choosing individuals, able to sign up to contracts and to accept responsibility for their agreements, do not exist in the state of nature. Popper himself acknowledges that magical ways of thinking, submission to dark forces and the desire to appease them, define the original position from which we humans must free ourselves. We become free individuals by a process of emancipation and this process is a *social* process, dependent on our interactions with others, and on the mutual accountability that shapes each of us as a self-choosing 'I.' The free individual is the product of a specific kind of social order, and the constraints necessary to perpetuate that order are therefore necessary to our freedom. If openness means freedom, then freedom cannot be extended so far as to unsettle the social order that produces it. But then the advocate of freedom must be an advocate of that kind of social order, and this means thinking in terms of something other than openness. We need to know what kinds of constraints are required by a free society and how far we can allow them to be eroded. As I see it, that defines the agenda of conservatism, from its foundation in the philosophy of Thomas Hobbes, through Burke, Smith, and Hegel to its frail and beleaguered advocates today.

Enlightenment

For some Enlightenment thinkers, individual freedom makes sense only in the context of a universal morality. Individual freedoms and universal values sustain each other, and are two sides of a coin. Such is the position advocated by Kant, in his theory of the categorical imperative. Morality, according to Kant, stems from our shared nature as rational agents, each of whom is governed by the same collection of imperatives. Humanity and free rational agency are ultimately the same idea, and to be human is to live under the sanction of the moral law, which tells us to will the maxims of our actions as universal laws, and to treat humanity always as an end in itself, and never as a means only.

The moral law, in Kant's view, follows immediately from the fact that we are free, in the sense of being guided by our own reason, independently of any threats or rewards that might be waved in front of us. This condition—which he described as the autonomy of the will—can be over-ridden by tyrants, but never destroyed. Even if we are constrained to do what the moral law forbids, we will inevitably know that we are doing wrong. A regime that maintains itself in being by threats therefore violates what for Kant was the basic condition of legitimate order, which is that rational beings, consulting their reason alone, would consent to it.

There are many complexities and subtleties involved in spelling out that position. But it has lost none of its appeal, and is the best argument ever produced for the very idea of human rights—the notion that there are universal rights which serve as a shield behind which we can all exercise the sovereignty over our lives that reason itself requires of us, and in doing so express and act out our consent to the political regime under which we live. Rights are equal and universal, and are the way in which the sovereignty of the individual is fitted into the same slot, as it were, as the sovereignty of the state.

Few doubt the importance of this idea, and all that it has inspired by way of constitution building. It is the foundation stone of the liberal order. For Popper, as for many others, it is the way to release reason into the community, and to produce a society open to innovation and experiment. But we should not neglect the difficulties associated with the human rights idea, of which two, in particular, stand out as especially relevant to the times in which we live. First, what exactly *are* our rights, and what prevents people from claiming as a right what they happen to want, regardless of the effect on the common good? Second, what are our duties, and to whom or to what are they owed?

The American Declaration of Independence told us that all human beings are endowed by their Creator with certain inalienable rights, including Life, Liberty, and the Pursuit of Happiness. That relatively innocuous summary leaves open as many questions as it answers, and when Eleanor Roosevelt set out to draft the UN Universal Declaration of Human Rights (1948), the list began to grow in ways that the American founders might very well have questioned, in particular the expansion from basic political and civic rights to embrace what have come to be called social and cultural rights. Human rights, which began life as fundamental freedoms, came to include elaborate claims to health, work, security, family life, and so on, which are available only if someone is prepared to provide them. Rights, initially conceived as a limitation to the power of the state, thus became a way of increasing state power, to the point where the state, as guardian and provider, occupies more and more of the space once allocated to the free acts of individuals. We have seen this process of 'rights inflation' everywhere in the post-war world, and much of it issues either from declarations such as that of the UN, or from the national or international courts established to adjudicate their application.

The expansion of rights goes hand in hand with a contraction in duties. The universalist vision of the Enlightenment, as classically presented in Kant, conceives duties as owed indifferently to all mankind. We have a general duty to do good, the beneficiaries of which are not bound to us by specific obligations but are simply equal petitioners for a benefit that cannot in fact be distributed to them all. No particular person comes before us as the irreplaceable object of our concern: all are equal, and none has an over-riding claim. In such circumstances, I can be easily forgiven if I neglect them all, being unable to fulfill a duty that will in any case make little difference to the net sum of human suffering.

If you look at recent literature on ethics stemming from thinkers such as Peter Singer (2019) and Derek Parfit (2013–17), you will get a fairly clear idea of what this Enlightenment morality has come to mean today: futile calculations of cost and benefit, from which all real human feeling and all lively sense of obligation and moral ties have been removed. Unless you have the good fortune to be switching the points in the path of a runaway railway trolley, giving to Oxfam is about all the moral life amounts to.

It should be said that Kant's own position by no means tends in that direction. For Kant, the fundamental moral concept was not right but duty. The free being is bound by the moral law, which imposes the duty to treat humanity always as an end in itself, and never as a means only. If there are universal rights, this is simply a consequence of the fact that there are universal duties: notably, the duty to respect each other as sovereign individuals, to tell the truth, and to keep our promises. As Onora O'Neill (1993, 2005) has persuasively argued, for a Kantian moral outlook, there is a necessary balance between rights and duties and an obligation to clearly cognize our specific moral ties, or at least to reflectively seek a path toward such a cognition and act on it. But without the underlying metaphysics, it is difficult to see how today's muddied version of the Enlightenment vision of the moral life will lead to anything other than enhanced claims for me, accompanied by reduced duties to you (Korsgaard 1996).

A Misconception

That imbalance can be observed in a radical misconception that seems to lie at the heart of much liberal politics in our day. The view adopted by many advocates of the open society is that Enlightenment universalism, once adopted, will *replace* all other social ties, providing a sufficient basis on which individuals can live together in mutual respect. Moreover, this replacement *ought* to occur, since universalist values are ultimately incompatible with those historical loyalties and rooted attachments that cause people to discriminate between those who are entitled to the benefits of social inclusion and those who are not. Enlightenment universalism requires us to live in an open and borderless cosmopolis, from which all forms of traditional obedience—whether tribal, national, or religious—are marginalized or banished.

This misconception results from identifying what is in fact a rare achievement, involving extensive trial and sacrifice, as the default position of humanity. Only take away the exclusive loyalties, it is supposed, and people will revert of their own accord to the universal values, having no particularist code to distract them. We saw the effect of this misconception in the so-called 'Arab spring,' when the Western powers acted on the assumption that we need only remove the tyrant, and democratic politics will emerge from beneath him, as the default position of any modern society. But the default position is neither democracy nor any other system expressive of Enlightenment individualism. As Ruth Wodak (2015) has argued, the default position in response to this is fear, and I would hasten to add, this is indeed a justified fear. For fear in the face of adversity and uncertainty is proper to creatures living side by side with the most dangerous of all existing animals. Hence, people flee toward the next offer of security, often provided by the army and/or a strongman leader since that is what armies are for (Chatterjee and Katznelson 2012).

Loyalty and Trust

Human beings have a primary need to trust those among whom they live, and to be settled side by side with them in a shared experience of belonging. Trust grows in small units like the family, in which the members experience each other's wellbeing as their own. But family-based communities are unstable, riven by the all-too-apparent contrast between the unbreakable trust that unites me to my family and the defeasible obligations that I acknowledge toward families other than mine. Under pressure, such communities break down along family lines, with vendettas of the Montague and Capulet kind. In general, kinship loyalties are more likely to sustain closed than open societies since each family holds its loyalty close to its chest.

Trust in an open society must extend to strangers: only then will it provide the foundation for an outgoing and experimental experience of belonging, one that guarantees free deals and consensual arrangements and which will not be undermined by favoritism and family ties. The question we need to ask ourselves is how trust between strangers arises, and what maintains it in the absence of personal affection or shared commitments? Trust, like affection, cannot be commanded. ('Trust me!' is not a command but an undertaking.) Trust extended to strangers is what enables people in a large modern society, referring to their neighbors, their countrymen, and their fellow citizens, to say 'we' and to mean it—to mean it as an expression of obligation and not just of fate.

It is important to recognize that most of us in Western democracies are living under a government of which we don't approve. We accept to be ruled by laws and decisions made by politicians with whom we disagree, and whom we often deeply dislike. How is that possible? Why don't democracies regularly collapse, as people refuse to be governed by those they never voted for? Clearly, a modern democracy must be held together by something stronger than party politics. As thinkers as ideologically variant as Francis Fukuyama (2018) and Jürgen Habermas (2001) have argued, there must be some sort of "civic" nationalism, a 'first-person plural' identity and a pre-political loyalty, that causes neighbors who voted in opposing ways to treat each other as fellow citizens, for whom the government is not 'mine' or 'yours' but 'ours,' whether or not we approve of it. This first-person plural varies in strength, from fierce attachment in wartime, to casual acceptance on a Monday morning at work. But at some level, it must be assumed if we are to accept a shared form of government.

A country's stability is enhanced by economic growth. But it depends far more upon the sense that we belong together, and that we will stand by each other during the real emergencies. Trust of this kind depends on customs and institutions that foster collective decisions in response to the problems of the day. It is the *sine qua non* of enduring peace, and the greatest asset of any people that possesses it, as the British have possessed it throughout the enormous changes that gave rise to the modern world. Whether the Hungarians possess it, after the disasters of Nazi and Soviet occupation, and all that has flowed from the Treaty of Trianon, is a real question today, and one that I am not competent to answer. But the evidence is that the Hungarian 'we' is just as strong, and just as full of conflicts and tensions as the British.

People acquire trust in different ways. Urban elites build trust through career moves, joint projects, and cooperation across borders. Like the aristocrats of old, they often form networks without reference to national boundaries. They do not, on the whole, depend upon a particular place, a particular faith, or a particular routine for their sense of membership, and in the immediate circumstances of modern life, they can adapt to globalization without too much difficulty. However, even in modern conditions, this urban elite depends upon others who do not belong to it: the farmers, manufacturers, factory workers, builders, clothiers, mechanics, nurses, carers, cleaners, cooks, policemen, and soldiers for whom attachment to a place and its customs is implicit in all that they do. In a question that touches on identity, these people will very likely feel differently from the urban elite, on whom they depend, in turn, for government.

Hence, the word 'we' in this context does not always embrace the same group of people or the same networks of association. David Goodhart (2017) has presented a dichotomy between the 'anywheres' and the 'somewheres': those who can take their business, their relations, and their networks from place to place without detriment, and those for whom a specific place and its indigenous lifestyle are woven into their social being. These two kinds of people will be pulled in different directions when asked to define the real ground of their political allegiance. This fact is beginning to cause radical problems all across Europe, as the question of identity moves to the center of the political stage.

Liberal individualism grants to each of us a great benefit: sovereignty over our lives, and a shield of rights in the face of all who seek to take that sovereignty away. But it also imposes on us a great burden, which is life among others who enjoy the same benefit, and who may very well use their sovereignty to our disadvantage. And because liberal individualism expands freedom and opportunities, it also amplifies society, bringing in more and more people who do not know each other personally, but who nevertheless want to sign up to the deal. Why and how should we trust them? To that question, liberal individualism gives no persuasive answer.

Forms of Belonging

In a religious community, people are bound together by a shared faith, and by traditions and customs that express the faith and are in some way authorized by it. The history of modern Europe is the history of our emancipation from that kind of community. Not that we have turned away from religion (though some people certainly have) but that we have privatized it, removed it from the foundations of our public life, and brought it into the house, as, classically, Jews have learned to do. In communities founded on religious obedience, such as Calvin's Geneva, the fear and hatred of the heretic will, in any emergency, destabilize loyalties. Like Muhammad's Medina, Calvin's Geneva made no distinction between secular and religious authority, and for both Muslims and Calvinists, the move toward purely secular government has been an uphill struggle, and also something that Islam, in some of its versions, actually forbids.

Whatever we think about the Enlightenment, a glance at 17th-century Europe prior to the Peace of Westphalia, and at the Islamic world today, must surely give credence to the opinion that a modern society needs another kind of first-person plural than that provided by religion. And down the centuries, people have always been aware of this. It is why religious communities morph into dynasties or military dictatorships. Those are the real default positions, and vestiges of them remain wherever religion is in retreat from its formerly dominant position.

The religious first-person plural should not be contrasted with those default positions but rather with the first-person plural that we in Western societies enjoy: the 'we' of political order. The American constitution was issued in the name of 'we the people'—i.e. of people bound together by political obligations in a place that they share. Any advocacy of the open society must begin from this conception, which is the *sine qua non* of open dealings. In summary, the 'we' of political order arises in the following conditions:

- There is an inclusive political process, i.e. one in which we all participate in one way or another, and which therefore legislates by consensus building, negotiation, and compromise.

- There are rules determining who is and who is not a member of the first-person plural: anyone who seeks the benefit of membership must also assume the cost.
- The cost includes that of belonging to a community of trust, which, in turn, involves acquiring the attributes that enable trust, such as a willingness to learn the language, to work, to put down roots, and to adopt the surrounding public culture.

Those conditions suggest that, under the bargain of secular authority and individual autonomy, political order rests on a pre-political identity, in which neighborhood rather than religion has become the foundation of belonging. This pre-political identity puts territory, residence, and secular law before religion, family, and tribe. And it is what makes true citizenship possible, as those who assume the burden of a man-made law acknowledge their right to participate in making it.

But who is included in such a bargain? This is the question of our time, and globalization has made it increasingly urgent (see Calhoun in this volume). People have wanted the benefit of the open society without the cost of providing a secure answer to that question. But can we have an open society without national sovereignty, and borders secured by a territorial jurisdiction? The European Union says yes; Mr Orbán says no. And in my own country, it is in part the pressure of migration from the European Union (Hungary included) that led to the Brexit vote, which was interpreted by many people as an affirmation of national sovereignty and a defense against inward migration.

What Is Openness?

Before deciding what a conservative defense of the open society would look like today, we must be clear about what openness actually consists in. There are, in fact, two rather different conceptions in the literature as to the nature and value of the open society: one epistemological, the other political.

Popper's conception is purely epistemological, and was critiqued for this reason by Aurel Kolnai (1995: xii–iii), among others. Only in conditions of open discussion and the free exchange of opinion, Popper argues, does human enquiry reliably tend toward knowledge. In such conditions, as he puts it, our hypotheses die in our stead. Without the open competition of opinions in the forum of free discussion, beliefs are chosen for their convenience rather than their truth: darkness and superstition reclaim their ancestral territory. The inspiration for Popper's view is the scientific revolution and the benefits that have flown from it, as much as the political philosophy of liberal individualism.

The epistemological benefits of openness have been emphasized by other central European thinkers, notably Michael Polanyi and Friedrich Hayek, for whom free association is the repository of social knowledge—the kind of knowledge that exists only in social networks and never in an isolated head. And we should not overlook the argument, due to Mises and Hayek, that a regime of free exchange is the necessary vehicle of the economic information on which a Great Society depends. But all these epistemological benefits might exist in a society, like modern China, in which personal liberties are seriously curtailed and, in some areas, non-existent.

Thus, a further and expressly political defense of the open society is needed. Such a defense values freedom not as a means to knowledge and information, but as an end in itself. This was the position defended by John Stuart Mill (2007 [1859]), and it raises the question of political order in a radical form. When do we jeopardize the social order by extending freedom, and what kind of order does freedom presuppose? Or does social order arise spontaneously from freedom, when individuals are released from traditional constraints? Those are the questions that underlie conservatism in politics, and I will conclude with a summary of what follows, when we take them seriously.

The Conservative Response

Conservatives have in general been suspicious of the liberal individualist idea, that society is, or can be, founded on a social contract. Deals and contracts *presuppose* trust and do not produce it. Trust is the long-term background condition that makes political order possible (Fukuyama 1995). Such trust comes to us as an objective fact, something that we inherit with our social membership. It is bound up with customs, traditions, and institutions that establish a continuous conversation linking past, present, and future. This conversation exists only where there is a confident sense of who belongs to it and who does not. It requires a conception of membership, and the knowledge that in emergencies, each will assume the duties that are needed for our collective survival.

This membership is not simply a matter of acquiring rights that will be protected by the community; it means acquiring duties toward the community, including the duty to inspire the trust on which the community depends. In the case of newcomers, this means displaying a willingness to belong; minimally, Habermas (2001), himself a left-liberal, has maintained an understanding of and commitment to the basic law/constitution of the host nation. Such an understanding and commitment has long been the norm among immigrants to the US, but it has not been the norm everywhere in Europe (Müller 2006).

The mobility of populations in the modern world is one reason why conservatives have leaned toward the national idea as their preferred first-person plural: it indicates a way of belonging that is accessible to the newcomer, to the stranger, and to the person who has nothing in common with you apart from residing in the place where you are. By contrast, the religious way of belonging presents an existential challenge. To adopt a religious form of membership is to convert, to change your life entirely, and to submit to strange gods and alien doctrines. Religious communities present a barrier to the migrant and the refugee, as well as an internal boundary within the nation, a fault line that will open at once in any conflict, as in the former Yugoslavia. As I have recently argued, national identity shapes a pre-political loyalty that is adapted to the most urgent of our political requirements today, which is that of a single system of law, defined over territory, and resting on a shared attachment to the place where we are, rather than on any religious or family-based imperative (Scruton 2017).

Of course, nationality is not enough to establish a viable first-person plural. The nation is a pre-political community that is turned by its nature in a political direction, and may find a political expression in many different ways. There are nations that are bound together under a unified sovereign order, as in Britain, and nations that are scattered across political borders, as in Hungary. Nevertheless, there is a trust between neighbors that comes from a shared attachment to territory and the language and customs that prevail there; and it is this kind of trust rather than shared religious obedience or the fall-out from global markets and cosmopolitan ideals that will sustain the truly open society. It is when people are settled side by side in a condition of neighborliness that they are most disposed to tolerate differences of opinion, freedom of speech, and a variety of lifestyles. It is, in my view, a mere illusion that societies become more open in those respects the more cosmopolitan they are.

In this connection, however, we must acknowledge that the nation-state, which seemed to open so tempting a path to democratic government in the 19th century, is no longer a clear conception in the minds of the young. At the same time, the question of what to be put in its place has received no consensual answer. On one interpretation, the European Union was such an answer, but in all issues in which national sovereignty has been at risk, the EU has slipped away into the realm of wishful thinking, and the nation has stepped forward in its stead. While the EU has tried by all available means to persuade Europeans to replace their national attachments with a new and cosmopolitan identity, the only effect has been to stir up other, narrower, and more emotional nationalisms, as with the Scots, the Flemings, and the Catalans. The conservative response to all this is to say: stop looking for something that has never previously existed, and think instead of adapting what we have. And what we have is a collection of historic settlements, in which national attachment sustains a liberal rule of law, and in which people can live together without conflict, agreeing about some things and disagreeing about others.

Liberal Doubts

Liberals and conservatives are united in accepting the epistemological argument for the market economy. And classical liberals will often go further along the road taken by conservatism, and acknowledge that tradition too might be an essential part of social knowledge, on which we depend in the unforeseen and unforeseeable circumstances of social change. But liberals, like many social conservatives, argue that markets must be controlled and that human ingenuity is constantly giving rise to new ways of abusing the trust on which markets depend, as in currency speculation, asset stripping, and similar ways of extracting value from everyone without adding value of one's own. Economic freedoms may impose a huge and unforeseen cost on people who had built their lives around a now defunct economic order. Under capitalism, the *Communist Manifesto* famously said, 'all that is solid melts into air.' Globalization vastly enhances this effect, as capital roams the world in search of those unexploited margins, detaching one economy after another from its protected enclave. In the face of this, it is normal, now, for governments to offer some protection to their citizens against the global storm. A free economy, it is therefore assumed, must be a regulated economy, if the citizens are to put their trust in it.

But that means that the economy should be regulated in the interests of the given first-person plural, the 'we' on which social trust depends. A free economy must be constrained by the national interest.

Liberal doubts about market freedoms are now widespread. More controversial are liberal doubts about religious freedoms. The first amendment to the US Constitution granted freedom of religion, or at least forbad the Federal government from imposing a religion of its own, and also forbad any interference with free speech and free assembly. But it should be clear to everyone that we have come a long way from those requirements. Does freedom of religion extend to the freedom to teach religion to the young, to wear religious symbols in public, to run an adoption agency that upholds the traditional Christian view of marriage, and which on these grounds accepts no applications from gay couples, to refuse to design a cake celebrating gay marriage, when trading as a provider of wedding cakes? Some of those freedoms are rejected by people who consider themselves to be defenders of the open society idea. Likewise, there is a growing view among people who declare themselves to be liberals that free speech should not extend so far as to protect hate speech, a term which is itself hostage to the one who chooses to define it.

To put it simply, we have witnessed a closing down of choices in those areas, such as religion and speech, where new interests are competing for space against the old and once-settled customs. It is no longer clearly true that self-styled liberals are unqualified in their support for the open society. Yes, they say: an open society, provided it is a society of liberals.

Conservative Doubts

Conservatives also have doubts about the open society idea, believing that the modern tendency to multiply options might damage the trust on which freedom ultimately depends. The case of marriage has been particularly important:

an institution that many believe to be the bedrock of society has been redefined, so as to offer same-sex marriage through the mediation of the state. Is this an addition to our freedoms, or an assault on them?

Many conservatives say that the state, by intruding into a sphere that is, in its true meaning, sacramental, has exercised a power that it cannot legitimately claim. If that is so, the enlargement of choices has been purchased at the cost of the institution that gives sense to them. What is offered to homosexuals by the state, therefore, is not marriage but something else. And by calling it marriage, the state downgrades the life-choice that previously went by this name. Conservatives who mount that argument do not, as a rule, seek to impose their view on those who disagree with it, since they are attached to the liberal conception of law, as the protector of individuals against those who would like to control them. But they also see the enlargement of the concept of marriage as restricting liberties since it takes away an institution that they would otherwise have wished to commit to. A new option is created, yes, they argue, but only by destroying the old option that meant so much more.

Conclusion

Responding to both sets of doubts concerning the open society and the fact of globalization, how can we articulate a conservative defense of the open society that can speak to the growing popularity of expressly illiberal ideas and illiberal policies on the political right? First, we must recognize that conservatism is not against openness and change; it is concerned with the conditions that must be kept in place if those things are to be possible. In this respect, it is attuned to liberal individualism's dangerous tendency to cast any and every constraint of an individual's freedom of movement or action as unjustified, until proven necessary. Such an onus of proof constantly in its own favor shields liberal individualism in the absolute protection of law while undermining the social trust on which liberal policies ultimately depend. Resisting this tendency in liberal individualism, a conservative defense of the open society will instead recognize that every increase in freedom (such as the freedom for an individual to marry a member of the same sex, or to be recognized as belonging to a sex other than that they were assigned at birth) is likely to have a cost attached to it, which might well involve a loss of freedom for others.

Given this trade-off, the second key feature of the conservative defense of the open society will be an insistence upon the dependence of the freedom of free individuals to live where and how they like upon the first-person plural context of mutual trust and shared identity, which alone can suffice for the maintenance of peaceful relations between us and guarantee the passing on of social capital. This trust must also be an *open* trust, one that does not depend on surrender to an authority or a custom that closes down those freedoms that are precious to us: freedom of association and opinion. Hence, it must help us to move away from the religious and tribal forms of society toward the condition of citizenship, and this entails replacing faith and kinship by neighborhood and secular law as the primary bonds of civil association. The two points, many conservatives will assert and celebrate, already have been the achievement of Europe: the creation of the nation as an object of loyalty and the secular state as its expression. Thus, the conservative defense of the open society seeks not to establish something new on the basis of abstract universal claims, but to preserve a heritage on the basis of mutual trust and a shared tradition.

Bibliography

Bergson, Henri. 1932. *Les deux sources de la morale et de la religion*. Paris: Felix Alcan.

Bialas, Wolfgang (ed.). 2019. *Aurel Kolnai's the War against the West Reconsidered*. London: Routledge.

Chatterjee, Partha and Ira Katznelson (eds.). 2012. *Anxieties of Democracy*. Oxford: Oxford University Press.

Fukuyama, Francis. 1995. *Trust: The Social Virtues and the Creation of Prosperity*. New York, NY: Free Press.

Fukuyama, Francis. 2018. *Identity: The Demand for Dignity and the Politics of Resentment*. London: Profile Books.

Goodhart, David. 2017. *The Road to Somewhere: The Populist Revolt and the Future of Politics*. London: Penguin Books.

Habermas, Jürgen. 2001. "Why Europe Needs a Constitution." *New Left Review* 11: 5–26.

Kolnai, Aurel (Francis Dunlop, ed.). 1995. *The Utopian Mind and Other Papers: A Critical Study in Moral and Political Philosophy*. London: Athlone.

Korsgaard, Christine. 1996. *The Sources of Normativity*. Cambridge: Cambridge University Press.

Mill, John Stuart. 2007 [1859]. *On Liberty*. London: Penguin Books.

Müller, Jan-Werner. 2006. "On the Origins of Constitutional Patriotism." *Contemporary Political Theory* 5: 278–96.

O'Neill, Onora. 1993. "Duties and Virtues." *Royal Institute of Philosophy Supplement* 35: 107–20.

O'Neill, Onora. 2005. "The Dark Side of Human Rights." *International Affairs* 81(2): 427–39.

Parfit, Derek. 2013–17. *On What Matters (Vols. 1–3)*. Oxford: Oxford University Press.

Popper, Karl. 1962 [1945]. *The Open Society and Its Enemies*. London: Routledge.

Scruton, Roger. 2017. *Where We Are: The State of Britain Now*. London: Bloomsbury.

Singer, Peter. 2019 [1998]. *Ethics into Action*. Lanham, MD: Rowman and Littlefield.

Wodak, Ruth. 2015. *The Politics of Fear*. London: Sage Publications.

6

THE FAILING TECHNOCRATIC PREJUDICE AND THE CHALLENGE TO LIBERAL DEMOCRACY

Roger Berkowitz

Introduction[1]

In 1990, I graduated college and did something I could not have done even one year earlier. I hoisted a pack on my back and instead of traveling through the glistening capital cities of Western Europe, I flew to Istanbul and made my way up through the cities of Eastern Europe. After stops in Athens and Santorini, I took the train to Skopje, Sarajevo, Zagreb, Prague, Pecs, Budapest, Cracow, Warsaw, and finally East Berlin. In each of these cities, newly freed from the Iron curtain, I encountered people hungry for contact with young Americans. The people of the former Eastern bloc were friendly and open. I never stayed in a hotel, choosing instead to board with one of the dozens of people who I met on every train and ferry I took hoping to earn some hard currency and also have encounters with someone from the West.

Those were heady times. The walls had come down and the Velvet Revolutions had brought the Cold War to an abrupt conclusion. Francis Fukuyama (1989) wrote a year earlier of the "end of history," and whatever one thought of his thesis, the world did suddenly seem more free, more open, and more full of possibility. Democracy had emerged victorious over the quasi-totalitarian and repressive tyrannies of the Soviet Bloc.

The world feels different in 2019. Liberal democracies around the world are in crisis. In Turkey, Hungary, Brazil, the United Kingdom, Italy, and the United States, the "people" are in revolt against governments run by elites. We are witnessing what Martin Gurri calls the "revolt of the public," a revolution against all manner of elite authority (Gurri 2018). There is a "revolution in the relationship between the *public* and *authority* in almost every domain of human activity" (Gurri 2018, 27). The public—better understood as multiple publics of self-informed amateur bloggers and activists—is angry at the mismanagement and arrogance of the elites; these publics are rebelling and seemingly would rather tear apart the system of elite governance than allow it to govern.

After more than five decades of increasingly technocratic rule by elites, we are seeing a rebellion of the publics against elite governance. The prejudices of liberal-democratic politics—that democracy is liberal and individualist, and that democracy should privilege technocratic governance over populist politics—are being upended. We are reminded, as Hannah Arendt argues, that politics is not about truth, but a plurality of opinions. In this essay, I argue that the technocratic prejudice of elite politics is no longer meaningful or feasible. This means that we need to re-imagine a pluralist politics free from the prejudices that have, for decades, bridled democracy by liberal and individualist ideals.

Elite Failures and Crisis of Democracy

The rise of modern society included the rise of management elites—the scientists, social scientists, journalists, social engineers, and governors—who promised to analyze and steer an increasingly complex mass society toward an infinite promise of progress. The world depends upon these elites; even now, the public must rely on experts and specialists to address economic, educational, environmental, and political challenges. But increasingly, the experts are seen to have failed. When schools are not improved, when health care makes you sick, when the CIA doesn't protect the country from terrorists, and when taxes go up and services go down, the elite claim to govern is suspect. Elites hurt their case more when they simply claim that the public needs to trust them to do better and give them more resources. And never do they lose their jobs. To the public, there appears to be a mutual protection pact among elites. The result is anger, distrust, and *ressentiment*.

For much of the industrial era, elite authority was protected by a generally rising standard of living and an elite monopoly on information. As Martin Gurri rightly sees, the daily newspaper was "an odd bundle of stuff—from government pronouncements and political reports to advice for unhappy wives, box scores, comic strips, lots of advertisements, and tomorrow's horoscope" (Gurri 2018, 26). This eclectic mix claimed to be authoritative, organized, and vouched for by elite gatekeepers. The newspaper—as also the politicians and scientists they relied upon—"pretended to authority and certainty" (Gurri 2018, 26). But the bundling has been met with a massive tsunami of information, a "digital revolution" that has overwhelmed the "artificial boundaries of information" and empowered plural public communities to question the narratives put forth by elite gatekeepers (Gurri 2018, 25–27). Every story is partial and leaves out some facts—facts that are irrelevant or inconvenient. In the age of unlimited information and misinformation, it is simply too easy to poke holes in elite narratives of climate change or the benefits of immigration.

And the result, Gurri convincingly argues, is uncertainty that dissolves elite authority.

> Uncertainty is an acid, corrosive to authority. Once the monopoly on information is lost, so too is our trust. Every presidential statement, every CIA assessment, every investigative report by a great newspaper, suddenly acquired an arbitrary aspect, and seemed grounded in moral predilection rather than intellectual rigor. When proof *for* and *against* approaches infinity, a cloud of suspicion about cherry-picking data will hang over every authoritative judgment.
>
> *(Gurri 2018, 24)*

The revolt of the public has upended journalism, education, business, and politics. It has created a society of distrust between elite and the public. And an

> exasperated public has countered by notching up the vehemence of criticism and the frequency of its interventions. At times, in some places, the public has abandoned all hope in modern society and lapsed into a permanent state of negation and protest.
>
> *(Gurri 2018, 119)*

There is a "tectonic collision between a public which will not rule and elite institutions of authority who are progressively less able to rule" (Gurri 2018, 119).

The danger is in the collision of the public with the elites who desperately want to cling to what they think they have earned. There is a mutual incomprehension between a public that simply loathes the elites and elites who have utter contempt for the public. The public sees the elites as talking funny, protected from reality, and out of touch. And the elites look at the public as a basket of deplorable, prejudicial, and uneducated troublemakers.

The danger from the elites is that there has maybe never been an elite class more detached from the social reality of everyday people. The sex scandals, the $4 lattes, the living in bubbles, and the contempt create an elite class that disdains the people and feels justified in its privilege. The elites just want to be elites. To be distant, protected, and insulated, that is the reward for having made it big. An out of touch elite is indifferent to the people like the aristocracies of the 18th century in France. The way elites maintain their authority is that they control the narrative. But with technology and information today, it is no longer possible to have and control authority; what Gurri makes clear is that the result is a loss of authority in institutions, including liberal democracy.

The more imminent danger is that the public in its hatred of elite institutions slips into nihilism. Driven by a frustration at their disempowerment, the publics easily move from resistance to destruction. Demagogic leaders such as Victor Orbán and Donald Trump are symptoms and stimuli to such nihilism. They are post-ideological and nationalist, but only in the sense of economic advantage for the nation. And yet when someone as unqualified as Donald Trump is elected President of the United States, it can only be as a "gesture of supreme repudiation, by the electorate, of the governing class" (Gurri 2018, 357). Trump's success is a result of his nihilism, an expression of "the public's surly and mutinous mood." He is hardly a great dictator or revolutionary. Rather, he is a sign of a major shift in politics, "away from the structures of representative democracy to more sectarian arrangements. The public craves meaning and identity" (Gurri 2018, 358). It is just such meaning and identity that the feeble and bureaucratic institutions of modern, elite, cosmopolitan government frustrate. Amidst an "institutional vacuum and an informational chaos" (Gurri 2018, 360), a plurality of decentralized, angry, and mobilized publics seeking meaning and identity find it more meaningful to bring down the institutions that frustrate their particular ambitions.

For most elites today, the rise of the publics is interpreted as a return to authoritarianism. Thus, Henry Giroux writes of Trump as the leader of a "dystopian ideology" who offers a "nostalgic yearning for older authoritarian relations of power" (cited in Gurri 2018, 369). But as Gurri responds, to be authoritarian, a government must do something. It must "trample on institutional checks, break the law, abuse established rights" (Gurri 2018, 370). And for the most part, Trump and Orbán and their brethren around the world are not acting as authoritarians so much as democratic demagogues.

Far from authoritarianism, we are witnessing a crisis of authority. If you look at the 1960s, trust in government in the United States was 60–70%. Today, trust in government is between 20 and 30%, and for Congress, it is in the teens (PEW 2019). Trust in the media is below 30%. The kind of authority that the industrial model bestowed on institutions is being destroyed. That governments are failing regularly in Britain, Israel, and Italy—and that coalitions of the mainstream parties in Germany, France, and Greece are being realigned and challenged—shows the widespread mood of chaos and rebellion that afflicts politics today.

The elites have failed to deliver the better world that was promised. In the United States, there is widespread agreement that public schools have failed. Health care has failed. Government has failed. And the elites say: give us another chance. Let us make it better. But the people have lost their trust in elites. And the revolt of the public has given rise to a democratic crisis.

For decades, many of us living in Western-liberal-representative democracies had thought such worries about liberal democracy were relics of a past age. We were, we now know, naïve to believe in the stability of modern liberal-representative democracies. We looked away as skyscrapers built by migrant laborers sprouted for cosmopolitan elites in Dubai. We turned a blind eye to resentment against illegal immigration and applauded as the European Union created a new constitution without a vote. All the while, we ignored how the working classes around the world were hollowed out, squeezed, disenfranchised, and abandoned; financial markets soared, CEOs paid themselves more than 300 times the salary of their average employee, and global cities became our playgrounds (Giang 2013). And while this was happening, we in the United States elected Bill Clinton, George W. Bush, and Barack Obama, three of the least politically experienced Presidents in our nation's history. American confidence in the stability of representative democracy now seems like a dangerous nostalgia for a "golden age of security" that lasted from the 1950s through to the first decades of the 21st century. American faith in representative democracy during the last 50 years could go on only because nobody cared.

The Origins of Crisis: The Technocratic Fallacy

In retrospect, it may be possible to mark the beginning of our democratic crisis. In 1962, President John F. Kennedy gave the commencement address at Yale University. The President told the graduates that they were entering a very different world. Past graduates had found themselves in a world beset by great questions. When John C. Calhoun graduated in 1804, the nation was divided over the questions of a national bank and slavery. When William Howard Taft graduated Yale in 1878, the nation was grappling with questions of reconstruction, the "cross of gold," and the progressive movement. In the 1930s, at the end of Taft's career, the United States was again buffeted by forces of political and economic division surrounding economic liberalism and the New Deal. For nearly 200 years, politics in the United States had been riven by dramatic disagreements "on which the Nation was sharply and emotionally divided" (Kennedy 1962). Such ideological and political divisions, Kennedy optimistically proclaimed in 1962, were specters of a distant past. He announced:

> Today these old sweeping issues very largely have disappeared. The central domestic issues of our time are more subtle and less simple. They relate not to basic clashes of philosophy or ideology but to ways and means of reaching common goals—to research for sophisticated solutions to complex and obstinate issues.
>
> *(Kennedy 1962)*

This was one of the worst-timed speeches in political history. Kennedy's confidence that major political questions were behind us—that political problems had transformed into "administrative or executive problem[s]"—quickly ran into the return of political disagreements of the highest order in the Vietnam War, the Cold War, the 60s counterculture, and the Civil Rights revolution. Soon after, in the 1980s, the Reagan Revolution reasserted the return of political and ideological contestation. And in the 21st century, the rise of the Tea Party and the outbreak of Occupy Wall Street once again set serious political disagreements front and center. And then there is Donald Trump. Contra Kennedy, we are not living in a period of post-political and post-ideological administration.

In spite of being so completely wrong, Kennedy's technocratic faith—his belief that "the kinds of problems" we face today are those "for which technical answers, not political answers, must be provided"—sounds eerily familiar (Kennedy 1962). The idea that expert analysis should and would replace political contestation is bipartisan boilerplate. Tony Blair offered a new free-market Labor Party. Emmanuel Macron, a former investment banker and founder of the Centrist *En Marche*, and Angela Merkel of the conservative Christian Democrats are beloved by educated elites because they elevate competence over ideology. Bill and Hillary Clinton built the former's presidency and the latter's campaigns on the promise of a third way that melded Blue Dog Democratic centrism with technocratic competence—which gave us the welfare to work program and other centrist policies (Lammert in this volume). George W. Bush, in the midst of a war, depoliticized major decisions in Iraq by saying that "our commanders on the ground will determine the size of the troop levels" (Clarke 2011). And President Barack Obama was deeply deferential to the "expertise of conventional authorities: generals and national-security professionals, political operatives like Rahm Emanuel, and, above all, mainstream economists and bankers such as Larry Summers and Tim Geithner" (Purdy 2016). Relying on administrators, Obama regularly bypassed Congress and governed to an unprecedented extent through the administrative state. Jedediah Purdy (2016) writes that President Obama personifies the technocratic style of our anti-political times. Modern politicians increasingly imagine themselves as administrative overseers who defer to and rely upon technocratic elites.

After Technocracy

It is my thesis that our crisis of democracy is deeply entwined with the rise of the technocratic and anti-political approach to politics. In a 2016 column, David Brooks sought to defend politics against what he called the anti-politics of populism. Brooks argued that politics is about the engagements among plural people who have different opinions in a common public sphere.

> Politics is an activity in which you recognize the simultaneous existence of different groups, interests and opinions [...]. The downside of politics is that people never really get everything they want. It's messy, limited and no issue is ever really settled [...]. But that's sort of the beauty of politics, too. It involves an endless conversation in which we learn about other people and see things from their vantage point and try to balance their needs against our own. Plus, it's better than the alternative: rule by some authoritarian tyrant who tries to govern by clobbering everyone in his way.
>
> *(Brooks 2016)*

Brooks's defense of the messiness of a pluralist politics gets something right. Politics is based upon what Arendt in *The Human Condition* calls the "human condition of plurality, [...] the fact that men, not Man, live on the earth and inhabit the world" (Arendt 1958, 7). Politics is that centripetal force, a magnetic or charismatic center, around which a diverse and chaotic multitude gathers and is held together.

> The polis, "Arendt argues," is not the city-state in its physical location; it is the organization of the people as it arises out of acting and speaking together, and its true space lies between people living together for this purpose, no matter where they happen to be.
>
> *(Arendt 1958, 198)*

Politics is that "space of appearance" in which individual actions acquire "an enduring quality of their own because they create their own remembrance" (Arendt 1958, 208). And the politician is that person who speaks or acts in such a way as to enable the people to say what they share in common in spite of their differences.

But even as he praises the messiness of politics, Brooks recoils from the tumultuous nature of populist politics. The problem with populists, he writes, is that they refuse to recognize expertise. They don't like the social scientists and technocrats that Brooks believes are most qualified to govern our democracy. He dislikes the Tea Party and the Bernie Sanders contingent of the left for the same reason: they want to elect people who are immature political actors, people who don't recognize restraints. The populists Brooks demeans are political precisely in the way that Kennedy thought was a thing of the past. They are pugilistic rather than bureaucratic. They have ideologies and they want total victories for themselves. They are not inclined to listen to experts. They prefer "soaring promises and raise ridiculous expectations" (Brooks, 2016).

Brooks is right that populism can be crude, coarse, and dangerous. Right-and-also-left-wing populisms threaten the stability of a liberal-democratic consensus around technocratic governance of stable, liberal-representative democracies. With the rise of populist politics in the United States, Russia, Turkey, and Hungary, traditional liberal democracies are experiencing a crisis. The weakening of that democratic consensus is scary and dangerous. This is especially so because it was the weakness of Western democracies in the 1930s that led to the rise of authoritarian and totalitarian regimes across Europe.

Driven by real fears, it is only natural to seek to defend the institutions and norms of liberal-representative democracies that are currently under attack. We should and must do so. But so much reflection on democratic crisis today assumes only the defensive posture of protecting our crisis-riddled democracies. It is my hope that we can take advantage of this crisis to make democracy stronger.

Four Elite Prejudices

A crisis, writes Hannah Arendt, "tears away façades and obliterates prejudices."

> The opportunity provided by the very fact of crisis—which tears away
> façades and obliterates prejudices—[is] to explore and inquire into what-
> ever has been laid bare of the essence of the matter [...]. A crisis forces
> us back to the questions themselves and requires from us either new or
> old answers, but in any case direct judgments. A crisis becomes a disas-
> ter only when we respond to it with preformed judgments, that is, with
> prejudices.
>
> *(Arendt 1968, 171)*

Populist and authoritarian movements have exposed the fantasy of peaceful,
stable, and just liberal-representative democracies. The forgotten middle class
has risen up and said enough; black Americans subject to police violence are
insisting that black lives matter. Around the world, millions of citizens in the
United States and other liberal democracies regimes are rebelling; they are
raising fundamental questions about previously taken-for-granted assumptions
concerning political inclusion and exclusion, ethnic and racial prejudice, and
economic and social inequality.

If Arendt is right and a crisis only becomes a disaster when we respond to it
with prejudices, we need to look upon our prejudices with open eyes. In what
follows, I suggest four prejudices that have been exposed by our democratic
crises. First, there is a prejudice held by many of the very elites that have come
to control liberal democracies that democracy by its very nature is liberal. Second, many liberal elites insist that modern representative democracy should be
individualist and cosmopolitan and is endangered by collectivist nationalism.
Third, there is a conviction that non-liberal political actors are evil. Finally,
these three prejudices coalesce in an overriding prejudice that democracy must
oppose populist politics in order to enforce its distinct liberal preference for
security over freedom. Together, these four prejudices form an overwhelming
prejudice that democracy must be liberal and thus must forsake democratic
disorder for the certain and technocratic control by a community of educated
elites.

At a moment in which liberal democracy in the United States and around
the world is in crisis, we who live within these democracies are confronted
with a choice. We can double down on our prejudices for liberal democracy
and insist that democracy must be liberal, while insisting that any deviance
from liberal-democratic principles is dangerous and evil. Or we can question
our own prejudices and seek to open ourselves to new democratic possibilities.
Such a path of openness is dangerous and even terrifying in a political culture
suffused with violence, bigotry, and propaganda. But in a crisis, Arendt argues,

we must not take the easy path and fall back on these prejudices. Instead, we must obliterate our prejudices and in doing so open the possibility for a new politics to emerge; at the very least, we must open ourselves to revisiting these questions.

The First Prejudice: Individual Rights Trump Conditions of Equality

First, populist movements have revealed the elitist prejudice that democracy by its very nature is liberal. By liberal, I don't mean left-wing or progressive. The liberal tradition has its source in the freedom from oppression, whether it be the oppression of tyrants, aristocrats, oligarchs, or the democratic majority. Liberalism speaks the language of civil and human rights. The nobility of the liberal tradition is that it recognizes that human beings and political citizens possess certain natural and political rights that are crucial to the thriving of human dignity.

Against the liberal tradition of plurality and individual rights, the democratic tradition has its foundation in the power and equality of the people. As Tocqueville understood, democracy is about the "equality of conditions" (Tocqueville 2002 [1835], Chapter XI). No one has the traditional, political, or God-given right to rule over me.

What is too often overlooked is that the liberal and democratic traditions are generally opposed to each other (Mouffe 2005, 53). Liberalism opposes and suppresses the coarser elements of democratic freedom. As Tocqueville observed,

> A very civilized society tolerates only with difficulty the trials of freedom in a township. The civilized community is disgusted at the township's numerous blunders, and is apt to despair of success before the experiment is completed.
>
> *(Tocqueville 2002 [1835], 67*

Tocqueville saw the spirit of the United States in townships governed by farmers, teachers, and shop owners. The township includes "coarser elements" who resist the educated opinion of the experts and politicians. Which is why township freedom is usually sacrificed to enlightened government. A government by elites and experts risks actively disempowering the people.

When liberalism triumphs over democracy, the people no longer feel that they have a meaningful opportunity for participation concerning important decisions. In part, this sense of powerlessness arises in the face of an elite-driven bureaucracy. "[T]he greater the bureaucratization of public life," Arendt saw, "the greater will be the attraction to violence" (Arendt 1970, 178). Much of the populist anger in the United States and around the world today results from a feeling of the betrayal of the democratic promise of self-rule. Since "in a fully developed bureaucracy there is nobody left with whom one can argue, to whom one can present grievances, on whom the pressures of power can be exerted" (Arendt 1970, 178), bureaucratic rule breeds resentment. It is what Arendt calls "The Rule of Nobody" and is "the form of government in which everybody is deprived of political freedom, of the power to act; for the rule by Nobody is not no-rule, and where all are equally powerless we have a tyranny without a tyrant" (Arendt 1970, 178). The very idea of democracy as "government of the people, by the people, and for the people" is too often opposed by elites who in the name of pluralism and civilization foreclose democratic possibilities and alternative ways of free peoples choosing to live in their own way.

We witness the populist and popular revolt against the rule of nobody today in jeremiads against the "system" or the "deep state." For nearly 50 years, popular opinion across ethnic and racial groups has opposed immigration, while liberal and even conservative elites in the United States have embraced immigration. As Eric Kaufmann writes,

> No one who has honestly analysed survey data on individuals—the gold standard for public opinion research—can deny that white majority concern over immigration is the main cause of the rise of the populist right in the West. This is primarily explained by concern over identity, not economic threat.
>
> *(Kaufmann 2019, 2)*

As Kaufmann sees, "The tug of war between white ethno-traditionalism and anti-racist moralism is redefining Western politics" (Kaufmann 2019, 23). In short, elites in the West insist on a policy of cosmopolitan anti-racism even reaching to the idea of open borders, which is deeply unpopular with white national majorities. Once we understand the contradictions between liberalism and democracy, we can understand how the victory of a particularly liberal idea of democracy carries with it a democratic deficit that can contribute to right-wing and also left-wing anti-establishment populist parties (Mouffe 2005, 53).

The Second Prejudice: For Individualism and Cosmopolitanism; against Collectivist Nationalism

A second prejudice exposed by our crises of democracy is that modern representative democracy should be individualist and cosmopolitan and is endangered by collectivist nationalism. Politics, Arendt reminds us, is the gathering of a group of diverse persons around certain common experiences and shared beliefs. Insofar as political elites—especially those political elites on the social-democratic left—have defined politics as the pursuit of individual interests, they either ignore or reject the political need to "mobilise passions and create collective forms of identifications" (Mouffe 2005, 53). Elite and technocratic democratic politicians recoil from arguments about rootedness, belonging, and fundamental questions about how to organize our common world and shared existence.

Technocratic democracy forgets that politics must not only feed the people bread but also must inspire and give them meaning. It is the rootlessness and homelessness of modern life, Arendt argues in *The Origins of Totalitarianism* (1951), that leaves people susceptible to totalitarian movements that satisfy their deep human need for belonging. Human beings need stories they can tell about themselves that give purpose and significance to their individual existences; only when our lives are understood to serve some higher purpose can we bear the pain of our insignificant human lives.

Especially in the modern age when religious and traditional explanations of collective purpose have lost their public impact, it is natural that large numbers of people seek to justify the tribulations of their lives with artificial but coherent collective narratives. It is because of their prejudice against collective religions, traditional, and national identities that liberal democrats cede the terrain of defining what it means to be an American to right-wing populists who are often the only ones eager to define a national vision of a people.

The Third Prejudice: The Moralization of Political Opposition

A third prejudice made evident by our worldwide democratic crises is that we imagine our political antagonists to be evil. Instead of understanding political opponents as people with different opinions and different interests, the moralists of the anti-political elite imagine the populists as violent outsiders who threaten the post-political consensus. So confident in their access to the truth, liberal, centrist, and even conservative elites refuse to engage in debate with those populists who disagree; instead, elites present both right-and-left-wing populists as moral enemies to be destroyed and eradicated; they are deplorables and anarchists.

The moralization of the political opposition as evil is much easier than having to consider them as political adversaries (Mouffe 2005, 58). What is more, the moralization of democratic politics makes democracy impossible insofar as democracy requires that we agree to share a common world with those who in their plurality are fundamentally different from ourselves.

When our opponents are evil, no common democratic world is possible. On all sides, we can retreat into our comfortable bubbles of affirmation; we live content in the echo chambers of our superiority. But we recoil from the hard work of democracy, of listening to and learning to find commonalities with those with whom we disagree.

The Fourth Prejudice: Prioritizing Security over Freedom

Taken together, these three prejudices—that democracy is liberal, that democracy is individualist, and that democracy moralizes our opponents as evil and undeserving of sharing in a liberal democracy—reveal a fourth and overriding prejudice underlying our democratic crisis: democracy today is prejudiced against politics by its distinct preference for security over freedom.

The prejudice against politics is governed by a profound fear: "the fear that humanity could destroy itself through politics and through the means of force now at its disposal" (Arendt 2005, 97). Having lived through totalitarianism, and having witnessed the dropping of nuclear bombs, we today are deeply aware that politics may well destroy the political and economic worlds we have built; it may also destroy the earth itself.

From out of the fear of politics comes, as Arendt writes, a horrible hope:

> Underlying our prejudices against politics today are hope and fear: the fear that humanity could destroy itself through politics and through the means of force now at its disposal, and linked with this fear, the hope that humanity will come to its senses and rid the world, not of humankind, but of politics. It could do so through a world government that transforms the state into an administrative machine, resolves political conflicts bureaucratically, and replaces armies with police forces.
>
> *(Arendt 2005, 97)*

Terrified by the danger of politics in an age of horrifying technical power, it is all-too-likely that democracies will seek to replace politics with technocratic and bureaucratic administration. But such a hope, Arendt argues, will more likely lead to

> a despotism of massive proportions in which the abyss separating the rulers from the world would be so gigantic that any sort of rebellion would no longer be possible, not to mention any form of control of the rulers by the ruled.
>
> *(Arendt 2005, 97)*

We will, in other words, trade our political and democratic freedom for the security of expert rule.

Hannah Arendt knew that democratic freedom is tenuous. She famously wrote in *The Crises of the Republic* in 1970,

> Representative government is in crisis today, partly because it has lost, in the course of time, all institutions that permitted the citizens' actual participation, and partly because it is now gravely affected by the disease from which the party system suffers: bureaucratization and the two parties' tendency to represent nobody except the party machines.
>
> *(Arendt 1972, 89)*

Arendt saw the weakness of representative democracy to be its basic idea, that citizens should turn over the time-consuming work of self-government to professional politicians. This fundamental anti-political prejudice of representative democracy is magnified in an age where technology brings the terror of massive political abuses.

Conclusion

Most liberal-minded people today are fearful of public power. We say power corrupts, and absolute power corrupts absolutely, but the insufficiency of this formula is lately all too apparent. We are scared of the power that emerges when people act together. So, we prefer a government of experts, not least because it frees us to spend our time on private pursuits like consumption and family. The disempowerment of the people in representative democracy embraces our bourgeois preference to be freed to pursue our individual interests, to be relieved of the duty of politics and public virtue. Much easier to leave governing to the experts.

For Arendt, the rise of massive technocratic bureaucracies leads to what she calls "the rule of nobody" (Arendt 1970, 178). The fact that politics is apolitical and governed by technocratic departments does not mean that it is less tyrannical or less despotic. On the contrary, "the fact that no world government—no despot, per se—could be identified within this world government would in no way change its despotic character." Such a bureaucratic government "is more fearsome still, because no one can speak with or petition this 'nobody'" (Arendt 2005, 97). Bureaucracy is anti-political because "any sort of rebellion would no longer be possible" (Arendt 2005, 97).

Note

1 This chapter is a longer version of a speech first given at the 2017 Hannah Arendt Center Conference "Crises of Democracy" and published in HA: The Journal of the Hannah Arendt Center v. 6 (2018).

Bibliography

Arendt, Hannah. 1951. *The Origins of Totalitarianism*. New York, NY: Schocken Books.

Arendt, Hannah. 1958. *The Human Condition*. Chicago, IL: University of Chicago Press.

Arendt, Hannah.1968. "The Crisis in Education." In *Between Past and Future*. New York, NY. Penguin Books.

Arendt, Hannah. 1970. *On Violence*. Boston, MA: Mariner.

Arendt, Hannah. 1972. "Civil Disobedience." In *The Crises of The Republic*. New York, NY: Harcourt Brace Jovanovich.

Arendt, Hannah. 2005. "Introduction to Politics," In *The Promise of Politics*. New York, NY: Schocken Books.

Brooks, David. 2016. "The Governing Cancer of Our Time." *The New York Times*, February 26. www.nytimes.com/2016/02/26/opinion/the-governing-cancer-of-our-time.html

Clarke, Richard A., "The President and His Generals." *The New York Times*, December 12, 2011. www.nytimes.com/2011/12/13/opinion/the-president-and-the-generals.html

Fukuyama, Francis. 1989. "The End of History?" *The National Interest* 16: 3–18.

Giang, Vivian. 2013. "13 CEOs Who Get Paid Shockingly More Than Their Employees." *Business Insider,* March 2013. www.businessinsider.com/ceos-who-get-paid-much-more-than-workers-2013-3.

Gurri, Martin. 2018. *The Revolt of the Public.* San Francisco, CA: Stripe Press.

Kaufmann, Eric. 2019. *Whiteshift. Populism, Immigration, and the Future of White Majorities.* New York, NY: Abrams.

Kennedy, John F. 1962."Commencement Address at Yale University." June 11, 1962. https://americanrhetoric.com/speeches/jfkyalecommencement.htm

Mouffe, Chantal. 2005. "The End of Politics and the Challenge of Right-Wing Populism." In *Populism and the Mirror of Democracy,* edited by Francisco Panizza, 50–71. London: Verso.

PEW. 2019. "Trust in Government 1958–2019." PEW. www.people-press.org/2019/04/11/public-trust-in-government-1958-2019/

Purdy, Jedediah. 2016. "America's Rejection of the Politics of Barack Obama." *The Atlantic.* www.theatlantic.com/politics/archive/2016/07/obamas-attempt-to-redeem-america/492710/

Tocqueville, Alexis de. 2002 [1835]. *Democracy in America.* The Complete and Unabridged Volumes I and II. New York, NY: Random House.

PART II

Democracy, Distorted

Cases of Illiberalism

7

GLOBAL TRUMPISM

Understanding Anti-System Politics in Western Democracies

Jonathan Hopkin and Mark Blyth

Introduction

Donald Trump is such a departure from the conventions of the US presidential politics that it is easy to treat him as an N of one. If he is compared at all, he is cast in with Brexit, which has its own peculiarities. But doing so would be a mistake. From a comparative perspective, Donald Trump is far from being an outlier on the global stage. Variants of Trump's populist rhetoric and refusal to play by the norms of democratic politics can be observed in most of the advanced industrial states. Trump is a manifestation of a global phenomenon, what has previously been called Global Trumpism (Blyth 2016). To see why this is the case, we need to place Trump in his proper context: the universe of advanced democratic countries that have all, to some degree, accepted a particular neoliberal understanding of the relationship between the market economy and the democratic polity over the past quarter-century. This policy consensus, in particular the externalities that it has generated, has produced not just Trump but a wholesale shift in the party systems of the advanced democracies. Trump is a data point. Global Trumpism is a structural shift.

Understanding what lies behind this new anti-system politics is crucial if Western societies are to understand how to respond to it. To do so, it is first of all necessary to understand what Trumpism is, and what it is not. Second, we need to understand the causes of Trumpism, and to do that, we need to recognize the real nature of the liberal democratic orthodoxy that he rails against. The backlash the Western democracies are witnessing is best understood as a reaction against a specific set of political and economic arrangements, which combine decreased competition in the political sphere and enhanced competition in the economic sphere. These arrangements have left many, perhaps most, citizens in Western democracies exposed to greater economic risk while reducing the scope for political action to cope with those risks. In circumstances of such sustained economic insecurity, any politician who offers to "root out" the politicians responsible for producing it, and offers protection from the unpredictability of globalized markets while doing so, has just cornered a ready electoral market.

The return of aggressive nationalism after a financial crisis and recession unlike any seen since World War II should not surprise anyone. Indeed, quantitative work predicts it (Jordà et al. 2015). At the very least, past experience should have warned that a policy of rescuing financial institutions while imposing harsh austerity on citizens would have consequences in a democratic political system. Indeed, in many respects, the policies pursued in Europe and North America since 2008 are uncomfortably similar to the defense of the Gold Standard in the 1920s—stabilization through high unemployment and balanced government budgets. Today, while living standards are much higher, and welfare protections more highly developed than in the inter-war period, the political response has taken longer. But the election of Trump and other similar cases across the developed West suggest that patience and protective institutions can both wear thin, and now have the potential to fundamentally change the global order.

While this chapter takes the financial crisis and the subsequent austerity policies imposed on populations in Europe at the regional level and in the US at the state level as an important short-term cause of the rise of anti-system politics, we also believe that these developments should be placed in a broader context of institutional change in the global economic order over the past half-century. In that regard, the work of Thomas Piketty (Piketty 2014) and others has revealed a dramatic shift in the balance of power between capital and labor since the 1970s, with major implications for the distribution of income between different social groups in Western democracies.

Recent scholarship on party politics also reveals that democracy has been weakened significantly over the same period by the organizational and intellectual decline of political parties, which has exposed democracy to an increasing degree of capture by wealthy interests, while the political influence of middle and lower-income groups has been curtailed (Palan et al. 2009). As such, we contend that the current institutional arrangements governing democracy and the market economy—what we call here the 'liberal order'—were actually quite fragile even before the crisis. The inadequate response to the crisis by mainstream political forces after the crisis laid bare the inability of established elites to govern in the interests of the broader public.

In short, the initially contained response of Western publics to the crisis has given way to a rising tide of anti-system politicians expressing voters' anger at how they are governed. But these politicians do more than rail against existing elites: they also demand a change in the existing political and economic order.

In particular, they articulate a social demand for protection from unfettered markets. Trump has much in common not only with Nigel Farage, Marine Le Pen, or Matteo Salvini, but also with Bernie Sanders, Pablo Iglesias, Alexis Tsipras, and Jeremy Corbyn. From different ideological perspectives, all these politicians express a demand for politics to intervene in markets, whether they be financial, labor, or for goods and services, to protect the interests of their voters. They can make such demands precisely because of the failings of the existing order to satisfy this demand for protection. As Karl Polanyi wrote 80 years ago, attempts to shoehorn human civilization into a market system would lead to resistance. He theorized a 'double movement' whereby the increasing encroachment of market relations on social life provoked a protective reaction or 'counter-movement' (Polanyi 1957, 79). If the incumbent political elites have appeared reluctant to act to protect society from the downturn, competitors offering a more aggressive approach can be expected to win support.

What Is Local about Trumpism? Anti-Globalization and Anti-Elitism

Trump is in many ways a classic populist. His appeal to the nation, his fear-mongering about its purported enemies, his demagogic railing against a corrupt elite, his demonization of minority populations and immigrants, his cavalier attitude to facts, and his vague but confident assertions of easy solutions to complex problems are all familiar components of populist rabble-rousing leadership (Müller 2017). His oft-repeated slogans reflect these familiar populist tropes. "America First" offers comfort to disgruntled voters that under his leadership, American citizens would be a priority, unlike under previous incumbents, all of whom, it was implied, favored foreigners (through a lax immigration policy or bad trade deals). His insulting dismissal of political opponents—'little Marco,' 'crooked Hillary,' 'lyin' Ted Cruz' (Itkowitz 2016)—capitalized on widespread popular dissatisfaction with incumbent elites and the workings of the political system, a system which was 'rigged,' a 'swamp' which had to be 'drained.' Unlike these 'losers,' Trump himself was a 'winner,' a gifted man with a magic touch, able to make things better by making "great deals" and telling incompetent elites "you're fired." In the face of criticism and uncomfortable facts, Trump retreats into a parallel world of "fake news." Trump's transparent racism and sexism; his amateurish, personalistic, and familistic interpretation of the office; and his dubious international connections (especially with Russia) have been front and center in the mainstream opposition to his presidency. But these critiques have been ineffective in shifting attitudes amongst most Trump supporters. To understand why, we need to examine what is appealing about his populism.

"America First" may seem a simplistic slogan, but its effectiveness derives from its ability to capture a feeling amongst many voters that mainstream governing elites have not, in fact, put "America First." Certainly, part of this stems from a xenophobic and racist view of America as a quintessentially white society, whose values are threatened both by the demands of minorities and migrants to take a greater share of the nation's resources (Hochschild 2016). But it also reflects resentment toward globalization, and in particular trade agreements, which have exposed many Americans in geographically concentrated and electorally important areas, to competition from workers in emerging countries willing to work for much lower wages (Autor et al. 2013). In short, it is not just nationalism, it is economic nationalism, an appeal for policies that would unapologetically protect Americans from market competition and favor American interests in the global economy.

Trump's rhetoric therefore represents a significant break not only from Republican discourse on economic policy but also from the consensus of close to the entire political establishment of the US, and Europe, over a quarter-century, that free trade is not only good for the world but essential for America. Trump directed particular ire at NAFTA, ultimately renegotiating the agreement in separate agreements with Canada and Mexico after threatening to quit it altogether, arguing that it is "unfair" to Americans (Campoy 2018). Similar invective has been directed at China, accused of the "rape" of the American economy and the "theft" of manufacturing jobs (Aleem 2018).

Instead, Trump campaigned on a slogan to "buy American, hire American," promising to revive American manufacturing and force the return of high-wage production jobs outsourced over the past quarter-century of globalization. Market liberals rushed to condemn this strategy as implausible and unworkable, but it had obvious appeal to lower-income Americans in areas of industrial decline and received the backing of Bernie Sanders (Mayeda 2017). In contrast, both Hillary Clinton and Trump's major rivals in the GOP primaries represented positions of broad continuity on trade, despite the former's equivocation on TTIP and similar agreements late in her electoral campaign.

The second main plank of Trump's populist appeal is his "outsider" status and anti-establishment rhetoric. By describing Washington, D.C. as a "swamp" that needed to be 'drained,' Trump was doing more than simply replicating the disdain for government regulation and federal overreach typical of Republican candidates from Reagan onward. He was also condemning a cross-party complicity with "special interests," which constituted "rampant government corruption" frequently associated with his opponents, especially "crooked Hillary Clinton." He has directly attacked individual companies that he regarded as betraying American workers by outsourcing production: for example, by threatening General Motors over Twitter with a border tax for its Mexican-made vehicles (Stewart 2018). The press and most mainstream media apart from Fox News—almost universally hostile to Trump—have also been a frequent target. In sum, by combining criticism of policies that have allowed American jobs to be shipped abroad with attacks on the political establishment that has presided over economic decline, Trump has channeled the anger and desire for change of large numbers of Americans.

Trump's rhetoric constitutes a concerted assault on the political establishment and the market liberal values it mostly represents. In this respect, his campaign rhetoric shared common themes with the other prominent outsider of the 2016 electoral season: Bernie Sanders. Both were deeply critical of free trade agreements and the role of special interests and campaign contributions, and both presented themselves as insurgents or outsiders against the Washington establishment. Neither were "insider" candidates, Trump self-identifying as a Democrat at various points in his life, Sanders an independent socialist caucusing with the Democrats. The obvious differences between them should not obscure their common status as challenger candidates with outsider credibility, a valuable credential at a time of legitimacy crisis, with public approval of Congress at record lows (Gallup 2018).

Locating Trumpism Ideologically

Something that was barely noticed at the time of the 2016 election was that the three key figures of the 2016 electoral season represented the three broad ideological options that have shaped political conflict in Western democracies, particularly in times of economic stress: liberalism, socialism, and nationalism (Luebbert 1991; Berman 2006), with the Democrats in particular typifying liberalism.

For all the debate around the increasingly partisan and polarized politics of the US in the recent period, on economic issues (see Keller and Kelly 2015), American politics has been marked by a high degree of consensus around market liberalism since the beginning of the Clinton presidency. Democrats eagerly embraced trade openness, financial deregulation, and welfare curbs, while Republicans were mostly reluctant to mobilize opposition to high levels of immigration, which provided a steady supply of both skilled and unskilled non-unionized labor. Both parties' leaderships converged around the need to bail out insolvent financial institutions in 2008, and Obama, despite presenting himself as an outsider candidate promising change, made continuity appointments in key economic policy positions. The 2012 election pitted Obama against an economically and socially liberal Republican, Mitt Romney, with close ties to the financial sector.

In 2016, Hillary Clinton was widely perceived as the candidate representing this continuity position. Both Sanders and later Trump attacked her for her ties to financial interests and complicity in a fundamentally corrupt political system that failed to represent ordinary Americans. The entirely unexpected degree of support for both the socialist and economic nationalist positions of the outsiders in 2016 derailed the Clinton strategy of cautious centrism, to almost universal surprise.

Yet it should not be so surprising that the candidate offering more of the same, when the same meant stagnant living standards for most, and decline and despair for many, would not carry the day. Indeed, putting the 2016 election in a broader comparative perspective, we can see how Trump's victory was in fact quite consistent with the pattern of electoral politics observed in the advanced democracies since the global financial crisis a decade ago. Continuity works when things are going acceptably well. America, as Trump consistently hectored, was "in terrible shape." For many Americans, Trump was the candidate that in the words formerly used by Bill Clinton in his first successful Presidential campaign "felt their pain."

What Is Global about Trumpism? The Rise of Anti-System Parties

The 2016 presidential election was not as unique as it might appear from an American perspective. Following on from the Brexit vote in the UK in June, it was not even the first unanticipated electoral result of the year. In fact, defeats of incumbent parties and successes of outsider candidates have become routine in the post-crisis period without much commentary from academics or journalists. The typical electoral cycle in crisis-hit democracies since 2008 has been for the incumbent party to lose the first post-crisis election to the mainstream opposition—a normal alternation—and then for (often new) anti-system political forces to make major gains in the second post-crisis election as voters vent their frustration at the slow pace of economic recovery.

Figure 7.1 provides some evidence of the dramatic shifts in electoral politics in Europe over the past decade. Average electoral volatility, as measured by the Pedersen index, has hit its highest levels in the democratic era, and there have been far more 'extreme' volatility events, with eight of the biggest 12 electoral shifts since World War II occurring after 2008.

This high level of volatility has meant more frequent incumbent defeats and alternation of partisan control of government. But electoral change is not limited to voters switching between political parties but extends to the growth of parties whose very raison d'être is to disrupt the existing political order. The share of the vote going to parties outside the usual governing coalitions has also grown markedly since the financial crisis. For example, in a sample of 39 European countries, populist parties have improved their share of the vote in national elections to an average of 24.1% in 2017—up from 8.5% in 2000, with most of that increase occurring since 2008. Figure 7.2 shows that these parties—which we will describe as "anti-system" parties (see Hopkin 2020)—have taken a significant share of the vote in several European countries in recent elections.

Anti-system parties have been present in many democracies since the 1970s, and have sometimes survived for long periods, but the levels of support

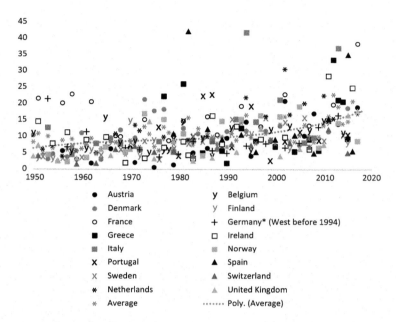

FIGURE 7.1   Electoral Volatility 1950–2018, Western Europe.
Source: Dassonville 2014.

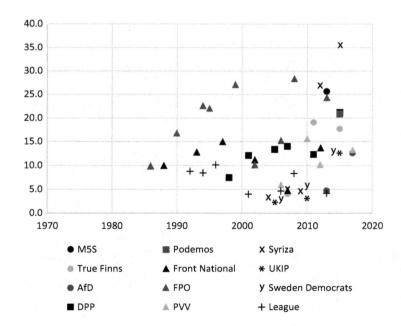

FIGURE 7.2   Anti-System Parties Vote Share 1975–2018, Western Europe.
Source: Dassonville 2014.

these parties have recently won, in some cases very soon after being founded, or after long periods in the wilderness, point unequivocally to systemic shifts in democratic politics. Moreover, these data only show us the shares of the vote won by anti-system forces in general elections, and do not include other clear signs of political disruption, notably the 2016 UK referendum in which voters narrowly voted to leave the European Union, and the large numbers supporting the secession of Catalonia and Scotland from their respective nation-states.

In a world where anti-establishment politics is surging, Donald Trump's electoral success no longer seems exceptional. The defiance of entrenched protocols of political competition Trump, and to a lesser degree Sanders, brought to the 2016 US election is in fact present in almost all of the advanced democracies. And Trump's success has encouraged anti-system forces in Europe, some of whom have imitated his slogans to promote their own campaigns.

If this kind of anti-system politics is happening across the developed democratic world at the same time, it is extremely likely that it has some kind of common cause. That means that the kinds of ad hoc, nationally focused explanations that dominate political debate in the US, which revolve around appeals to partisan and racial identities, and the defense of parties' specific policy commitments to their core constituencies, are probably not where we should be looking. After all, they cannot be generalized to other similar cases.

In particular, the very specific, short-run factors that receive disproportionate attention during election campaigns, such as the FBI's investigation into Hillary Clinton's emails and the hacking of the DNC, may have effects at the margin, but they cannot explain how an unusual candidate such as Donald Trump could have been positioned to win the presidency in the first place. In particular, it cannot explain why similar electoral earthquakes have been happening across a range of different democracies in the last decade.

Two broad structural explanations have dominated more comparative accounts of these changes. One popular account focuses on the prevalence of immigration in the campaigns of anti-system politicians, and the sometimes-overt racism and xenophobia present in the discourse of Trump and the right-wing populists in Europe. This amounts to what could be described as a culturalist explanation of the anti-system vote, drawing on the strong associations between support for right-wing populist candidates and authoritarian values, and the weak evidence for income levels dictating anti-system voting.

For example, Trump voters on average had higher income levels than Clinton voters, but were far more likely to be white and have socially conservative and authoritarian values (Inglehart and Norris 2016, Sides et al. 2017). Similarly, support for Brexit in the UK was strongly correlated with authoritarianism: one study found that the strongest predictor of Leave voting was support for the death penalty, and age was more correlated with the Leave vote than income (Clarke et al. 2017). Opposition to immigration has been associated with the vote for right-wing populist parties in several democracies (Oesch 2008).

Another version points to the financial crisis of 2008 and the harsh austerity meted out by governments in the 2010s, which in many countries led to stagnant or even negative income growth over a much longer period than is usual for the democratic era. Building on the established economic voting literature, defeats of incumbent parties that open the space for anti-system alternatives to prosper are the result of voters blaming the established parties for their income and wealth losses resulting from the crisis. This research identifies regions and localities suffering economic decline as particularly likely to support anti-system candidates (Colantone and Stanig 2016; Che et al. 2017; Malgouyres 2017). For example, Trump's victory has been attributed to his unexpected success in counties in the rustbelt states that had previously reliably supported Democrats. Similarly, support for Brexit in the UK was strongest in small towns and rural areas outside the prosperous South-East of England, with growth since the financial crisis lower than the UK average.

Both of these explanations offer only a partial understanding of the global reach of Trumpism. To move beyond these explanations, we need to both properly conceptualize the phenomenon we are trying to explain and consider the ways in which this phenomenon and the variables purported to explain it vary over time. Failure to correctly define what we are trying to explain will limit our ability to capture the causes of variation. This is particularly important because political instability has been rising recently across many countries, but it has taken different forms in different places, so focusing our attention solely on support for right-wing populism, while excluding other forms of anti-system politics from the analysis, as is often done, overstates the importance of immigration in driving change. Moreover, we need to account for the quite sudden nature of the shift in electoral behavior in several countries in recent years, which implies that slow-moving variables such as the presence of authoritarian attitudes or hostility to immigration among Western publics are unlikely to be the sole cause, as cultural explanations try to maintain.

Here, we take a more global view and argue that recent political shocks are best understood as the result of the exhaustion of a particular set of political and economic ideas, policies, and institutions that can broadly be described as the neoliberal "growth model" or "macroeconomic regime". Our argument develops in two stages. First, we outline the nature of the neoliberal growth model, and show why it has undermined political stability across Western democracies. We then show how the anti-system politics that is emerging across the democracies can be causally connected to the collapse of this regime. Finally, we analyze some of the differences in the characteristics and magnitude of anti-system politics in different democracies.

The Neoliberal Growth Model: The Political Consequences of Putting Capital First

The political and economic institutions that constituted Western capitalism in the immediate pre-2008 period were themselves the product of the collapse of the prior post-war order, variously described as "managed capitalism," the "mixed economy," or "embedded liberalism." That immediate post-war order was built out from a recognition by liberal elites, in the US and the UK in particular, that liberal democracy and the market economy were threatened not only by the nationalist forces that had been defeated in World War II but by the communist forces that had emerged out of it ever stronger. The reconstruction of the market economy was therefore accompanied by the development of international institutions that protected national economies from financial risk—the Bretton Woods arrangements—and domestic institutions that protected labor from economic and social risk—welfare state institutions that established long-term policy commitments over full employment and income replacement.

These risk-sharing institutions were extraordinarily successful in delivering both high growth and relative income equality. But doing so was predicated upon constraining the investor class significantly by entrenching capital controls, redistributive taxation, and corporatist practices in the workplace. As a result, when the Bretton Woods arrangements collapsed and the 1974 oil shock compounded already high wage-led inflation, political forces inimical to the post-war order mobilized to dismantle the institutions protective of labor and remove constraints on capital, leading to a fundamental shift in bargaining power and an increasing privatization of economic and social risk. The ideas and institutions associated with this neoliberal turn, and their consequences for the distribution of income are well documented and understood (Piketty 2014). What is less appreciated is that the neoliberal model had implications for democracy too.

The liberal order that emerged out of what Jacob Hacker has called the "great risk shift" prides itself on its democratic credentials, and its advocates have been quick to condemn anti-system politics as a threat to democratic values (Mounk 2018). However, neoliberalism is only consistent with a very specific vision of democracy, one that gives primacy to the protection of individual rights, especially property rights, over the ability of a majority of voters to assert claims to represent the popular will. Not coincidentally, this 'liberal constitutionalist' vision of democracy is articulated most clearly in the political arrangements of the US, the country which developed the most limited welfare arrangements in the post-war period, and which has traditionally tolerated much higher levels of economic inequality than most other Western countries.

In the neoliberal vision of democracy, one that spread widely during the 1990s and 2000s, with center-left parties in particular being the carriers, popular movements demanding constraints and taxes on capital, or policies to share the national product and protect labor from economic and social risk, needed to be curbed (MacLean 2017). These arguments, associated with the public choice school of political economy and the emergent new classical macroeconomics, carried particular force in a period of high levels of labor mobilization like the 1970s (Crozier et al 1975, King 1975). Governments were diagnosed as suffering from "overload" as citizen demands outstripped the capacity of the political system to supply the public goods that were promised in ever greater numbers by post-war parties.

Freeing capital from controls that limited its ability to move across borders was an effective way of shifting the balance of power away from labor by enhancing the "recoil mechanism" of a capital strike, where investment would fall and unemployment would rise until more capital friendly policies became normalized (Lindblom 1982). In this new environment, national governments became far more restrained in their use of monetary and fiscal policy to affect employment levels and expand social protection. As a result, democratic elections since the late 1980s became less powerful tools for the implementation of the popular will, becoming instead instruments for the disciplining of competing elites, a function in keeping with the thin liberal conception of democratic participation associated with scholars such as Schumpeter and Riker (Riker 1982; Schumpeter 2013).

This liberal model of democracy became entrenched through a gradual extension of the role of non-majoritarian institutions that protected monetary policy and market regulation from democratic incursions. Central bank independence became the norm through the 1980s and 1990s and was finally entrenched as a requirement of European Monetary Union membership in the Maastricht Treaty. The remaining hold-outs, such as the UK, adopted it by the late 1990s.

Central bank independence was explicitly based on the theory that democratic participation in monetary policy-making was a threat to stability, and hence profitability, and delegated this key tool of macroeconomic management to representatives of the financial industry and the economics profession subscribed to such views. Trade policy was likewise made safe from democracy by legalizing it globally through the GATT agreements and the WTO, and regionally in Europe through the jurisdiction of the European Court of Justice. The increasingly close oversight of European Union member states' fiscal policies by the supranational authorities, which seeks to ensure that governments have a severely limited scope to affect demand, has compounded these tendencies.

These institutional changes effectively removed a large part of the key decisions around the economy and the division of the surplus that it generated from direct democratic scrutiny and control, "hollowing out" the nation-state (Rhodes 1994) in the process. What were once objects of policy, such as the employment level, the price level, and trading arrangements, were no longer contested in elections, leaving citizens with no formal channel through which they could influence them. Democratic politics became, as party system theorists noted, "cartelized," as the main political parties ceased competing over the basic institutional structure of the economy (Blyth and Katz 2005; Mair 2013). National parliaments and governments had increasingly less and less influence over macroeconomic policy, and a significant part of regulatory policy. This delegation of policy-making to technocratic institutions, some of them supranational, was matched by a progressive decentralization of the remaining nation-state powers (Hooghe et al. 2010), such as the rise of devolved assemblies, which fragmented political authority and made major challenges to economic policy orthodoxy even more difficult.

The Economic Origins of the Democratic Deficit

These institutional changes, in turn, coincided with a decline in the organizational presence of political parties in society, and their embedding into the structure of the state (Katz and Mair 1995, 2009). Party membership and voter turnout declined steadily from the 1970s, as elections became less and less meaningful in terms of fundamental policy change, and political parties became ideologically more similar. An extensive literature has examined a variety of organizational and societal causes of party decline but it has largely ignored the consequences of the much more constrained role reserved for elected politicians in the post-Bretton Woods era in terms of their ability to either govern the economy or be seen to "do anything" about distribution. The neoliberal macroeconomic regime successfully shifted power from political parties to technocrats and capital markets, leaving politicians to perform the task of securing citizen consent for the outcomes they no longer directly controlled. But such success comes at a price the moment there is a crisis.

This hollowing out of democratic decision-making made collective risk insurance weaker while leaving citizens to rely on decentralized market mechanisms to secure their wellbeing. This was particularly the case in the US and the UK, where a concerted assault on worker organization and redistribution through the welfare state was launched as early as the 1980s, leading to an increasing privatization of risk, reflected in the highest levels of inequality and income insecurity amongst the democracies. In Western Europe, the marketization of social life was a more gradual process as such policies had to erode more entrenched labor market and welfare institutions,

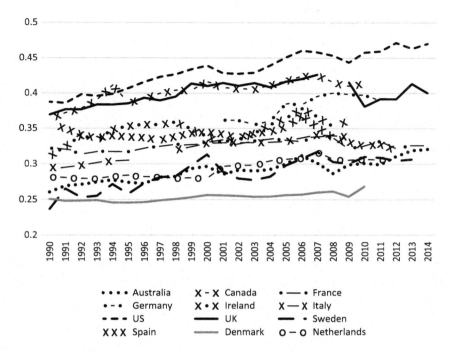

FIGURE 7.3   Top 10% Income Share 1990–2014 (World Inequality Database).

but here too, we observe a clear 'neoliberal trajectory' as reforms at the margin have undercut labor power (Baccaro and Howell 2017). The consequence is rising inequality in almost every advanced democratic state, as Figure 7.3 illustrates:

This increasing inequality between households was reflected in increasing inequality between regions within nation-states. Across countries, economic growth has become more and more concentrated around a small number of regions, leaving others increasingly dependent on redistributive policies for income growth (Rodríguez-Pose 2018). As government spending was reined in after the 2008 financial crisis, this redistribution essentially halted, leading to quite sharp decline in incomes in some regions (Becker et al. 2017, Davidson and Ward 2018).

This trend of rising inequality varies according to the degree to which protective national institutions have been entrenched enough to survive the pressures of marketization. The differing levels of inequality in countries equally exposed to marketizing pressures show that American or British income distributions are not inevitable but are instead the result of the growing bargaining power of capital translating into unmediated influence over the policy process (Hacker and Pierson 2010, Hopkin and Alexander Shaw 2016). In countries where welfare states and labor power were more entrenched, inequality remained at much lower levels, and citizens remained more protected from economic risk, although these arrangements have been coming under pressure almost everywhere. Indeed, as these more egalitarian countries have aged, what shows up as sustained welfare spending in the aggregate in fact masks an intra-generational inequality as pensions are protected, if not expanded, while other decommodifying programs are increasingly curtailed (Emmenegger et al. 2012). The German Hartz IV reforms and subsequent pension reforms of the 2000s show this asymmetric dynamic clearly.

Financialization Covered This Up—Until the Growth Model Failed and Was Bailed

Economic risk is driven not only by position in the income distribution within a society. The expansion of the financial sector has added a further layer of risk to households, especially in the US, but also across much of Western Europe. As the newly liberalized financial sector extended credit more and more liberally, often riding bubbles in housing markets, household debt rose spectacularly, exposing parts of society to the consequences of dramatic changes in credit availability. With wages stagnant and money cheap, households' balance sheet explosions became the 'assets' on the Banks' balance sheets. But with wages stagnant and then suffering a sharp drop since 2008, the ability to service these debts turned assets into liabilities.

Debt crises are thus threatening to both creditors and debtors as the latter's repayment problem can and indeed has translated into the former's default problem. Bailing out this system is 2008–10, and again in Europe in 2012–15, set up debtor-creditor standoffs all over Europe that populist parties, especially in the left such as Syriza and Podemos, capitalized upon. These tensions have been reproduced at the global and regional levels as countries occupy different positions in the various creditor-debtor relationships that have emerged as capital markets have become more integrated and global imbalances have grown. Creditor-debtor conflicts are likely to compound, as household imbalances match those in national accounts. In countries such as Greece, large numbers of households face servicing onerous debts as their countries are also forced into a net saving position to meet their international obligations.

In sum, the liberal order post-Bretton Woods by design placed democratic politics in a subordinate position to capital markets and delivered growing inequality and insecurity to the majority of its citizens, even if these inequalities were masked by cheap credit. After 2008, it ceased to deliver growth to the majority and the credit that masked the income and wealth skew became more expensive while wages fell still further. The centrist politicians who alternated in power in this immediate post-crisis period shared a common response to the crisis focused on maintaining private asset values through monetary engineering while offloading the burden of fiscal adjustment onto wage-earners. Creditors were supported and debtors were squeezed to find repayment out of falling incomes. The historical experience of such situations indicates that political crises will soon follow. In our view, the operational dynamics of this "capital friendly" growth regime made a protective reaction inevitable, and the severity of the financial crisis and the subsequent imposition of austerity explain the timing of that reaction.

Having identified the failings of the neoliberal regime and suggested how its operational dynamics made a populist reaction on both the left and the right more or less inevitable, we now show that the anti-system forces that have prospered in the post-crisis period are a direct response to the trails of this growth regime. We assess two kinds of evidence for our contention. We first examine the ideas and discourses of these new anti-system parties to show that they are articulating more than a simple demand for elite turnover. They are in fact challenging the foundational institutions of the extant growth regime. Then we examine the support bases of these movements to show that they receive support predominantly from the groups that have borne the greatest costs of the crisis of this growth model.

The Rise of Anti-System Politics and the Distribution of Risk: Right and Left Responses

In assessing the ideological and discursive identities of anti-system parties and politicians, we take our cue from the last major episode of regime breakdown, the depression of the 1930s. Scholarship of the inter-war period identifies three broad ideological currents that were articulated in Western countries at that time: liberalism, the pro-market, pro-Gold standard orthodoxy preferred by political and economic elites in the early phase of the depression, nationalism (in some cases articulated through fascism), and socialism or social democracy. The same broad positions can be identified in the current post-crisis environment in several democracies. Liberalism in the contemporary period implies support for the key institutions of the neoliberal regime: open capital, product, and labor markets, monetary policy favoring low inflation and creditor interests, and constraints on redistribution and active demand management through restrictions on taxation and spending. The anti-system forces expressing hostility to these institutions articulate broadly nationalist or socialist alternatives (see Figure 7.4).

Trump's discourse is a good example of what we could describe as the nationalist, or right-wing, attack on neoliberalism. Nationalist anti-system movements target open product and labor markets as threats to the interests of

	Nationalism	Cosmopolitanism
Capitalism	Right-wing populists Regionalists/Secessionists Economic nationalism Welfare chauvinism (Trump, Brexit, National Front, Alternative for Germany etc)	Cartel/mainstream parties Neoliberal challengers (eg Macron, Citizens)
Anti-capitalism	Secessionist left More welfare Anti-euro (eg Catalan Left)	Anti-system left More welfare Internationalism (eg Podemos, Syriza)

FIGURE 7.4 Types of Anti-System Parties.

workers in Western countries, demanding protectionist measures in the form of restrictions on trade openness and, most prominently, restrictions on labor market competition through immigration. Right-wing anti-immigrant parties have grown their votes in all the major West European democracies, with the sole exceptions of Ireland and Portugal, where left populists predominate. Monetary sovereignty is also a major issue. In member states of the Eurozone, where monetary sovereignty has been pooled, nationalist parties protest at the forms of burden-sharing that have emerged out of the debt crisis, which is particularly the case of right-wing populists in the creditor countries of Northern Europe, where the True Finns, the Dutch PVV, and the German AfD have all mobilized around opposition to bailouts of debtor countries in the South. Less commonly, nationalist movements in debtor countries of the Eurozone mobilize in protest at the onerous conditions imposed on them after their bailouts by supranational authorities. More often, as the Italian election showed clearly, proximity to migration flows united right and left populists in opposition to Europe.

The main alternative critique of the liberal order comes from the left and focuses on the excessive political power of financial capital, and the austerity policies that placed the burden of adjustment disproportionately on lower-income citizens. The anti-system left is critical of globalization and its institutions, but mostly refuses to blame immigrants for the crisis, advocating decisive action through the democratic institutions to curb finance and revive the public sector. In Europe, these forces are mostly pro-European, seeing cooperation at the supranational level as a route to fiscal and monetary burden-sharing which could alleviate austerity in the weaker economies. The anti-system left has performed best in debtor countries, particularly in Southern Europe, where the Eurozone crisis led to harsh austerity and the imposition of often unpopular structural reforms.

The broad positioning of democracies on two dimensions of exposure to economic risk predicts which types of anti-system parties are most likely to prosper. Western democracies can be located in three broad positions, according to their current account position, which acts as a proxy for their degree of exposure to the financial crisis, and the commodification of labor, measured as the degree of internal burden-sharing through protective labor market and welfare institutions (Figure 7.5). These two variables capture the two main drivers of individual-level risk of economic distress.

Current account position is a predictor of the type and extent of anti-system politics. Debtor countries have carried most of the burden of adjustment, particularly in Europe, and therefore individuals in debtor countries are more exposed to economic losses and have greater incentives to challenge existing arrangements. We expect therefore that electoral instability and anti-system party vote share will be higher in those countries with the greatest losses in income growth.

Figure 7.6 shows that major party system changes after 2008 are correlated with negative income growth for the median. However, creditor countries also face internal tensions as policy toward debtors can easily provoke resentment, both amongst savers angry at default risks and low interest rates, and amongst citizens resentful of the outlay of public funds to bail out banks and foreign governments. In the context of the relatively slow income growth and growing inequality observed even in the creditor countries, anti-system politicians can mobilize to offer protection from the risks to accumulated assets, or the labor market competition and welfare burden resulting from increased migration from debtor states.

Welfare and labor market arrangements are important determinants of how the failure of the growth model affects different groups. Western European democracies have relatively developed welfare systems, but the extent to which

	Less commodified labour	More commodified labour
Creditor	Right-wing populist (Germany, small Northern European states)	Right-wing populist (Switzerland)
Debtor	Anti-system left (Southern Europe)	Right-wing populist Anti-system left (UK, US)

FIGURE 7.5 Dominant Forms of Anti-System Politics.

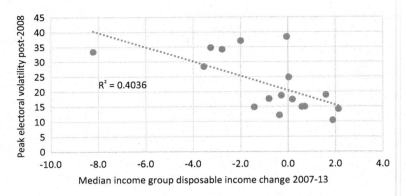

FIGURE 7.6 Median Income Change and Critical Elections after 2008.

Source: OECD Income Distribution Data Base http://www.oecd.org/social/income-distribution-database.htm.

they protect citizens from economic risks—their degree of decommodification (Esping-Andersen 1990; Scruggs and Allen 2006)—varies. The English-speaking democracies mostly have limited welfare protection and more open labor markets, implying a more commodified labor force facing a higher individualization of risk. Most Western European countries in contrast have highly developed welfare and labor market institutions that cushion citizens from economic risk and equalize incomes, but risks are still unevenly distributed and skewed by spending on the vote rich elderly. The main distinction here is between the highly dualized forms of social protection that have developed in the mixed market economies of Southern Europe, and the more comprehensive coverage typical of the coordinated market economies of Northern Europe.

In the Southern European case, 'outsider' groups, especially younger citizens, are much more exposed to risk than older 'insider' groups, and economic shocks manifest themselves particularly through very high levels of youth unemployment, which affect skilled and less-skilled workers alike. An anti-system left appeal, which demands more government spending and curbs on financial sector excesses, but avoids nationalistic blame-shifting, has the potential to mobilize the most affected groups in these states. In the creditor countries of Northern Europe, where insider-outsider dynamics are less severe, a nationalistic appeal to preserve the welfare state for citizens while protecting savers from financial threats through monetary burden-sharing has more chance of being successful. These broad differences in exposure to the crisis determine the constituencies available to be mobilized and by extension the types of political messages that anti-system politicians can use to capture them. This is seen and illustrated schematically in Figure 7.7, which shows how creditor/debtor status and welfare regime type correspond reasonably well to the extent and variance of the anti-system response in Western democracies.

Type of Economic System	Mobilized Groups	Anti-System Type
Debt crisis + residual welfare (US, UK)	Most outside top 10%: Indebted working-age households, insecure youth Pensioners, small savers, older low-skill workers	Strong -> Anti-System Left (Sanders, Corbyn) -> Right-wing populism (Trump, Brexit)
Debt crisis + dualized welfare and labour market (Greece, Spain, Italy, Portugal, France)	'Outsiders'. Indebted working-age households, insecure youth	Strong -> Anti-System Left (Syriza, Podemos, Five Stars Movement, Left Bloc)
Creditor country, strong welfare (Austria, Denmark, Sweden, Germany, Netherlands, Finland)	Pensioners, small savers, older low-skill workers	Moderate -> Right-wing populism (Alternative for Germany, Dutch and Austrian Freedom Parties, Finns Party)

FIGURE 7.7   Nature of Crisis and Variations in Anti-System Politics.

Global Trumpism and the Global Economic Order

The anti-system wave reflects the deep crisis afflicting the liberal order that emerged out of the disembedding of the post-war regime from the 1970s onward. To locate our argument in terms of Dani Rodrik's influential trilemma of globalization (Rodrik 2011), an attempt to combine democracy with globalization at the expense of national self-determination has collided with the explicit withdrawal of consent on the part of a large share of Western electorates. The elite-led project of closing off the democratic state from popular pressure could perhaps be sustained in a context of consistent economic growth, or at least credit-led growth, but with the need to impose painful austerity on the lower-income majority to rescue the assets of the wealthy, this model's fundamental lack of legitimacy has been exposed. Instead, voters are demanding that politics be put at the service of defending society from economic threats. Focusing on the race-baiting of the Trump campaign, or the apparent proximity of some populist leaders to Putin's Russia, obscures the underlying dynamics of the crisis and misleads as to the possibilities of restoring the liberal regime without institutional changes to regain the authority to govern.

In the longer run, this latest attempt to make the liberal order more capital friendly reflects the unstable relationship between democracy and the market economy. Economists and public choice theorists developed a cogent and influential critique of post-war managed capitalism, arguing that popular democracy inevitably placed governments under irresistible pressure to interfere with markets for partisan purposes, by manipulating monetary policy, taxing productive social forces to redistribute to electoral constituencies, or suppressing market competition to reward favored industries. Their response was to limit the scope of government to protect the market, to free capital of regulatory constraints, and to remove important powers from elected politicians. Politicians were complicit in this exercise, since the "logic of no alternative" implied by globalized economy with free capital flows liberated governments from the need to compete in policy terms for voters, establishing a cozy 'cartel' of parties offering fundamentally similar approaches to managing the market.

This arrangement survived for several decades, in part because the established parties could live off the inertia of large numbers of partisan identifiers, which only slowly declined, in part because of institutional advantages they leveraged to exclude challenger parties from access to power (public financing of parties, electoral system thresholds, control over the state machinery). The financial crisis and the shock to incomes exposed the vulnerability of this arrangement, particularly when traditional alternation between government and opposition failed to produce any major changes in policy.

The anti-system wave can therefore be seen as a return of politics to the governance of the economy on a global scale. Trump's threats to impose unilateral tariffs and reluctance to observe conventional protocols regarding the Federal Reserve have been described as a fundamental threat to the American liberal order, but they can also be located in the tradition of populist demands to subordinate the interests of capital to those of citizens lower down the income scale, which is part and parcel of that America's multiple political traditions, as Rogers Smith put it (Smith 1993). Trump is not the first populist America has seen. Neither is Salvini Italy's.

Trump may be an inarticulate and unreliable ally of the poor, but anti-system politicians in many other Western democracies have adopted similar discourses, from supporters of Brexit in the UK claiming to speak for a down-trodden population threatened by inflows of cheap labor from Eastern Europe, to the anti-system left in Southern Europe railing against the euro and the imposition of harsh austerity measures that served only to bail out what many see as corrupt governments working with greedy bankers.

The liberal order always faces a fundamental difficulty in that it cannot entirely protect the market from political interference without the consent of the electorate, and the electorate's patience may be tested when the share of income reserved for the bottom 90% of the population has declined substantially in most Western democracies. If democracy is to uphold rather than subvert the market, then governments will have to act in order to ensure the market economy distributes income and wealth in a fashion deemed fair by a large majority of voters. If it does not, we can expect more Trumpets to sound and more populists to follow.

Bibliography

Autor, David, David Dorn, and Gordon H. Hanson. 2013. "The China Syndrome: Local Labor Market Effects of Import Competition in the United States." *American Economic Review* 103(6): 2121–68.

Baccaro, Lucio, and Chris Howell. 2017. *Trajectories of Neoliberal Transformation: European Industrial Relations Since the 1970s*. New York, NY: Cambridge University Press.

Becker, Sascha, Thiemo Fetzer, and Dennis Novy. 2017. "Who Voted for Brexit? A Comprehensive District-Level Analysis." *CAGE Working Paper* 305, University of Warwick, October.

Berman, Sheri. 2006. *The Primacy of Politics*. New York, NY: Cambridge University Press.

Blyth, Mark. 2016. "Global Trumpism: Why Trump's Victory Was 30 Years in the Making and Why It Won't Stop Here." *Foreign Affairs* 15.

Blyth, Mark, and Richard Katz. 2005. "From Catch-All Politics to Cartelisation: The Political Economy of the Cartel Party." *West European Politics* 28(1): 33–60.

Campoy, Ana. 2018. "The Definitive Guide to Trump's Positions on NAFTA." *Quartz* 23 January. https://qz.com/1185878/nafta-negotiations-the-consequences-of-trumps-positions/.

Che, Yi, Yi Lu, Justin Pierce, Peter Schott, and Zhigang Tao. 2016. "Did Trade Liberalization with China Influence U.S. Elections?" *NBER Working Paper* No. 22178.

Colantone, Italo, and Piero Stanig. 2016. "Global Competition and Brexit." *BAFFI CAREFIN Working Paper* No.2016–44, Bocconi University.

Dassonneville, Ruth. 2015. *Net Volatility in Western Europe: 1950–2014*. Dataset. KU Leuven: Centre for Citizenship and Democracy.

Davidson, Mark and Kevin Ward (eds.). 2018. *Cities under Austerity: Restructuring the US Metropolis*. Albany, NY: SUNY Press.

Emmenegger, Patrick, Silja Häusermann, Bruno Palier, and Martin Seeleib-Kaiser (eds.). 2012. *The Age of Dualization. The Changing Face of Inequality in Deindustrializing Societies*. Oxford: Oxford University Press.

Esping-Andersen, Goesta. 1990. *Three Worlds of Welfare Capitalism*. Cambridge: Polity.

Gallup. 2018. "Congress and the Public." Gallup. http://news.gallup.com/poll/1600/congress-public.aspx (retrieved October 31, 2019)

Hacker, Jacob S., and Paul Pierson. 2010. "Winner-Take-All Politics: Public Policy, Political Organization, and the Precipitous Rise of Top Incomes in the United States." *Politics & Society* 38(2): 152–204.

Clarke, Harold D., Matthew Goodwin, and Paul Whiteley. 2017. *Brexit: Why Britain Voted to Leave the European Union*. Cambridge: Cambridge University Press.

Hochschild, Arnie Russell. 2016. *Strangers in Their Own Land: Anger and Mourning on the American Right*. New York, NY: The New Press.

Hooghe, Liesbet, Gary Marks, and Arjan H. Schakel. 2010. *The Rise of Regional Authority. A Comparative Study of 42 Democracies 1950–2006*. London: Routledge.

Hopkin, Jonathan. 2020. *Anti-System Politics. The Crisis of Market Liberalism in Rich Democracies*. New York, NY: Oxford University Press.

Hopkin, Jonathan, and Kate Alexander Shaw. 2016. "Organized Combat or Structural Advantage? The Politics of Inequality and the Winner-Take-All Economy in the United Kingdom." *Politics & Society* 44(3): 345–71.

Inglehart, Ronald, and Pippa Norris. 2016. "Trump, Brexit, and the Rise of Populism: Economic Have-Nots and Cultural Backlash." *HKS Working Paper* No. RWP16–026. https://papers.ssrn.com/sol3/papers.cfm?abstract_id=2818659.

Itkowitz, Colby. 2016. "'Little Marco,' 'Lyin' Ted,' 'Crooked Hillary:' How Donald Trump Makes Name Calling Stick.'" *Monkey Cage*, April 20. www.washingtonpost. com/news/inspired-life/wp/2016/04/20/little-marco-lying-ted-crooked-hillary-donald-trumps-winning-strategy-nouns/?utm_term=.0135f5b3f724.

Jordà, Òscar, Moritz Schularick, and Alan M. Taylor. 2015. "Leveraged Bubbles." *Journal of Monetary Economics* 76: S1–S20.

Katz, Richard, and Peter Mair. 1995. "Changing Models of Party Organization and Party Democracy: The Emergence of the Cartel Party." *Party Politics* 1(1): 5–28.

Katz, Richard, and Peter Mair. 2009. "The Cartel Party Thesis: A Restatement." *Perspectives on Politics* 7(4): 753–66.

Katz, Richard S. 2014. "No Man Can Serve Two Masters: Party Politicians, Party Members, Citizens and Principal–Agent Models Of Democracy." *Party Politics* 20(2): 183–93.

Keller, Eric, and Nathan J. Kelly. 2015. "Partisan Politics, Financial Deregulation, and the New Gilded Age." *Political Research Quarterly* 68(3): 428–42.

King, Anthony. 1975. "Overload: Problems of Governing in the 1970s." *Political Studies* 23(2–3): 284–96.

Lindblom, Charles. 1982. "The Market as Prison." *The Journal of Politics* 44(2): 324–36.

Luebbert, Gregory. 1991. *Liberalism, Fascism, or Social Democracy. Social Classes and the Political Origins of Regimes in Interwar Europe*. New York, NY: Oxford University Press.

MacLean, Nancy. 2017. *Democracy in Chains: The Deep History of the Radical Right's Stealth Plan for America*. New York, NY: Viking.

Mair, Peter. 2013. *Ruling the Void. The Hollowing of Western Democracy*. London: Verso Books.

Malgouyres, Clement. 2017. "Trade Shocks and Far-Right Voting: Evidence from French Presidential Elections." *Robert Schuman Centre for Advanced Studies Research Paper* No. RSCAS 2017/21.

Mayeda, Andrew. 2017. "Bernie Sanders Tells Trump to Keep His Promise on Nafta." *Bloomberg*, December 13. www.bloomberg.com/news/articles/2017-12-13/bernie-sanders-to-trump-on-nafta-for-once-keep-your-promise.

Mayer, Jane. 2016. *Dark Money: The Hidden History of the Billionaires behind the Rise of the Radical Right*. Harlow: Anchor.

Michel Crozier, Samuel Huntington, and Joji Watanuki. 1975. *The Crisis of Democracy*. New York, NY: New York University Press.

Mounk, Yascha. 2018. *The People vs. Democracy: Why Our Freedom Is in Danger and How to Save It*. Cambridge, MA: Harvard University Press.

Müller, Jan-Werner. 2017. *What Is Populism?* London: Penguin.

Oesch, Daniel. 2008. "Explaining Workers' Support for Right-Wing Populist Parties in Western Europe: Evidence from Austria, Belgium, France, Norway, and Switzerland." *International Political Science Review* 29(3): 349–73.

Palan, Ronen, Richard Murphy, and Christian Chavagneux. 2009. *Tax Havens: How Globalization Really Works*. Ithaca, NY: Cornell University Press.

Piketty, Thomas. 2014. *Capital in the Twentieth-First Century*. Cambridge, MA: Belknapp/Harvard.

Polanyi, Karl. 1957. *The Great Transformation: The Political and Economic Origin of Our Time*. Boston, MA: Beacon Press.

Rehm, Philipp, Jacob S. Hacker, and Mark Schlesinger. 2012. "Insecure Alliances: Risk, Inequality, and Support for the Welfare State." *American Political Science Review* 106(2): 386–406.

Rhodes, Rod. 1994. "The Hollowing Out of The State: The Changing Nature of the Public Service in Britain." *The Political Quarterly* 65(2): 138–51.

Riker, William. 1982. *Liberalism versus Populism*. San Francisco, CA: WH Freeman.

Rodríguez-Pose, Andrés. 2018. "The Revenge of the Places That Don't Matter (and What To Do About It)." *Cambridge Journal of Regions, Economy and Society* 11(1): 189–209.

Rodrik, Dani. 2011. *The Globalization Paradox. Why Global Markets, States and Democracy Cannot Coexist.* New York, NY: Oxford University Press.

Schumpeter, Joseph. 2013. *Capitalism, Socialism and Democracy*. London: Routledge.

Scruggs, Lyle, and James Allan. 2006. "Welfare-State Decommodification in 18 OECD Countries: A Replication and Revision." *European Journal of Social Policy* 16(1): 55–72.

Sides, John, Michael Tesler, and Lynn Vavreck. 2017. "Donald Trump and the Rise of White Identity Politics." Paper presented at 'The 2016 U.S. Presidential Election: Tumult at Home, Retreat Abroad?' conference at the Mershon Center, Ohio State University, November. https://mershoncenter.osu.edu/media/media/publications/misc-pdfs/sides.pdf.

Smith, Rogers M. 1993. "Beyond Tocqueville, Myrdal, and Hartz: The Multiple Traditions in America." *American Political Science Review* 87(3): 549–66.

Stewart, Emily. 2018. "How Wall Street Learned to Stop Worrying and Love Trump." *Vox* January 17. www.vox.com/policy-and-politics/2018/1/17/16897656/trump-wall-street-stock-market.

Zeeshan Aleem. 2018. "Trump's Moment of Truth on China Has Arrived." *Vox* January 22. www.vox.com/world/2018/1/22/16850100/trump-china-trade-steel-intellectual-property.

8

THE CRISIS OF DEMOCRACY

The United States in Perspective

Christian Lammert

Introduction

Populist parties and politicians are on the rise in Europe as well as in the US. Donald Trump in the US, Boris Johnson in the UK, Viktor Orban in Hungary, as well as electoral successes by the Rassemblement National in France and the Alternative for Germany: anti-establishment politicians and parties are successfully mobilizing an electorate that lost trust and confidence in established democratic procedures, actors, and institutions. Democracy seems to be on the decline, at least if we follow the Economists Intelligence Units ranking of democratic systems all over the world. Altogether, Western European's average score in the democracy index declined sharply for the third consecutive year, to 8.35, from 8.38 in 2017 and 8.42 in 2014. A more extreme development can be seen in the US. The US fell below the threshold for a "full democracy" in 2016, primarily because of a serious decline in public trust in US institutions. In 2018, the US fell further in the global ranking, to 25th place, from 21st in 2017. Even in the latest Economics Intelligence Unit report, the US continues to be rated as a "flawed democracy."

How can we explain the deterioration in the quality of democracies in the transatlantic region? What are the common denominators that might explain the success of populist and anti-establishment forces at nearly the same point in time? And what are more country-specific reasons that help explain those developments? I will argue in this chapter that the successes of anti-establishment forces are the result of a specific set of policies that were implemented in nearly all democracies in Western Europe and the US starting in the late 1980s and early 1990s. These policies have been supported by left-wing and right-wing political forces stating that "There is No Alternative" (TINA) to those policies (see Scruton in this volume for a critique of "TINA" politics from a conservative perspective). At its core, this neoliberal policy agenda is built around two main blocks: welfare state retrenchment and restructuring on the one side and a massive deregulation of market activities, especially in the financial markets on the other side (see also Vormann and Lammert 2019).

Illiberalism in the Transatlantic Context: Broader Factors

Anthony Giddens coined the term "third way" to describe a position akin to centrism that tries to reconcile right-wing and left-wing policies by advocating a varying synthesis of center-right and centrist economic policies, on the one hand, and some center-left social policies, on the other hand (Giddens 1998). In the context of broader globalization processes, this set of policies led to growing economic inequality within countries and triggered in large parts also the financial crisis from 2008. The neoliberal policy agenda that we do find on both sides of the Atlantic put the market above the state by stating that the welfare of the people and the society is best served by the efficiency of private actors and market instruments. It denigrates public goods as a waste of taxpayers' money, and regards state intervention as a clumsy interference. Economic and social policy, according to this way of thinking, must adapt to the givens of globalization. Everyone is responsible for him- or herself. Individualism and self-responsibility are core concepts to understand this strand of policies.

On both sides of the Atlantic, those changes had two major consequences: first, retrenchment and restructuring of the welfare system have affected the visibility of the welfare state. 'Visibility' means that citizens identify the state as the provider of welfare (Howard 1999; Morgan and Campbell 2011). Trends toward privatization of social policy and the idea of self-responsibility are shifting the focus away from the state and the public as the producers of social benefits toward non-state actors, individuals, and the market more generally. This leads to the second consequence: those shifts also affect the relationship between the state and its citizens in general. Different studies have shown that the visibility of social programs produces legitimacy for the political system and at the same time encourages political participation among its citizens (Campbell 2003). If the people don't perceive the state as a producer of economic security and social goods anymore, the system is losing legitimacy and trust in established political institutions will decline (Lammert and Vormann 2020).

Populism and illiberal tendencies in North Atlantic states are therefore not the cause of a crisis of governance, but its result. This crisis has been many decades in the making, and it is intricately linked to the rise of a certain type of political philosophy and practice that has extended across both sides of the Atlantic. This dominant political dogma has seen marketization as the only possible and legitimate way of organizing societies in the context of globalization processes. The shift from responsive governmental institutions to processual and semi-private governance bodies has contributed to a depoliticization of all things political (Vormann and Lammert 2019). Populism in Europe and the US is an expression of this immanent crisis of liberalism in which economic rationalities have hollowed out political values and have led to an impoverishment of the political sphere. The promises of the neoliberal revolution—individual freedom and self-determination—have failed to materialize for too many. Societies no longer pursue common projects but are reduced to the sum of their individuals.

TINA Policies: Retrenchments and Restructuring of the Welfare State

In the last three decades, social welfare and tax-related changes in the US and several European countries have played a central role in the increase of income inequality and the rise of poverty rates. Recent studies (Piketty 2014) indicate clearly that taxes and transfers have frequently become much less successful at reducing widening income gaps and that social policy reforms were at least partly responsible for widening household-income gaps (OECD 2011). Political elites described and justified those changes as policies without alternatives, because the process of globalization and the integration into world markets, so the argument, turned welfare states incrementally into 'competition states' (Genschel and Seekopf 2012). These competition states differ from the welfare state in the sense that they promote increased marketization by liberalizing cross-border movements of goods and people, re-commodifying labor, and privatizing public services. Whereas the welfare state tried to domesticate capitalism, the competition state tries to be attractive for capital and investments first (Cerny 1997). In order to be competitive in this sense, the state needs to deregulate the market and lower tax rates on corporations. As a consequence, this leads toward a downward spiral in social and public spending.

The origins of the transformation from the welfare to the competition state in the US can be traced back at least to the 1990s. Criticism of the social welfare system was so strong at the time that President Clinton, as a Democrat, began his term in office with the call to "end welfare as we know it" (Weaver 2000), which he then also did, with support from Republicans in Congress. The core of this reform was to repeal and replace the family support program known as Aid for Families with Dependent Children (AFDC). According to AFDC, certain persons, especially mothers with children, had a right to social benefits. With the elimination of AFDC and its replacement by a new program of temporary assistance, Temporary Assistance for Needy Families (TANF), this right was revoked and a time limit for receiving benefits from this program was imposed. Welfare as a right was abolished. Welfare reform has become possible in the 1990s because the dominant public discourse constantly made references to globalization so as to point out that international competition simply made it necessary to cut down public spending on welfare. The discussion focused on welfare because conservative think tanks were successful in stigmatizing welfare recipients in the 1980s as lazy and portraying the welfare system as paternalistic and expansive. Further, racial connotations in the reform debate further delegitimized welfare at that time. All in all, these factors made a sufficient majority of the public support cutting back welfare programs.

Parallel to this, another mantra of neoliberal critique was integrated into the social welfare realm: activation. The central idea here was that the programs, above all, should re-integrate benefit recipients into the labor market. The fetish of wage labor is clearly identifiable in all these programs and reforms. But it is founded on the assumption that the market, specifically the labor market, is actually able to carry out these functions—in other words, that it is capable of providing everyone with a wage and sustenance. If someone fails, this is a matter of personal responsibility. Overall, these ideas have led to a situation where the US, in general and especially in times of economic crisis, can protect its citizens only in the most rudimentary way from the failures of the market. In situations where a person loses a job, and in cases of illness, there is the real threat of a rapid loss of social position; indebtedness; and even, in many cases, personal bankruptcy.

The US certainly does have a system that helps people facing specific social risks. But compared to European welfare models, it differs in two specific respects that also magnify the problem of a faltering labor market. First, there is the significantly greater proportion of private social insurance. This is especially true of retirement and illness, as reflected in total expenditures for these programs. In the US, in 2013, according to figures provided by the OECD (OECD 2019), the percentage of GDP devoted to private social expenditures was 11.4%. By comparison, in Germany, only 3.3% was spent on private social expenditures, and in the OECD countries, the average was a mere 2.6%. Furthermore, the US relies much more heavily than many European governments on the tax system to generate social benefits. This happens in two ways. On the one hand, private social expenditures receive massive tax subsidies—from the purchase of a house to the cost of private retirement or health insurance. On the other hand, social benefits are also disbursed directly through the tax system. The most prominent example of the latter is the Earned Income Tax Credit (EITC), in other words a tax credit on income.

And the result of the transition into competition states? According to OECD data (2011), income inequality rose in 17 of the 22 OECD countries for which long-term data is available, climbing by more than four percentage points in countries like Germany, Sweden, and the US. We can see different patterns across OECD countries over time. Income inequality started to increase in the late 1970s and early 1980s in some English-speaking countries, notably the UK and the US. Starting in the 1980s, the increase in income inequality became more widespread. The latest trends since the 2000s showed a widening gap between the rich and the poor, not only in some already high-income inequality countries like the US, but also in traditional low-income inequality countries like Germany, Denmark, and Sweden, where inequality grew more than anywhere else since the 2000s.

Wages and incomes in the US are currently as unevenly distributed as they have not been since the era of the Great Depression, in the 1930s. Things are looking great, above all, for the top earners, who have done better and better in comparison to the rest of society. French economist Thomas Piketty (Piketty 2014) and his colleagues have made clear that it is the top 1%, in particular, who have benefitted most from economic development since the 1970s. Deregulation policies pursued by both the Clinton and Bush 43 administrations, starting in the 1990s, did stimulate free market forces for a certain period, but it was the rich, above all, who profited. The middle class and lower-income groups saw hardly any rise in income.

The bottom 50% of income earners in the US have been more or less shut out of the market for the last 40 years when it comes to increases in income. Their average annual income in 2014, at $16,197, was a mere 2.7% greater than their income in 1974. Over the same period, the income of the highest 10% jumped by a staggering 231%. The government, via its tax and transfer system, did very little during this period to balance out this unequal distribution of market forces. On the contrary, tax reductions, for example, under George W. Bush in the years after 2000, made the spread between rich and poor even more extreme (Bartels 2005).

Precisely this toxic mixture of deregulation, privatization, tax reductions for the rich, and cuts in welfare programs created the basis for dissatisfaction and a loss of trust among broad sectors of society. Combined with the national ideological overemphasis on individualism and self-reliance, ideas and ideologies were able to take root in the public discourse that ultimately led to social division and also, quite concretely, to the 2008 financial and economic crisis. This crisis was as serious as it was because it brought an already porous social system, which is dependent on growth, to the edge of collapse. If we wanted to tie it to a specific development, we could say that today's crisis of democracy is an aftershock of this same financial crisis.

Political Inequality, Money in Politics, Gridlock, and Polarization

The economic and financial crisis of 2008 made very clear the extent to which the American socio-economic model is dependent on a dynamic labor market, and, more specifically, on a constantly growing low-wage sector. If the latter is no longer able to absorb as many people, as happened during the recent economic crisis, the country's already quite fragile social balance comes under threat. The 2016 presidential campaign demonstrated this very clearly. In the camps of both political parties, candidates mobilized based on the difficult economic situation. Bernie Sanders led a primary campaign among Democrats that was mainly based on the growing social and economic inequalities, and Donald Trump was able to mobilize voters and win votes especially in those regions where the economic recovery was least felt and the unemployment rate had climbed far above the national average.

Fundamental distrust in government has turned into an attitude of refusal that makes the administration responsible for everything that goes wrong—but that simultaneously also fails to acknowledge that it was precisely the cutbacks in public social support systems that lit the fire under the crisis and then blew on it. In the economic liberals' thought model, it is not just that government plays a subordinate role; rather, in both politics and public affairs, there is virtual amnesia about the role that the American government has played up until now. This, at least, is the conclusion drawn by American political scientists Jacob Hacker and Paul Pierson in their recent book, *American Amnesia* (Hacker and Pierson 2017). This memory loss is not somehow accidental. It derives from the political culture of the US, and has been used strategically by powerful special interests to advance their agendas. This includes mega-actors in private enterprise, above all Wall Street finance capital, which has been able to impose its interests by means of massive lobbying.

It was primarily the economic crisis that again turned inequality into a problem for the meritocratic style of American liberalism. But there is also a political crisis that explains the crisis of democracy in a wider sense. Economic inequalities transitioned into political inequalities. Against the background of polarization, the structure of the political system itself has become a problem: built-in blocking mechanisms, which are actually supposed to guarantee democracy, have led to a democratic standstill instead.

Martin Gilens and Benjamin Page also ask whether the category "oligarchy" would not be more apt for the US at this time (Gilens and Page 2014). Their concerns center on the opportunities citizens have to influence politics: for example, the extent to which elected officials, in their actions and policies, act in accordance with the interests of the people who elected them. Political scientists call this responsiveness. In the US, Gilens and Page find, elected representatives are no longer attuned to the interests of the middle class or of low-income groups. They now listen only to the interests of the super-rich and the organized special interests that, with their campaign contributions and lobbying, succeed in influencing politics.

Under these circumstances, democracy's correction mechanism—elections—is ineffective. The only way to break open this circle seems to be either to carry out a political revolution (Sanders) or to drain the swamp (Trump). This perspective also makes abundantly clear that the neoliberal politics of the last 30 years in America were not policies without alternatives, but a concession to the super-rich and the powerful interest groups that succeeded in getting the ear of the political system. All this at the expense of the middle class and low-income groups, whom no one listened to anymore, and who now wanted to make themselves heard again by voting for radical political forces.

The influence of money in politics plays a decisive role in the lack of responsiveness. Elections in the US are expensive, and the politicians have to get this money from somewhere or someone. In 2012, more than 40% of all private contributions to the election came from the richest 0.01% in terms of income (Open Secrets.com). In the 1980s, this percentage from the super-rich was still only 10%! Generally speaking, both parties profited from the contributions, although the Republicans had a significant advantage: 62% of these campaign contributions ended up in their election accounts. The system of electoral finance is generally strictly regulated and formally transparent—at least where the specific electoral team is concerned. In this case, there are firm rules about how much money you can give to candidates, parties, and other groups during an election. But alongside this, since 2008, another realm of election financing has grown up, which is concerned not with the expenditures of the various candidates and their campaigns, but with third parties that are not permitted to be directly linked to the campaigns. This area is known as "independent expenditures," and here we again encounter influential and financially powerful actors and special interest groups that seek to influence elections. In 2010, the Supreme Court gave these actors the constitutional right, under the hallowed concept of freedom of expression, to spend as much money as they want to (see Dowling and Miller 2014).

But the influence of money is not the only problem bedeviling the American political system, even if it is certainly one of the gravest when it comes to the quality of democracy. The buzzwords "polarization" and "gridlock" are often used to describe other aspects of the political crisis that have resulted from the inequalities. Compromises no longer seem possible, and a politics of ideological extremism is taking over—among progressives as well as conservatives. This phenomenon is not entirely new, but it has become institutionally fixed and threatens to explode the political discourse altogether.

As early as the 1990s, the phenomenon of polarization was being talked about as a "culture war"—the buzzword for a cultural battle being waged by the two political camps (Hartman 2019). At the center of this "war" were abortion, the right to bear arms, the separation of church and state, drugs, and homosexuality. Around these questions, two poles formed within the political discourse. These two poles can no longer discuss things with each other on a common basis. Since the 1990s, the split in society has expanded beyond the above-named issues. At the core of the division, once again, we often find the familiar question what role the central government should play in the US.

This division of society into two camps becomes problematic because in the meanwhile the media landscape has adapted it. Under the pressure to sell their news programs, in other words to attract stable consumer groups that will generate advertising income, the media come up with exactly those messages their consumers want to hear. Right-leaning media like Fox News complain about the government and democratic politicians, in particular. Obama, for the right-wing media, was the incarnation of evil. Now, left-leaning media, for example, MSNBC, see Trump the same way. After his 2012 electoral victory, Obama said that if he watched Fox News all day, he would not have voted for his reelection (Hayden 2017).

Stations that once used to be politically neutral, like CNN, are ground down by this competitive struggle. They carry on 24/7 with "breaking news," as a means of maintaining their market share among media consumers. Scandal-mongering and one-sided reportage are the result. Now the only media outlet that is trusted is the one that broadcasts the messages a person wants to hear; people scarcely venture out of these echo chambers. Everything the other side reports is disqualified as "fake news." In Germany, right-wing populists refer to comparable but still noticeably tamer developments as "Lügenpresse," or "lying press"—a term that has unmistakable Nazi overtones.

Naturally, such a media environment is not inconsequential for the work of Congress. This is a big problem especially for a presidential system, where the party infrastructure plays a weaker role. The political system in the US is candidate-focused. This means, first of all, that individual candidates, not parties, get elected. Party lists of the kind that exist in Germany are unknown in the US. Candidates organize their own run for office, raise their own funds, and are ultimately responsible to their constituencies. Parties usually only get involved in supportive ways, by offering a broader, philosophical, or ideological framework within which voters can place their candidates. This system, naturally, also makes the elected official more independent from the party organization or legislative fraction. This is the tradition.

No wonder, then, that in the 1960s, a Republican congressman only voted with his party about 60% of the time (Stonecash 2018). Among the Democrats, this even occurred only half the time. The electoral district at home was much more important, in keeping with the politician's interest in being reelected two or six years hence. In this sense, members of Congress in the US have been like "church steeple" politicians, who have seen only their home district and thus looked no farther than they could see from the church steeple of their own congregation. Questions of ideology played a secondary role in their voting behavior.

But the situation has undergone a massive change. Today, coalitions or compromises with political opponents are as good as impossible, especially when it comes to the kinds of issues that also divide society. In the House of Representatives, today, 90% of Democrats and Republicans vote with their party bloc (Stonecash 2018). Some commentators see the polarization of the political elites as a direct consequence of the polarization of society. Others, though, make reforms within Congress partly responsible for it—reforms that led to the exercise of stronger control by party leaders. In this way, they argue, a more informal discipline has developed within the party factions, which makes non-partisan compromises hugely more difficult. Yet others explain the polarization of the political elites by the structure of electoral districts. In recent years, thanks to gerrymandering and sorting, electoral districts have become more and more homogenous and hence less politically contested. As a result, moderate candidates are no longer as successful. Radicalism pays, because the actual electoral decisions are no longer made in the election itself, but rather in the primaries, since it is quite certain that one party—or the other—will win the district.

Probably, the best explanation is one that takes all these factors into account. What is important, though, is that these developments have very definitely led to a gridlock of the political system. The established mechanisms within the political system no longer correspond to the polarization of the parties. Media polarization both mirrors this problem and renders it more acute, making it more and more difficult to put together successful policies.

Trump: Draining the Swamp

In his election campaign, Trump was able to mobilize a broad voter coalition of frustrated people, people left behind by TINA policies. 'Make American Great Again,' 'Draining the Swamp,' and 'bringing government back to the people' resonated well with a lot of people, providing an alternative to the policies of no alternatives. In his inauguration speech in 2017, Trump declared, "Today, we are not merely transferring power from one administration to another, or from one party to another," peering out at a sea of supporters, "but we are transferring power from Washington, D.C., and giving it back to you, the people" (White House 2017). But so far, Trump could not deliver on what he promised. Polarization and gridlock prevented major policy reforms to happen in Washington, D.C. So far, the only legislative success is a major tax reform bill that benefitted corporations and the wealthy, leaving behind the middle classes and lower-income groups (Slemrod 2018).

Instead of draining the swamp in D.C., Trump brought a lot of millionaires and billionaires into the administration, thereby fostering special interest policies, massive deregulation, and further privatization (Tindera 2019). Shortly after Donald Trump launched his reelection campaign, he announced that former Raytheon head lobbyist Mark Esper would replace former Boeing executive Patrick Shanhanan as acting defense secretary. Interior Secretary David Bernhardt is a former lobbyist for the coal and gas industry. Environmental Protection Agency Administrator Andrew Wheeler is a former lobbyist for, among other interests, the coal industry. Along with lobbyists, Trump has also named numerous former Goldman Sachs executives, the former head of ExxonMobil, and billionaire investors Betsy DeVos and Wilbur Ross to lead government agencies like the State Department, the Department of Education, and the Department of Commerce. Health and Human Services Secretary Alex Azar is also a former drug company executive who oversaw its lobbying efforts, although he is not a registered lobbyist.

Already in the first week of his administration, Donald Trump signed an executive order requiring all of his political hires to sign a pledge saying that they would never lobby foreign interests, and they would never engage in other lobbying for five years. But former administration officials have found ways around that rule. As of February 2019, Pro Publica identified 33 former officials from the Trump administration who were connected to lobbying in some capacity. The most prominent is former Interior Secretary Ryan Zinke, who resigned in December 2018 after a series of ethics investigations. He announced a couple of months later that he is joining a lobbying firm, Turnberry Solutions, which was started in 2017 by several former Trump campaign aides (Kravitz 2019).

But the mere presence of lobbyists in Trump's cabinet doesn't raise the alarm of government ethics experts. No doubt, the revolving door is a basic part of the Washington establishment, and it is not hard to see why: government agencies regularly deal with lobbyists when they are crafting regulations, so that they tend to hire professionals who are familiar with the process. The Trump administration does, however, seem particularly comfortable stacking high-level posts with former lobbyists. As Pro Publica revealed in March 2018, "At least 187 Trump political appointees have been federal lobbyists, and despite President Trump's campaign pledge to 'drain the swamp,' many are now overseeing the industries they once lobbied on" (Kravitz 2018). With seven lobbyists named to Cabinet-level positions, not to mention former industry executives, Trump is far outpacing former President Obama, who named five former lobbyists to his cabinet over two full terms, and George W. Bush, who named three former lobbyists to Cabinet-level posts during his eight years in office (Lardner 2019).

Furthermore, Trump is using the administration for personal and family benefits, acting more like a medieval monarch than a modern democratic president. That points to what critics call a troubling trend in the Trump administration: a tendency to rely on friends and family for policy advice and action. In a robust, well-functioning democracy, there are many checks against the abuse of power. There are institutions that establish procedures to regulate decision-making and set limits. These institutions are run by people loyal not to any particular leader, but rather to the rule of law itself. They understand, in theory, that their job is to protect the citizens and the constitution, not their bosses. When leaders rely on their friends and relatives to take key jobs, they can subvert the power of institutions because those individuals (who often aren't experts coming into a position with a particular set of objectives) aren't loyal to the institution. They are loyal to the person in power.

Trump, who swept into office as an outsider with no government experience, has largely surrounded himself with people who are also light on government experience but heavy on personal loyalty. As political scientist Henry F. Cary said:

> The U.S. presidency has always been prone to sultanistic tendencies, but under a Trump presidency what were once isolated incidents have predictably become a way of governing. When the closest advisers, both institutional (like his daughter Ivanka Trump and his son-in-law Jared Kushner) and informal (in the case of his two adult sons), are dominated by family members, the decision-making process will not only be erratic and possibly influenced by private family interests but also tend to ignore legal procedures that have also met the test of time.
>
> *(Cary 2017)*

His constant attacks on the press and his aggressive communication style via Twitter destroy a rational and open public discourse that is essential for a democratic representative system to function. Fake news and mere opinions trump facts. Trust in the public discourse is disappearing. In order to mobilize his core voter base, Trump is constantly attacking his political opponents, thereby further fostering polarization and politicization of the public discourse. For sure, criticism of the political opponent is part of politics, especially in a context of massive polarization. But Trump, unlike former presidents, never tried to be a president for all Americans. He used his attacks on political opponents just in order to mobilize his own political base. After Democrats announced to start an impeachment process, Trump called it a Coup D'état on Twitter. What we do see is a massive radicalization of political communication in the US and more and more pundits fear what might happen if Trump has to leave the White House, by an impeachment or through elections.

One way to understand Trump's rhetoric and actions is populism and its tendency to accuse corrupt elites (in this case, the Democrats) of betraying "the people" by empowering their enemies: in this case, migrants allegedly involved in criminal activities against law-abiding American citizens. As Müller (2016, 22–23) suggests, a key aspect of populism is the claim that "only the populist authentically identifies and represents […] real or true people." Trump's populism is mainly based on mechanisms of exclusion and criticizing political elites, and at the same time blaming specific groups—in most cases, minorities. This distinguishes Trump's populism from more progressive variants that focus on inclusion (see also the Introduction to this volume). Clearly, Trump draws on a right-wing version of this populism to label Democrats and those who disagree with him on immigration as enemies of a narrowly defined "American people."

Trump used this populist and nationalist rhetoric to motivate his base to vote for Republican candidates in the midterm elections of 2018, urging them to defeat Democrats and the threat to the American people he claims they represent.

In the specific case of Trump, preying upon the collective anxieties of his majority white base is a way to create a sense of urgency. His goal, prior to the midterms in 2018, was to mobilize his supporters to show up at the polls to thwart a purported assault on the US engineered by allegedly unpatriotic Democrats who let migrants in and don't stand up for America. What we're witnessing is a convergence of nationalism, populism, and the politics of insecurity. The exacerbation of collective insecurity stemming from seemingly uncontrolled immigration is coupled with nationalist claims about the existence of an enemy within (the Democratic Party) depicted as being soft on crime and on immigration.

Trump also promised deep cuts in regulations and bureaucracy to spur economic growth. Early in his presidency, an executive order was issued to freeze hiring in the executive agencies, not including Homeland Security and Veterans Affairs. Data shows that the order accomplished its objective. OpenTheBooks.com found 34,640 positions eliminated within the traditional paper-pushing, tax, and regulatory agencies: Education, Health & Human Services, EPA, IRS, Interior, and 114 others. Statistically speaking, the Trump re-prioritization of the government occurred without a material increase in the number of employees. Compared against the peak year of 2016, the payroll at the Education Department, for example, is down 657 employees, or 15% (OpenTheBooks.com). And the hiring freeze is still in place. Perceived as one of the most entrenched parts of the administrative state, a house cleaning in the State Department has been underway. In 2016, there were 13,108 employees, and by 2018, only 11,582 remained. "Foreign Affairs" staffers were cut back from 2,571 to 2,135. However, cuts have been across the board with 60 fewer office secretaries and 20 less public relations officers (OpenTheBooks.com).

In his campaign for the US presidency, candidate Donald Trump advocated widespread deregulation of the US economy. It was a central plank of his national economic and energy plans. He called for both a moratorium on new regulations and an explicit process whereby Cabinet departments would review existing regulations and repeal each one that was not necessary. Trump has followed through with an aggressive program of deregulation. Operationally, deregulation has meant first slowing the flow of new federal regulations, second collaborating with Congress on the repeal or scaling back of selected existing regulations, and third using executive power to repeal or curb the scope of selected existing regulations. The Trump Administration's most recent Regulatory Agenda reports that 514 deregulatory rulemakings are ongoing. This number is small compared to the huge stock of existing regulations but larger than what the Reagan administration tackled over a similar time frame. The deregulatory ambitions of the Trump administration are particularly large in the environmental arena. One set of deregulatory proposals seeks to simplify burdensome permitting processes for economic projects under the National Environmental Policy Act and the Endangered Species Act. A second set seeks to ease costly pollution-control requirements on energy developers and producers, especially in the coal, oil and gas, and biofuels industries. A third set is designed to limit future federal clean-water regulations that might adversely impact small businesses, construction, manufacturing, and agriculture (Spangler and Bomey 2018; Vogt 2018).

Another set of deregulations going on under the Trump administration can be found in the financial markets and banking sector. Trump has signed a massive rollback on bank regulations. The measure eases restrictions on all but the largest banks. It raises the threshold to $250 billion from $50 billion under which banks are deemed too important to the financial system to fail. Those institutions also would not have to undergo stress tests or submit so-called living wills, both safety values designed to plan for financial disaster. Trump has announced further deregulations, but so far, the main policies implemented under the Dodd-Frank Act in 2010 are still in place.

Conclusion

So far, Trump has transformed the crisis of democracy into a constitutional crisis that threatens the very foundations of the political system in the US. Trump and his administration are not willing to play by the constitutionally established rules of the game. He does not accept the system of separate branches of government sharing power. His zero-sum political style just knows winners and losers, thereby fully ignoring the procedural mechanism of a representative democracy like the US that is built on the condition and possibility of bipartisan cooperation. Opposition to his illiberal style of governance is growing, within the democratic institutions and on the streets. Massive protests and marches in the streets, Democrats winning a landslide in the midterm elections, and impeachment procedure are visible developments in this regard. But so far, it is not clear if that will build up trust again in the political system, or if the people will get more divided and frustrated about the way politics is done in D.C.

Until mid-2019, the administration was benefitting from a powerful economic development that already started under the Obama administration, but was further pushed by the Trump administration by massive deregulation and tax cuts. The bad awakening will come with the next economic downturn. Nearly 40 years of neoliberal restructuring of the welfare system and Trump's massive deregulation destroyed an important number of social buffers that are meant to prevent growing poverty rates and income inequality in the next recession. People will get more frustrated with politics in D.C.

In this chapter, I argued that the rise of illiberalism in the US and Western Europe is primarily the result of a specific set of policies that Anthony Giddens summarized under the term "Third way politics" that dominated the policy agenda in Western countries at least since the 1990s. This is the common denominator, explaining the rise and success of anti-establishment parties and politicians on both sides of the Atlantic. If the welfare system is less and less able to help poor people by redistributing market incomes from the top to the bottom, the material base and legitimacy for political participation are threatened. An increasing number of people—especially the poor, minorities, and immigrants—will be disconnected from the political process, making the system less democratic. That's what has happened to different degrees in the US and in Europe as well. As a result, people's trust in the political system and its major institutions declined massively. The crisis of democracy in the US is exceptional because economic liberalism was already so pronounced there. The culture of individualism, the drastically increased inequalities that followed the financial crisis, and the growing polarization have driven the existing political structures to the brink of dysfunctionality, much more than this is the case in Western European democracies. Voters were looking for alternative policy approaches, both on the left and the right. Illiberalism à la Trump seemed to be a successful alternative. But so far, Trump was not able to provide a real alternative.

Bibliography

Bartels, Larry M. 2005. "Homer Gets a Tax Cut: Inequality and Public Policy in the American Mind." *Perspectives on Politics* 3(1): 15–31.

Bartels, Larry M. 2009. *Unequal Democracy: The Political Economy of the New Gilded Age.* Princeton, NJ: Princeton University Press.

Campbell, Andrea Louis. 2003. *How Policies Make Citizens. Senior Political Activism and the American Welfare State.* Princeton, NJ: Princeton University Press.

Cary, Henry F. 2017. "Do Ivanka Trump and Jared Kushner Have Too Much Power?" *Huffington Post,* April 12, www.huffpost.com/entry/do-ivanka-trump-and-jared-kushner-have-too-much-power_b_58ee454ae4b07557c4858687?guccounter=2

Cerny, Philip G. 1997. "Paradoxes of the Competition State: The Dynamics of Political Globalization." *Government and Opposition* 32(2): 251–74.

Dowling, Conor M., and Michael G. Miller. 2014. *Super Pac! Money, Elections and Voters after Citizen United.* New York, NY: Routledge.

Esping-Andersen, Gøsta. 1990. *The Three Worlds of Welfare Capitalism.* Cambridge: Polity Press.

Genschel, P., and L. Seekopf. 2012. *Did the Competition State Rise? Globalization, International Tax Competition, and National Welfare.* Bremen: Jacobs University (mimeo).

Giddens, Anthony. 1998. *The Third Way: The Renewal of Social Democracy.* Cambridge: Polity Press.

Gilens, Martin, and Benjamin I. Page. 2014. "Testing Theories of American Politics: Elites, Interest Groups, and Average Citizen." *Perspectives on Politics* 12(3): 564–81.

Hacker, Jacob S., and Paul Pierson. 2017. *American Amnesia: How the War on Government Led Us to Forget What Made America Prosper.* New York, NY: Simon and Schuster.

Hartman, Andrew. 2019. *A War for the Soul of America: A History of the Culture Wars.* Chicago, IL: University of Chicago Press.

Hayden, Sara. 2017. "Obama Says: I Wouldn't Vote for Me If I Watched Fox News." *The Independent*, December 2, www.independent.co.uk/news/world/americas/barack-obama-fox-news-donald-trump-india-hindustan-times-leadership-summit-a8088356.html

Howard, Christopher. 1999. *The Hidden Welfare State: Tax Expenditures and Social Policy in the United States*. Princeton, NJ: Princeton University Press.

King, Aaron. 2018. "No, Dodd-Frank Was Neither Repealed Nor Gutted. Here's What Really Happened." Brookings Report, www.brookings.edu/research/no-dodd-frank-was-neither-repealed-nor-gutted-heres-what-really-happened/

Kravitz, Derek. 2018. "What We Found in Trump's Drained Swamp: Hundreds of Ex-Lobbyists and D.C. Insiders." Pro Publica, www.propublica.org/article/what-we-found-in-trump-administration-drained-swamp-hundreds-of-ex-lobbyists-and-washington-dc-insiders

Kravitz, Derek. 2019. "Former Trump Officials Are Supposed to Avoid Lobbying. Except 33 Haven't." Pro Publica. www.propublica.org/article/the-lobbying-swamp-is-flourishing-in-trumps-washington

Lammert, Christian, and Boris Vormann. 2020. "When Inequalities Matter Most: The Crisis of Democracy as a Crisis of Trust." In *Mobilization, Representation, and Responsiveness in the American Democracy*, edited by Michael Oswald, 139–56. Basingstoke: Palgrave Macmillan.

Lardner, Richard. 2019. "Trump Outpaces Obama, Bush in Naming Ex-lobbyists to Cabinet." *The Associated Press*, September 17. www.apnews.com/08 dce0f5f9c24a6aa355cd0aab3747d9

Ledyard King, Ledyard. 2018. "Trump's Plan for Coal-Fired Power Plants: Key Takeaways about the EPA Clean Air Proposal." *USA Today*. August 22.

McLaughlin, Patrick. 2018. Regulatory Data on Trump's First Year. Mercatus Center at George Mason University. January 30.

Morgan, Kimberly J., and Andrea Louise Campbell. 2011. *The Delegated Welfare State. Medicare, Markets and the Governance of Social Policy*. New York, NY: Oxford University Press.

Müller, Jan-Werner. 2016. *What Is Populism?* Philadelphia: University of Pennsylvania Press.

OECD. 2011. "Divided We Stand – Why Inequality Keeps Rising," *OECD*. www.oecd.org/berlin/publikationen/dividedwestand-whyinequalitykeepsrising.htm.

OECD. 2019. "Social Expenditure Database." *OECD*. www.oecd.org/social/expenditure.htm

Open Secrets. 2019. "Costs of Elections." www.opensecrets.org/overview/cost.php OpenTheBooks.com

Piketty, Thomas. 2014. *Capital in the Twenty-First Century*. Cambridge, MA: Harvard University Press.

Slemrod, Joel. 2018. "Is This Tax Reform, or Just Confusion?" *Journal of Economic Perspectives* 32(4): 73–96.

Spangler, Todd, and Nathan Bomey. 2018. "Trump Administration Wants to Freeze Gas-Mileage Standards, Reversing Obama." *USA Today*. August 2.

Stonecash, Jeff. 2018. *Diverging Parties: Social Change, Realignment, and Party Polarization*. New York, NY: Routledge.

Tindera, Michela. 2019. "The Definitive Net Worth of Donald Trump's Cabinet." Forbes, July 25. www.forbes.com/sites/michelatindera/2019/07/25/the-definitive-net-worth-of-donald-trumps-cabinet/#42f486926a15

Vogt, Heide. 2018. "EPA Announces Proposal to Roll Back Obama-Era Rules on Methane Emissions." *Wall Street Journal.* September 11.

Vormann, Boris, and Christian Lammert. 2019. *Democracy in Crisis. The Neoliberal Roots of Popular Unrest.* Philadelphia: University of Pennsylvania Press.

Weaver, R. Kent. 2000. *Ending Welfare As We Know It.* Washington, DC: Brookings Institution Press.

White House. 2017. "Statement by President Trump on the Paris Climate Accord." June 1. www.Whitehouse.gov.

9

THE EUROPEAN UNION AND ITS CHANCES FOR DEMOCRATIC REVITALIZATION

Claudia Wiesner

Introduction

Criticism of the EU's democratic deficits is notorious at least since the 1990's (see below for an overview on the "democratic deficit" debate, see Follesdal and Hix 2006). The European Union is regularly included into critical or pessimistic accounts on the state of democracy in general and the risks of its deterioration. These critical accounts relate to the negative impact of economic liberalism and its consequences on democratic standards. The EU has been regularly criticized for the downsides of internal trade liberalization, as expressed in the pronounced concept of negative integration, i.e. the abolition of market obstacles, and its negative effects on democracy and social standards (Scharpf 1999, see also below). Moreover, the creation of the inner market went along with cutting down the powers of directly legitimized national democratic institutions—a point classically mentioned in the democratic deficit debate is power shifts from directly legitimized legislatives to executives, and pertinent legitimation problems. During the financial crisis, criticisms on the EU's democratic deficits intensified, as new EU-related governance setting were introduced that bypassed existing democratic structures (see Streeck 2014; Offe 2015; White 2015, Wiesner 2019, 261–279)—a special issue of the *European Law Journal* in this context raised the question if "authoritarian liberalism" was pushed by the EU (Menéndez 2015).

In this context, I argue that the EU is—rather than an international organization—a political system that has continuously been democratized and relates to a multi-level system, including the current 28 member states and their democracies. In this system, four core dimensions of democratic quality are insufficient: agenda control as well as horizontal and vertical accountability, responsiveness, and equality. These deficiencies are related to an accumulation of seven problem fields: (1) over-bureaucratization, (2) expert bodies, (3) over-constitutionalization, (4) differentiated integration, (5) negative integration, (6) the question of the EU's common good, and (7) the split between the EU citizens being citizens in a legal sense but only a limited sovereign and a limited *demos*. In order to recognize these problem fields and chances to remedy them, I start with a conceptual reflection on the basic principles of representative democracy and a short summary of central arguments concerning the EU democratic deficit debate, followed by a critical analysis of the problem fields. In conclusion, I will discuss the possibilities for democratic revitalization of the EU's political system, focusing especially on the development of a demos and its politicization.

Conceptualizing Democracy and Democratic Deficits in the EU

My argument relates to a basic set of conceptual and normative premises on representative democracy (see Wiesner 2019, 1–49). If we try to distill the general elements that classify most concepts of representative democracy (see Dahl 2000; Diamond and Morlino 2004; Palonen 2016), and if we also take into account how representative democracy developed (Manin 1997; Urbinati 2006; Pitkin 2009) in parliamentary democracies, there is a typical interrelation between three elements, or conceptual clusters: *citizens* vote for parliament and hence legitimize it; *parliament* represents the citizens and elects the government; *government* is responsible to parliament. I have termed this the *triad of representative democracy* (Wiesner 2019, 7). Obviously, in presidential systems, the triadic relations work differently, especially regarding the relation between government and parliament, and the role of head of state. The European Union has similarities to a semi-presidential system where the executive is dual and the role of head of state is ambiguously split between either the European Council (EC) or its permanent president (Wiesner 2019, 165–84).

Irrespective of the type of political system at stake, following Lincoln's well-known formula (Lincoln 1863), democracy can be furthermore understood as being government of, by, and for the people. Following this idea, three decisive directions and components of the relations between citizens, their representatives, and the government can be outlined for any of these types of systems. The first is the input dimension: the citizens need rights and possibilities for participation and contestation (government of the people), and they need the right to elect their representatives (government by the people). Second, the representatives must be accountable: election procedures of governance in the representative system must be organized transparently and following the rule of law, and the system should stick to the ideal of the separation of powers. This is what has been termed "throughput" (Schmidt 2013). Third, representative democracy has an output dimension: the decisions taken by the representatives should satisfy the majority of the represented (government for the people).

Citizens constitute the *demos*, the core body that is at the base of the democratic practices, the sovereign. A *demos* should be active, since democracy from a normative point of view must consist not only in rights to vote or democratic institutions, but also in democratic practices. A core characteristic of most conceptions of representative democracy therefore is that it must allow and open up spaces for debate, participation, and contestation. As elections take place only at relatively long intervals, it is an essential condition that representative democracy is completed by such spaces and arenas for political participation, debate, and contestation. Parliamentary debates are public, and issues can hence be debated in parliament and also publicly. There must also be the possibility to contest and protest against government measures. Citizens thus can express their political opinions in between elections.

There are many good reasons to argue that these basic premises of representative democracy need to be thickened: for instance, by deliberative mechanisms or social rights (see Barber 1984; Merkel 2004). But the question in this chapter is not how we can institutionalize a strong, participatory, or even deliberative democracy in the EU and its multi-level system. My goal is to discuss how the basic premises of representative democracy that were just sketched can be safeguarded and revitalized. It is important to underline once more that representative democracy in the EU context includes the multi-level system, i.e. the EU member states. Adding the political level of the EU has at the same time challenged the classical conception of a representative legitimation chain ranging from citizens to parliaments, politicians, their decisions, and back. In the classical conception, the sovereign *demos* elects a national parliament and legitimates a national government, which is accountable to the sovereign via the parliament. But in the EU multi-level system, legitimization chains become longer, more indirect, and less transparent: national sovereigns still elect national parliaments and thus legitimate national governments—but many policy decisions are now taken at the EU level, where neither the Commission nor the Council is directly legitimized by EU citizens, even if the European Parliament (EP) has by and by obtained the right to vote upon the Commission's approval and also to influence the Commissioner setting to a certain degree (see Tiilikainen and Wiesner 2016).

The EU: A Short Summary of the Democratic Deficit Debate

The EU's democratic deficits have been intensively discussed in the last decades regarding the institutional setting related to the treaties from Maastricht to Lisbon. Controversy in this debate starts with the question what the EU actually is. Should it be defined as a "polity sui generis," i.e. as a kind of new polity without precedent that accordingly cannot be grasped with the established categories? Is it an international organization (see Magnette 2005)? As sketched above, my argument is based on the position that (a) the EU is to be seen as a political system (see Hix and Høyland 2011; Tömmel 2014) that (b) has continuously been and still can be further democratized and (c) relates to a multi-level system, including the current 28 member states and their democracies. From that standpoint, and based on the normative and conceptual premises that have been lined out above, a number of critical points have been raised in the "democratic deficit" debate.

EU institutions increased their competencies over the last decades without adding a representative-democratic legislative component that equals the ones in the nation-states. As at the same time national legislatives lost competencies, executive powers increased on the whole in the EU multi-level system, and legislative powers decreased (Mény 2003; Føllesdal and Hix 2006). Moreover, powers also shifted to the judiciary realm. In sum, decision-making powers in the EU multi-level system are constantly withdrawn from the realm of representative democracy and political participation (Habermas 2001). The balance switches in favor of an executive and judiciary dimension of the classical balance of powers, at the expense of the legislative (Mény 2003; Diez Medrano 2009).

For many EU institutions, except the EP, not only are legitimation chains still long and rather untransparent, but accountability is also not easily claimed. Input legitimacy is thus still weaker on the EU level than in the democratic structures of member states (Beetham and Lord 1998; Bellamy and Castiglione 2003). Since these continually lost competencies to the EU level by different ways and means, European integration has led to a net loss of input legitimacy in the multi-level system (Beetham and Lord 1998, 17–19; Habermas 1999, 186–87).

A New Perspective on the EU's Democratic Deficits

Beyond this brief restatement of the arguments about the democratic deficit in the EU, it must be stated that, actually, four core dimensions of democratic quality are insufficient in this context: (i) agenda control (Dahl 2000); (ii) horizontal and vertical accountability; (iii) responsiveness; and (iv) equality (Diamond and Morlino 2004). All in all, the EU thus appears as a kind of defective democracy (Merkel 2004). These deficiencies are decisively linked to the complexity of the EU's system, which leads to an accumulation of the seven problem fields described above and which can be briefly analyzed as follows (for an expanded discussion, see Wiesner 2019, 281–301):

1. Over-bureaucratization: Consensus-building and bureaucracy dominate in decision-making processes in the EU system (see in detail Tömmel 2014, 171) at the expense of democratic deliberation and publicity. Processes

such as trilogues (see below) and comitology that largely take place behind closed doors and in expert circles depoliticize the EU and withdraw decision-making from the realm of public and/or parliamentary deliberation.

2. Expert bodies: There are a number of expert bodies with executive competencies that have been created over the years, and they are also largely withdrawn and decoupled from the realm of public representative decision-making. EU agencies, as well as private consultancy firms that work for the Commission are examples here, but so are the Troika and involvement of the International Monetary Fund (IMF, see below).

3. Over-constitutionalization: The treaties in themselves limit the possible realm for democratic deliberation and decision-making, as they limit the policy areas that are subject to it well beyond the extent that is usual in national representative democracies (see Grimm 2017).

These three problem clusters have a strongly de-democratizing and depoliticizing effect. They limit the realm for public deliberation and politicized decision-making, and they limit accountability in both horizontal and vertical directions, as well as transparency. The case of trilogues—informal negotiations between EP, Commission, and Council representatives on legislative projects taking place before the parliamentary readings—illustrates what I mean here. The introduction of legislative co-decision between the EP and the Council has led to an extensive usage of such trilogues (Farrell and Héritier 2007; Rasmussen 2012). Committees or the plenary send a draft law to the trilogue body, where it is negotiated between the representatives of the three institutions. In most cases, trilogues lead to so-called early agreements on legislation. The legislation in question is then usually prepared so that it is approved in the first EP reading (European Parliament 2017; European Parliament 2018b, 2018c). In other words, an agreement has been reached between Commission, Council, and EP in the trilogue meetings, and parliamentary deliberation serves the purpose of adding a rubber stamp. The number of legislative acts thus adopted on the basis of the first reading has increased remarkably since the introduction of co-decision, that is, in the legislature 2009–14, when 85% of the legislative files were accepted on first reading (European Parliament 2018c). The degree of first reading decisions has been going down slightly since. Between July 1, 2014 and April 5, 2017, 75% of legislative projects were decided upon in first readings (European Parliament 2018a). While the EP claims that trilogues are linked to a need for efficiency (European Parliament 2018c), non-governmental organizations see it much more critically (EDRI) and so does the academic literature (Reh 2014; Roederer-Rynning and Greenwood 2015). In short, parliamentary deliberation, transparency, and publicity, principles embodied in the procedure of having several parliamentary readings of a law in plenary, are decisively reduced by early agreements and trilogues. Decision-making is thus taken away from the public nature of parliamentary debates and pushed into the realm of non-public bodies without direct legitimation. This reduces the deliberative function of parliament, as well as its control of, and responsibility for, decisions ultimately taken.

The fourth problem cluster regards a diversification of governance modes in the EU:

4. Differentiated integration: There are different degrees of integration in different policy areas, and there are different degrees of integration among different groups of member states. The EU is hence dispersed into a great variety of different regulatory regimes and schemes, ranging from co-decision in the common market to the intergovernmentally structured Common Foreign and Security Policy, the Euro Group that simply unites the Euro-Countries, to the Schengen System that is another structure half apart. This dispersion of a polity as big as the EU also creates differing patterns of legitimization and control. The diverse governance modes in the EU and different modes of decision-making in the different fields hamper transparency and accountability because it is unclear who actually has taken a decision and who is included, and how the decision-making process went, even to experts.

The case of financial crisis governance illustrates the problem here: depending on which level is concerned (EU or member states), which kind of measure and instrument (European Stability Mechanism (ESM), Six-pack, Two-pack), and which status the respective state has (debtor or creditor), the effects of crisis governance on representative democracy vary. First, there are measures that fall under the regime of the Lisbon Treaty and have been voted upon with the participation of the EP, such as the Six-pack and Two-pack measures. Second, other measures are excluded from the treaty framework, such as the ESM and its predecessors and the Fiscal Compact. Those are based on new intergovernmental treaties and decisions and hence fall outside the official realm of the Lisbon Treaty and the checks and balances it establishes. Third, implementation of financial aid legislation has led to different kinds of attempts by governments and executives to strengthen their powers at the expense of legislatures: for instance, by using fast-track procedures in decision-making. These attempts have been successful in several cases; in others, such as in Germany, they failed: in the German case, the Constitutional Court stopped the executive attempt to introduce fast-track procedures in financial aid decision-making (for an overview on these dynamics, see Maatsch 2017).

All this means that a system of supervision and new bodies emerged that decisively limited the competence of national legislatures, leading to the deterioration or circumvention of national democratic institutions. The new institutions amplify existing EU accountability and transparency problems: it is difficult to determine who is to be held accountable for budgetary decisions and austerity. Moreover, all crisis governance institutions brought a power shift from legislatives to executives and experts. In addition, the new inter-governmental institutions bypass the progresses to supranational representa-tive democracy obtained in the EU over the last decades by excluding the EP. It is a decisive legitimization problem to have shifted substantial parts of the decision-making competencies both outside EU and most of the national representative institutions. Accordingly, crisis governance has been severely judged in the academic debate (see Crum 2013; Majone 2014; Bellamy and Weale 2015; in the following, see also Wiesner 2017b; Wiesner 2019, 261–79) and in the public debate.

The fifth problem is also one that harms national democratic standards. Eco-nomic liberalism, i.e. the creation of the internal market and the abolition of market obstacles, led to cutting them down.

5. Negative integration: In the EU, negative integration dominates over positive integration (Scharpf 1999). With this concept, Scharpf wants to emphasize the fact that market creation in the European Union, much more than on the creation of new rules and common standards ("positive integration"), was based on what he terms "negative integration," i.e. the abolition or reduction of national social standards because they were con-sidered as obstacles to market integration (Scharpf 1999).

The reasons for this dominance are manifold: on the one hand, negative integra-tion has corresponded to policy preferences of governments and EP majorities. On the other hand, the discrepancies between richer and poorer EU member states favor negative integration. Negative integration is wished for by both as it facilitates market access and trade. Positive integration, that is, raising new standards, is not wished for by the poorer states, as they tend to profit from social dumping and a race to the bottom (Hix and Høyland 2011, 209–15). This leads to regulatory diversity and hinders the setting up of common new standards, for instance, regarding social rights. Judgments of the Court of Justice of the EU (CJEU) have added up into this panorama. In numerous cases, they have led to abolishing social and democratic standards, such as in the notorious cases of Rüffert and Laval. In the Laval case, the ECJ decided that national governmental actors and also trade unions can only take action in the few cases touched upon by a specific EU legal act, the posted workers directive. In all other cases, legal action or strike against companies that sidetrack national social standards is legally excluded (see in detail Wiesner 2019: 249–260).

The points discussed, finally, hint at two more problem fields that will be discussed in the concluding section of this chapter:

6. The EU's common good: All this underlines that, so far, there is no agree-ment about what, if anything, constitutes the EU's common good. There is not even an agreement on the basic goals of the EU. Should it just continue

to create a common market? Should we rebuild and cut back the EU? Or should it become a truly supranational federation?

These questions have been contested since the first conceptions of integration were put forward (Wiesner 2019), and it seems necessary to open the debate yet again. Besides a lack of debate, the institutional setting favors dissensus in this respect. While the EU's supranational bodies, the EP and Commission, are oriented toward the EU, its intergovernmental bodies, the Council and EC, are oriented toward the particular national interests (see Tömmel 2014, 324–30). Moreover, while national governments work on the basis of a short-term logic, as they want to be re-elected, EU institutions are much more independent of electoral choices (see Hix and Høyland 2011, 334). This situation creates a tension and a tendency in the EU's system that, in a very general way, hinders an overall orientation toward an EU common good. Such an orientation, however, should be a basic principle of all institutions of a polity.

7.   The split between the EU citizens being citizens in a legal sense, but only a limited sovereign and a limited *demos*, further accentuates these problems.

Approaching Possible Solutions

Having discussed the complex setting of the EU's democratic deficits, what can be done to safeguard and revitalize democracy in the EU? Regarding the problem cluster of over-bureaucratization and expert dominance (1 and 2 above), its weight could be drastically reduced by just filling the democratic bodies that there are with active life. The problem of trilogues, for example, is not that they withdraw decisions from parliament, as parliamentary committees and the plenary are involved in trilogues from the beginning to the end. The problem is one of weights and substance: if the most decisive part of the decision-making process is carried out behind closed doors by experts in non-transparent negotiating circles, transparency and democratic accountability are decisively cut down, even if, in the end, parliament and its committees are involved just as they should be formally and legally. But nobody, then, prohibits the EP from using its co-decision powers to the fullest extent possible and shifting the substantial weight of parliamentary debates and decisions back to the parliamentary and public bodies and arenas. Such a shift would also increase the EP's horizontal accountability and legitimacy, as well as its responsiveness.

(3) Regarding over-constitutionalization, more room for democratic deliberation is possible and needed at the EU level and within the multi-level system. This closely refers to the dimension of agenda control mentioned. A broad solution here would be to de-constitutionalize the EU and to turn a large part of the EU's primary law into secondary law. Thus, economic policy goals, which

are currently largely fixed by the treaties, would be made subject to political debate and politicized decision-making—just as it is usual in most representative democracies, by having public debates and several parliamentary readings on an issue. But this change would be a major treaty change, and in the EU's current situation, it seems highly unlikely that it could be obtained, especially as not all the member states' governments (and Germany first in rank) would subscribe to the goal of politicizing, democratizing, and regulating economic policy-making in the EU. Nevertheless, there are a number of policy areas that are already potentially subject to political and controversial deliberation and decision-making, both at the EU and at the national level. Existing differentiated and non-transparent decision-making structures, in combination with the preferences of national governments, hinder open debate in many cases. Why shouldn't we, for instance, debate austerity policies in all Euro Group member states, in a similar vein as we debate national pension scheme reforms? And why shouldn't debates about EP decisions on the budget be subject to EU-wide political discussion? Similarly, it can be asked why Council and EC do not have more controversial and more public political debates: they are, on the one hand, similar to governments that, according to the classical tradition of both parliamentarism and presidentialism, do not meet in public. But, on the other hand, they take on parliamentary functions when they discuss the EU's budget or EU laws. Accordingly these debates should be public as they are in parliaments. But currently, Council sessions are only public when the Council acts as a legislator, and EC meetings are never public.

The next two problem clusters, (4) differentiated integration and (5) negative integration, require solutions within the multi-level system. The question is how to restore transparency and accountability, and how to limit the effects of negative integration, especially when it comes to achievements that are crucial for democratic standards such as social citizenship rights. In brief (for detailed discussions, see Wiesner 2017a, 2017b), there are two possible ways to approach the problem of keeping up democratic standards in the multi-level system, one that is narrow and one that is wider.

In the narrow solution, the EU continues to rule only part of the policies that are carried out within the multi-level system and the member states, and hence only part of those policies are regulated in accordance with the EU treaties and the checks and balances they establish. The solution then is to defend what there is to be defended, that is, to hedge the backfire effects on national representative democracies and to protect transparency, accountability, and vertical balances of powers. There would be a mechanism to safeguard and protect national representative systems, for example, by defining a broad set of core national social standards and a broad range of core rights for national parliaments.

In the further reaching solution, the EU would be fully integrated. The EU would then decide or co-decide on all, or almost all, of the policies that are currently ruled by democratic nation-states. Differences between fully and partly integrated policy fields and different modes of regulation, law-making, and policy-making would be reduced and finally abolished. At the same time, co-decision should become the legislative procedure in all of the EU's policy fields. This system of full integration would stop differentiated integration and submit all policy areas to one mode of legitimation. Governance of financial aid and the Euro Group would then need to be submitted to the EU treaties' framework. But this, again, would require a thorough treaty change that is neither realistic nor workable at the moment. When discussing which of these solutions is realistic, it thus becomes apparent that the first one, the narrow solution, will be much easier to obtain than the second.

Demos-Building via Politicization?

All this leads to the last two problem fields mentioned above. These merit further substantial discussion, namely, how the EU common good could be determined, how the distance between EU citizens and elites could be reduced, and how the EU citizenry could turn into a stronger *demos*. On the one hand, these problems are emphasized by the reaction of the citizens of EU member states to the crisis and their withdrawal of support. The outcomes of problem clusters (1)–(5) have clearly diminished national democratic standards and achievements; equally apparently, these outcomes are also less and less in tune with citizens' policy preferences. Decreasing support rates during the financial crisis are just one indicator here, while the increase in support for EU-critical parties throughout all EU member states is another. Simply put, EU citizens in many member states disagree more and more with their elites' way of ruling the EU, especially in the crisis (Offe 2015).

But, as was described regarding the problem clusters (6) and (7), the problem goes still deeper. Insofar as democratic practices are from a normative point of view at least as important as democratic institutions for democracy, it will be decisive for the democratic character of the EU to strengthen an EU-related *demos*. This means that if EU citizens continue to participate in elections but do not identify much with the polity they are voting on, and therefore would probably not engage in much other political activity, then EU democratization in general will stay weak. If we want more democratic practice and deliberation in and about the EU, a *demos* that accounts for all this is needed. But how can a positive interrelation between *demos* development and strong EU democratization be conceptualized? One obvious step to both decrease the distance between EU citizens and elites, and lay a ground for further EU democratization by defining a common good is to open up the spaces and opportunities for political debate and contestation and to allow for and enhance an open debate on what is, what should be, the EU common good. Following what was said above, if the institutional system of the EU were further democratized, and the

EP gained more parliamentary competencies, if the EU were more politicized, this would increase the chances of an EU demos developing. The other way around, it has to be said that every political activity directed to the EU will actively contribute to the development of an active *demos* and stronger democratization. As Ankersmit has emphasized, the political act of representation creates the represented (Ankersmit 2002). This means that the actions of electing representatives and then the representatives representing the citizens not only establish a legitimizing link but also define both the representatives and those represented in their roles.

This means, as I have said, that we need more EU-directed participation, deliberation, and contestation. Other than remaining limited to expert circles, EU decision-making procedures, as well as the course of integration itself, should become a subject of political and public debate and political and democratic decision-making. This, speaking generally, is what has been referred to as politicization of the EU, or European integration, in the academic debate (see Statham and Trenz 2013; Hutter et al. 2016; see also the discussion in Wiesner Ed. 2019 and 2020b, as well as Kauppi and Wiesner 2018).

Conceptualizing the Link between Politicization and Democratization of the EU

In a very general sense, the academic debate on EU politicization describes a change in the actors and arenas that shape EU integration, switching from being an elite-driven project to a process that is influenced by different political stakes in different arenas. The link between democratization and politicization in this context is controversially discussed (on the following see in detail Wiesner 2020a). An argument that discusses EU politicization as a potential obstacle for EU integration stems from Hooghe and Marks (Hooghe and Marks 2009), who discuss the effects of politicization on national party systems. They describe politicization as a key mechanism that has changed public support for integration into "constraining dissensus": as citizens no longer want to follow and support the elite project without questions, their support for integration declines; they want explanations for integration as well as political conflict about it. For Hooghe and Marks, this endangers the integration process because parties and governments now tend to take into account their citizen's preferences and hence their EU-critical attitudes (Hooghe and Marks 2009, 9). This is why Eurosceptic parties gain support, decisions in integration policy get more public and more contested, political parties position themselves more publicly with regard to integration, and last but not least, even the EU institutions become internally politicized because the new cleavages are carried into what formerly was the realm of experts. Possible consequences of politicization that are discussed by Hooghe and Marks, finally, are two: either a differentiated integration of the EU or its disintegration.

Hooghe and Marks conceptualize a negative interrelation between EU politicization and effective EU integration—the end of permissive consensus leading to politicization linked to citizen dissatisfaction, which enhances euroscepticism, and this hinders EU integration. Their account presents part of the reactions on EU politicization quite well, as the results of the Brexit vote underline. In conceptual terms, however, this politicization model depicts only one possible relation between EU politicization and EU integration that I suggest to term a pessimist top-down model of EU politicization: dynamics are conceptualized to work top-down (citizens are not active but they grant or withdraw support and parties drive the politicization process) and the interrelation between politicization and integration is a negative one (politicization hinders integration). The trade-off that is implicitly claimed is one between ongoing EU integration and politicization of the EU, or, more sharply put, one between a continued integration and democracy and its possible effects—citizens being interested, criticizing the EU, and eventually voting for Eurosceptic parties.

Still, even if in reality, we have seen an outcome along the lines of this pessimistic top-down model of EU integration—Brexit being the most prominent current example—there is no necessary cause-effect relation. More concretely: it is not a causal relation (in the sense of (a) entails (b)) that elites will necessarily face opposition when integration becomes politicized, i.e. an issue of political debate and conflict. Accordingly, politicization does not necessarily create anti-EU opposition. Conceptually, there is a *potential*, but not a *causal* link between the two—elites *may* face opposition with the end of permissive consensus, but they also may not face such opposition. As such, there are several possibilities as a result of the politicization of EU integration and attempts to create more of an EU *demos*:

1. Elites continue the established train of integration—in that case, citizen support will probably shrink more. This is very much what we saw happening in the peak of the financial crisis.
2. Elites stop integration.
3. There is increasing political debate on integration and this leads to increased legitimacy and increased citizen support.

Classical functionalist and neofunctionalist accounts on politicization underline these arguments further. It is very useful to look at these classical texts of EU integration theory that were written at a time when the integration process was in its beginnings, as they contain fruitful reflections on the effects of EU politicization. Three key texts by Schmitter (Schmitter 1969), Haas (Haas 1968), and Lindberg and Scheingold (Lindberg and Scheingold 1970) open different possibilities, dynamics, and directions of EU politicization. Following the accounts by both Lindberg/Scheingold and Haas, we also encounter the idea that upon the end of permissive consensus, elites will, or at least may, face opposition. But this is not to say, and this is important to underline, that this will cause problems for integration as Lindberg and Scheingold explicitly state (Lindberg and Scheingold 1970, 41). Ernst Haas even sees rising economic dissatisfaction as a possible source of *more* demands for political integration (Haas 1968, 13). He mentions several possible pathways and positive linkages between EU politicization and the continuation of integration. And Philippe Schmitter's (Schmitter 1969) account on politicization even conceptualizes a potentially positive interrelation between politicization and demos-building: if EU integration becomes more controversial, this leads to a widening of the audience and more debate, and in consequence a manifest redefinition of mutual objectives. As a consequence, we experience a shift in actor expectancies and loyalty toward the new regional organization, i.e. the EU.

Schmitter, moreover, conceptualizes an interactive and dynamic relationship between citizens and elites: instead of citizens being limited to granting or withdrawing support, citizens can become audience, and they can redefine mutual objectives (at least his model opens up the possibility). This political process reminds us of what happens in nation-state representative democracies as well: if citizens do not like a policy, they can debate and try to change it. Hence, rather than a politicization, this account could also be termed a normalization of EU politics toward the standards of representative democracy. I suggest to term the ideas that were just sketched an optimist dynamic model of politicization.

Four Politicization Models

What has been discussed above underlines that we cannot assume a pre-established path for politicization and its effects on the EU—these can very well be either detrimental for the EU or beneficial for its democratization (on the following see in detail Wiesner 2020a). Politicization can lead to creating new public spaces and enhance public debate, which will lead to more transparency of policy debates and decisions, and enable an inclusion of civil society actors (see also Statham and Trenz 2013).

In addition to a positive dynamic model and a pessimist top-down model of politicization, I would like to argue that a pessimist dynamic model and an optimist top-down model are also possible, as the directions and pathways in EU politicization can be various: in an optimist top-down model, actor involvement into EU affairs might remain unchanged, but still—for example, because the EU's policy outputs were deemed more satisfactory by the citizens—EU support could increase. Change in that model would be introduced top-down, i.e. in the established way of EU elites making and implementing policy decisions. In a pessimist dynamic model, which represents the downside of the optimist dynamic model, citizens would engage much more actively in EU affairs than used to be the case—but this would lead to them increasing not their identification with the EU or their EU support but their EU criticism, for instance, because EU policies still would not satisfy them.

I do not claim either of these models to be more realistic than another—politics is marked by contingency, and one never knows the outcome of a process before it ended. To look once more at the Brexit case, the Brexit referendum was an outcome mostly of a process fitting the pessimist top-down model, in a mix with the pessimist dynamic model. But while, in October 2019, we still wait for a decision on when (or whether) Brexit will ultimately take place, British turnout in the EP elections in 2019 decisively increased as compared to 2014, which can be explained in terms of the two optimist models of politicization. However, nearly one-third of the British voters voted for a party that advocates Brexit, and this again fits the pessimist dynamic model.

Conclusion

To conclude, it is decisive to politicize the EU and to enhance political debates about EU policies and the course of integration. This is not something that can be declared or institutionalized, but it is something that can be done purposefully by political parties, politicians, even bureaucrats, and also by interested and active citizens and NGOs. In the same way that ideas and concepts on the EU were brought forward by thinkers, intellectuals, politicians, and activists before and in the early days of integration (Wiesner 2019), it can and should happen anew today. There is no reason not to have an open, public, and political debate about the EU and its political goals. On the contrary, if defenders of representative democracy do not want to have this debate, it will only be led by extremists, populists, and anti-democrats. After what has been said, it does not seem an option just to wait and see. Lingering disintegration (Britain might not have been the last candidate to exit), rising EU criticism, increasing problems of governance and cooperation at the EU level (as in the field of migration and refugees), and increasing inequalities both among citizens and among EU member states rather put pressure to act on all the actors named—member states governments and parliaments, the EP, the Commission, and even the CJEU and the European Central Bank (ECB). It is time for a new debate on the EU and its democratic future.

Bibliography

Ankersmit, F. R. 2002. *Political Representation. Cultural Memory in the Present*. Stanford, CA: Stanford University Press.

Barber, Benjamin R. 1984. *Strong Democracy: Participatory Politics for a New Age*. Berkeley: University of California Press.

Beetham, David, and Christopher Lord. 1998. "Legitimacy and the European Union." In *Political Theory and the European Union*, edited by Albert Weale and Michael Nentwich, 15–33. London: Routledge.

Bellamy, Richard, and Albert Weale. 2015. "Political Legitimacy and European Monetary Union: Contracts, Constitutionalism and the Normative Logic of Two-Level Games." *Journal of European Public Policy* 22(2): 257–74.

Bellamy, Richard, and Dario Castiglione. 2003. "Legitimizing the Euro-'Polity' and Its 'Regime': The Normative Turn in EU Studies." *European Journal of Political Theory* 1(2): 7–34.

Crum, Ben. 2013. "Saving the Euro at the Cost of Democracy?" *JCMS: Journal of Common Market Studies* 51(4): 614–30.

Dahl, Robert A. 2000. *On Democracy*. New Haven, CT: Yale University Press.

Diamond, Larry Jay, and Leonardo Morlino. 2004. "The Quality of Democracy. An Overview." *Journal of Democracy* 15(4): 20–31.

Diez Medrano, Juan. 2009. "The Public Sphere and the European Union's Political Identity." In *European Identity*, edited by Jeffrey T. Checkel, 81–107. Cambridge: Cambridge University Press.

EDRI. 2018. "Trilogues: The System That Undermines EU Democracy and Transparency – EDRi." EDRi. https://edri.org/trilogues-the-system-that-undermines-eu-democracy-and-transparency/.[accessed February 7th, 2018]

European Parliament. 2017. "Handbook on the Ordinary Legislative Procedure." European Parliament. www.epgencms.europarl.europa.eu/cmsdata/upload/10fc26a9-7f3e-4d8a-a46d-51bdadc9661c/handbook-olp-en.pdf.

European Parliament. 2018a. "Conciliations and Codecision – CODE." European Parliament. www.europarl.europa.eu/code/about/statistics_en.htm. [accessed February 7th, 2018]

European Parliament. 2018b. "Interinstitutional Negotiations for the Adoption of EU Legislation." European Parliament. www.epgenpro.europarl.europa.eu/static/ordinary-legislative-procedure/en/interinstitutional-negotiations.html. [accessed February 7th, 2018]

European Parliament. 2018c. "Trilogue_Negotiations." European Parliament. www.europarl.europa.eu/the-secretary-general/resource/static/files/Documents%20section/SPforEP/Trilogue_negotiations.pdf. [accessed February 7th, 2018]

Farrell, Henry, and Adrienne Héritier. 2007. "Codecision and Institutional Change." *West European Politics* 30(2): 285–300.

Føllesdal, Andreas, and Simon Hix. 2006. "Why There Is a Democratic Deficit the EU: A Response to Majone and Moravscik." *Journal of Common Market Studies* 44(3): 533–62.

Grimm, Dieter. 2017. *The Constitution of European Democracy*. With the assistance of J. Collings. Oxford: Oxford University Press.

Haas, Ernst B. 1968. *The Uniting of Europe: Political, Social, and Economic Forces 1950–57*. Stanford, CA: Stanford University Press.

Habermas, Jürgen, ed. 1999. "Braucht Europa eine Verfassung? Eine Bemerkung zu Dieter Grimm." In *Die Einbeziehung des Anderen*, 185–91. Frankfurt am Main: Suhrkamp.

Habermas, Jürgen. 2001. "Euroskepsis, Markteuropa, oder Europa der (Welt-)Bürger." In *Zeit der Übergänge*, edited by Jürgen Habermas, 85–103. Frankfurt am Main: Suhrkamp.

Hix, Simon, and Bjørn Kåre Høyland. 2011. *The Political System of the European Union*. Basingstoke: Palgrave Macmillan.

Hooghe, Liesbet, and Gary Marks. 2009. "A Postfunctionalist Theory of European Integration: From Permissive Consensus to Constraining Dissensus." *British Journal of Political Science* 39(1): 1–23.

Hutter, Swen, Edgar Grande, and Hanspeter Kriesi (eds.). 2016. *Politicising Europe: Integration and Mass Politics*. Cambridge: Cambridge University Press.

Ihalainen, Pasi, Cornelia Ilie, and Kari Palonen (eds.). 2016. *Parliament and Parliamentarism. A Comparative History of Disputes on a European Concept*. New York, NY: Berghahn Books.

Kauppi, Niilo, and Claudia Wiesner. 2018. "Exit Politics, Enter Politicization." *Journal of European Integration* 40(2): 227–33.

Lincoln, Abraham. 1863. "The Gettysburg Address." *American Writers*. www.americanwriters.org/classroom/resources/tr_lincoln.asp.

Lindberg, Leon N., and Stuart A. Scheingold. 1970. *Europe's Would-be Polity: Patterns of Change in the European Community*. Englewood Cliffs, NJ: Prentice-Hall.

Maatsch, Aleksandra. 2017. *Parliaments and the Economic Governance of the European Union: Talking Shops or Deliberative Bodies?* New York, NY: Routledge.

Magnette, Paul. 2005. *What Is the European Union? Nature and Prospects*. New York, NY: Palgrave Macmillan.

Majone, Giandomenico. 2014. "From Regulatory State to a Democratic Default." *Journal of Common Market Studies* 52(6): 1216–23.

Manin, Bernard. 1997. *The Principles of Representative Government*. Cambridge: Cambridge University Press.

Menéndez, Agustín José. 2015. "Hermann Heller NOW." *European Law Journal* 21(3): 285–94.

Mény, Yves. 2003. "De la démocratie en Europe: Old Concepts and New Challenges." *Journal of Common Market Studies* 41(1): 1–13.

Merkel, Wolfgang. 2004. "Embedded and Defective Democracies." *Democratization* 11(5): 33–58.

Offe, Claus. 2015. *Europe Entrapped*. Cambridge, Malden, MA: Polity.

Palonen, Kari. 2016. "Political Theories of Parliamentarism." In *Parliament and Parliamentarism. A Comparative History of Disputes on a European Concept*, edited by Pasi Ihalainen, Cornelia Ilie, and Karl Palonen, 219–27. New York, NY: Berghahn Books.

Pitkin, Hanna Fenichel. 2009. *The Concept of Representation*. Berkeley: University of California Press.

Rasmussen, Anne. 2012. "Twenty Years of Co-Decision Since Maastricht: Inter- and Intrainstitutional Implications." *Journal of European Integration* 34(7): 735–51.

Reh, Christine. 2014. "Is Informal Politics Undemocratic? Trilogues, Early Agreements and the Selection Model of Representation." *Journal of European Public Policy* 21(6): 822–41.

Roederer-Rynning, Christiana, and Justin Greenwood. 2015. "The Culture of Trilogues." *Journal of European Public Policy* 22(8): 1148–65.

Scharpf, Fritz W. 1999. *Governing in Europe*. Oxford: Oxford University Press.

Schmidt, Vivien A. 2013. "Democracy and Legitimacy in the European Union Revisited: Input, Output and 'Throughput.'" *Political Studies* 61(1): 2–22.

Schmitter, Philippe C. 1969. "Three Neo-Functional Hypotheses about International Integration." *International Organization* 23(1): 161–66.

Statham, Paul, and Hans-Jörg Trenz. 2013. *The Politicization of Europe: Contesting the Constitution in the Mass Media*. New York, NY: Routledge.

Streeck, Wolfgang. 2014. *Buying Time: The Delayed Crisis of Democratic Capitalism*. Brooklyn, NY: Verso.

Tiilikainen, Teija, and Claudia Wiesner. 2016. "Towards a European Parliamentarism?" In *Parliament and Parliamentarism. A Comparative History of Disputes on a European Concept*, edited by Pasi Ihalainen, Cornelia Ilie, and Karl Palonen, 292–310. New York, NY: Berghahn Books.

Tömmel, Ingeborg. 2014. *The European Union: What It Is and How It Works*. Houndsmills: Palgrave Macmillan.

Urbinati, Nadia. 2006. *Representative Democracy Principles and Genealogy*. Chicago, IL: University of Chicago Press.

White, Jonathan. 2015. "Emergency Europe." *Political Studies* 63(2): 300–18.

Wiesner, Claudia. 2017a. "Möglichkeiten und Grenzen repräsentativer Demokratie in der EU-Finanzhilfenpolitik." *Integration* 40(1): 33–47.

Wiesner, Claudia. 2017b. "Representative Democracy in Times of Austerity. New Challenges in the EU Multi-level System." In *Austerity: A Journey to an Unknown Territory*, edited by Roland Sturm, Tim Griebel, and Thorsten Winkelmann. Special issue, *Zeitschrift für Politik*. (special issue 8): 287–304.

Wiesner, Claudia. 2019. *Inventing the EU as a Democratic Polity: Concepts, Actors and Controversies*. Cham: Springer Science and Business Media; Palgrave Macmillan.

Wiesner, Claudia. 2020a. "Politicisation, Politics, and Democracy." In *Rethinking Politicsation in Politics, Sociology and International Relations*, edited by Claudia Wiesner. Palgrave Macmillan.

Wiesner, Claudia, ed. 2020b. *Rethinking Politicsation in Politics, Sociology and International Relations*. Palgrave Macmillan.

10

EASTERN EUROPE'S ILLIBERAL REVOLUTION

The Long Road to Democratic Decline

Ivan Krastev

Introduction[1]

In 1991, when the West was busy celebrating its victory in the Cold War and the apparent spread of liberal democracy to all corners of the world, the political scientist Samuel Huntington issued a warning against excessive optimism. In an article for the *Journal of Democracy* titled "Democracy's Third Wave," Huntington (1991) pointed out that the two previous waves of democratization, from the 1820s to the 1920s and from 1945 to the 1960s, had been followed by "reverse waves," in which "democratic systems were replaced [...] by historically new forms of authoritarian rule." A third reverse wave was possible, he suggested, if new authoritarian great powers could demonstrate the continued viability of nondemocratic rule or "if people around the world come to see the United States," long a beacon of democracy, "as a fading power beset by political stagnation, economic inefficiency, and social chaos" (Huntington 1991, quoted in Li 2016).

Huntington died in 2008, but had he lived, even he would probably have been surprised to see that liberal democracy is now under threat not only in countries that went through democratic transitions in recent decades, such as Brazil and Turkey, but also in the West's most established democracies. Authoritarianism, meanwhile, has reemerged in Russia and been strengthened in China, and foreign adventurism and domestic political polarization have dramatically damaged the United States' global influence and prestige.

Perhaps the most alarming development has been the change of heart in eastern Europe. Two of the region's poster children for postcommunist democratization, Hungary and Poland, have seen conservative populists win sweeping electoral victories while demonizing the political opposition, scapegoating minorities, and undermining liberal checks and balances. Other countries in the region, including the Czech Republic and Romania, seem poised to follow. In a speech in 2014, one of the new populists, Hungarian Prime Minister Viktor Orban, outlined his position on liberalism: "A democracy is not necessarily liberal. Just because something is not liberal, it still can be a democracy."[2] To maintain global competitiveness, he went on to say, "we have to abandon liberal methods and principles of organizing a society." Although Orban governs a small country, the movement he represents is of global importance. In the West, where the will of the people remains the main source of political legitimacy, his style of illiberal democracy is likely to be the major alternative to liberalism in the coming decades.

Why has democracy declared war on liberalism most openly in eastern Europe? The answer lies in the peculiar nature of the revolutions of 1989, when the states of eastern Europe freed themselves from the Soviet empire. Unlike previous revolutions, the ones in 1989 were concerned not with utopia but with the idea of normality—that is, the revolutionaries expressed a desire to lead the type of normal life already available to people in western Europe. Once the Berlin Wall fell, the most educated and liberal eastern Europeans became the first to leave their countries, provoking major demographic and identity crises in the region. And as the domestic constituencies for liberal democracy immigrated to the West, international actors such as the EU and the United States became the face of liberalism in eastern Europe, just as their own influence was waning. This set the stage for the nationalist revolt against liberalism seizing the region today.

People Power

Many have found the rise of eastern European populism difficult to explain. After Poland's populist Law and Justice party (known by its Polish abbreviation, PiS) won a parliamentary majority in 2015, Adam Michnik, one of the country's liberal icons, lamented, "Sometimes a beautiful woman loses her mind and goes to bed with a bastard." Populist victories, however, are not a mystifying one-off but a conscious and repeated choice: the right-wing populist party Fidesz has won two consecutive parliamentary elections in Hungary, and in opinion polls, PiS maintains a towering lead over its rivals. Eastern Europe seems intent on marrying the bastard.

Some populist successes can be attributed to economic troubles: Orban was elected in 2010, after Hungary's economy had shrunk by 6.6% in 2009. But similar troubles cannot explain why the Czech Republic, which enjoys one of the lowest unemployment rates in Europe, voted for a slew of populist parties in last year's parliamentary elections or why intolerance is on the rise in economically successful Slovakia. Poland is the most puzzling case. The country had the fastest-growing economy in Europe between 2007 and 2017, and it has seen social mobility improve in recent years. Research by the Polish sociologist Maciej Gdula has shown that Poles' political attitudes do not depend on whether they individually benefited from the postcommunist transition. The ruling party's base includes many who are satisfied with their lives and have shared in their country's prosperity.

The details of eastern Europe's populist turn vary from country to country, as do the character and policies of individual populist governments. As Dalibor Rohac (2017) reports, in Hungary, Fidesz has used its constitutional majority to rewrite the rules of the game: Orban's tinkering with the country's electoral system has turned his "plurality to a supermajority," in the words of the sociologist Kim Lane Scheppele. Corruption, moreover, is pervasive. David Frum (2017) quoted an anonymous observer who said of Fidesz's system: "The benefit of controlling a modern state is less the power to persecute the innocent, and more the power to protect the guilty."

Poland's government has also sought to dismantle checks and balances, especially through its changes to the constitutional court. In contrast to the Hungarian government, however, it is basically clean when it comes to corruption. Its policies are centered less on controlling the economy or creating a loyal middle class and more on the moral reeducation of the nation. The Polish government has tried to rewrite history, most notably through a recent law making it illegal to blame Poland for the Holocaust. In the Czech Republic, meanwhile, Prime Minister Andrej Babis led his party to victory last year by promising to run the state like a company.

Yet beneath these differences lie telling commonalities. Across eastern Europe, a new illiberal consensus is emerging, marked by xenophobic nationalism and supported, somewhat unexpectedly, by young people who came of age after the demise of communism. If the liberals who dominated in the 1990s were preoccupied with the rights of ethnic, religious, and sexual minorities, this new consensus is about the rights of the majority.

Wherever they take power, conservative populists use the government to deepen cultural and political polarization and champion what the American historian Richard Hofstadter termed "the paranoid style" in politics. This style traffics heavily in conspiracy theories, such as the belief, shared by many PiS voters, that the 2010 plane crash that killed President Lech Kaczynski—the brother of the PiS leader Jaroslaw Kaczysnki—was the product of an assassination rather than an accident. This paranoia also surfaces in Fidesz's assertions that Brussels, aided by the Hungarian-born billionaire George Soros, secretly plans to flood Hungary with migrants. Wherever they take power, conservative populists use the government to deepen cultural and political polarization.

Eastern Europe's populists also deploy a similar political vocabulary, casting themselves as the authentic voice of the nation against its internal and external enemies. As the political scientist Jan-Werner Müller has argued, "Populists claim that they and they alone represent the people," a claim that is not empirical but "always distinctly moral." Fidesz and PiS do not pretend to stand for all Hungarians or all Poles, but they do insist that they stand for all true Hungarians and all true Poles. They transform democracy from an instrument of inclusion into one of exclusion, delegitimizing nonmajoritarian institutions by casting them as obstacles to the will of the people.

Another common feature of eastern European populism is a Janus-faced attitude toward the EU. According to the latest Eurobarometer polls, eastern Europeans are among the most pro-EU publics on the continent, yet they vote for some of the most Euroskeptical governments. These governments, in turn, use Brussels as a rhetorical punching bag while benefiting from its financial largess. The Hungarian economy grew by 4.6% between 2006 and 2015, yet a study by KPMG and the Hungarian economic research firm GKI estimated that without EU funds, it would have shrunk by 1.8%. And Poland is the continent's biggest recipient of money from the European Structural and Investment Funds, which promote economic development in the EU's less developed countries.

Support for illiberal populism has been growing across the continent for years now, but understanding its outsize appeal in eastern Europe requires rethinking the history of the region in the decades since the end of communism. It is the legacy of the 1989 revolutions, combined with the more recent shocks delivered by the decline of United States power and the crisis of the EU, that set in motion the populist explosion of today.

Liberty, Fraternity, Normality

Although eastern European populism was already on the rise by the beginning of the current decade, the refugee crisis of 2015–16 made it the dominant political force in the region. Opinion polls indicate that the vast majority of eastern Europeans are wary of migrants and refugees. A September 2017 study by Ipsos revealed that only 5% of Hungarians and 15% of Poles believe that immigration has had a positive impact on their country and that 67% of Hungarians and 51% of Poles think that their countries' borders should be closed to refugees entirely.

As Elizabeth Collett (2017) discusses, during the refugee crisis, images of migrants streaming into Europe sparked a demographic panic across eastern Europe, where people began to imagine that their national cultures were under the threat of vanishing. The region today is made up of small, aging, ethnically homogeneous societies—for example, only 1.6% of those living in Poland were born outside the country, and only 0.1% are Muslims. In fact, cultural and ethnic diversity, rather than wealth, is the primary difference between eastern and western Europe today. Compare Austria and Hungary, neighboring countries of similar size that were once unified under the Habsburg empire. Foreign citizens make up a little under 2% of the Hungarian population; in Austria, they make up 15%. Only 6% of Hungarians are foreign-born, and these are overwhelmingly ethnic Hungarian immigrants from Romania. In Austria, the equivalent figure is 16%. In the eastern European political imagination, cultural and ethnic diversity is seen as an existential threat, and opposition to this threat forms the core of the new illiberalism.

Some of this fear of diversity may be rooted in historical traumas, such as the disintegration of the multicultural Habsburg empire after World War I and the Soviet occupation of eastern Europe after World War II. But the political shock of the refugee crisis cannot be explained by the region's history alone. Rather, eastern Europeans realized during the course of the refugee crisis that they were facing a new global revolution. This was not a revolution of the masses but one of migrants; it was inspired not by ideological visions of the future but by images of real life on the other side of a border. If globalization has made the world a village, it has also subjected it to the tyranny of global comparisons. These days, people in the poorer parts of the world rarely compare their lives with those of their neighbors; they compare them instead with those of the most prosperous inhabitants of the planet, whose wealth is on full display, thanks to the global diffusion of communications technologies. The French liberal philosopher Raymond Aron was right when he observed, five decades ago, that "with humanity on the way to unification, inequality between peoples takes on the significance that inequality between classes once had." If you are a poor person in Africa who seeks an economically secure life for your children, the best you can do for them is to make sure they are born in a rich country, such as Denmark, Germany, or Sweden—or, failing that, the Czech Republic or Poland. Change increasingly means changing your country, not your government. And eastern Europeans have felt threatened by this revolution.

The great irony is that although eastern Europe today is reacting with panic to mass migration, the revolutions of 1989 were the first in which the desire to exit one's country, rather than to gain a greater voice within it, was the primary agent of change. After the fall of the Berlin Wall, many in the former communist bloc expressed their wish for change by immigrating to the West rather than staying home to participate in democratic politics. In 1989, eastern Europeans were not dreaming of a perfect world; they were dreaming of a normal life in a normal country. If there was a utopia shared by both the left and the right during the region's postcommunist transition, it was the utopia of normality. Experiments were forbidden. In 1990, Czech Finance Minister Vaclav Klaus (who later became prime minister and then president) said of finding a middle ground between capitalism and socialism, "The third way is the fastest way to the Third World." Eastern Europeans dreamed that European unification would proceed along the same lines as German reunification, and in the early 1990s, many Czechs, Hungarians, and Poles envied the East Germans, who were issued German passports overnight and could spend the deutsche mark immediately.

Revolutions as a rule cause major demographic disruptions. When the French Revolution broke out, many of its opponents ran away. When the Bolsheviks took power in Russia, millions of Russians fled. But in those cases, it was the defeated, the enemies of the revolution, who saw their futures as being outside their own country. After the 1989 revolutions, by contrast, it was those most eager to live in the West, those most impatient to see their countries change, who were the first to leave. For many liberal-minded eastern Europeans, a mistrust of nationalist loyalties and the prospect of joining the modern world made emigration a logical and legitimate choice. It was the legacy of the 1989 revolutions that set in motion the populist explosion of today.

As a result, the revolutions of 1989 had the perverse effect of accelerating population decline in the newly liberated countries of eastern Europe. From 1989 to 2017, Latvia lost 27% of its population, Lithuania 23%, and Bulgaria almost 21%. Hungary lost nearly 3% of its population in just the last ten years. And in 2016, around one million Poles were living in the United Kingdom alone. This emigration of the young and talented was occurring in countries that already had aging populations and low birthrates. Together, these trends set the stage for a demographic panic.

It is thus, as Fareed Zakaria (2016) argues, both emigration and the fear of immigration that best explain the rise of populism in eastern Europe. The success of nationalist populism, which feeds off a sense that a country's identity is under threat, is the outcome of the mass exodus of young people from the region combined with the prospect of large-scale immigration, which together set demographic alarm bells ringing. Moving to the West was equivalent to rising in social status, and, as a result, the eastern Europeans who stayed in their own countries started feeling like losers who had been left behind. In countries where most young people dream of leaving, success back home is devalued.

In recent years, a rising desire for self-assertion has also caused eastern Europeans to chafe at taking orders from Brussels. Although during the 1990s, the region's politicians, eager to join NATO and the EU, had been willing to follow the liberal playbook, today, they wish to assert their full rights as members of the European club. Eastern Europe's integration into the EU mirrors at a national level the experience of integration familiar from the stories of immigrants around the world. First-generation immigrants wish to gain acceptance by internalizing the values of their host country; second-generation immigrants, born in the new country, fear being treated as second-class citizens and often rediscover an interest in the traditions and values of their parents' culture. Something similar happened to eastern European societies after joining the EU. Many people in those countries used to view Brussels' interference in their domestic politics as benevolent. Over time, they have started to see it as an intolerable affront to their nations' sovereignty.

The Return of Geopolitics

The final ingredient in eastern Europe's illiberal turn is the deep current of geopolitical insecurity that has always afflicted the region. In 1946, the Hungarian intellectual Istvan Bibo published a pamphlet called *The Misery of the Small States of Eastern Europe*. In it, he argued that democracy in the region would always be held hostage to the lingering effects of historical traumas, most of them related to eastern European states' history of domination by outside powers. Poland, for instance, ceased to exist as an independent state following its partition by Austria, Prussia, and Russia in the late 18th century; Hungary, meanwhile, saw a nationalist revolution crushed in 1849, before losing more than two-thirds of its territory and one-half of its population in the 1920 Treaty of Trianon.

Not only did these historical traumas make eastern European societies fear and resent external powers, but they also, Bibo argued, secured these countries in the belief that "the advance of freedom threatens the national cause." They have learned to be suspicious of any cosmopolitan ideology that crosses their borders, whether it be the universalism of the Catholic Church, the liberalism of the late Habsburg empire, or Marxist internationalism. The Czech writer and dissident Milan Kundera captured this sense of insecurity well when he defined a small nation as "one whose very existence may be put in question at any moment." A citizen of a large country takes his nation's survival for granted. "His anthems speak only of grandeur and eternity. The Polish anthem, however, starts with the verse: 'Poland has not yet perished.'"

If one effect of eastern Europe's post-1989 emigration was to kick-start the demographic panic that would later take full form during the refugee crisis, another, equally important effect was to deprive countries in the region of the citizens who were most likely to become domestic defenders of liberal democracy. As a result, liberal democracy in eastern Europe came to rely more and more on the support of external actors, such as the EU and the United States, which over time came to be seen as the real constraints on the power of majorities in the region. Bucharest's desire to join the EU, for instance, was primarily responsible for its decision to resolve a long-running dispute with Hungary about the rights of ethnic Hungarians in Romania. And the EU's eligibility rules, known as the Copenhagen criteria, make legal protections for minorities a precondition for membership in the union.

The central role of the EU and the United States in consolidating eastern Europe's liberal democracies meant that those democracies remained safe only so long as the dominance of Brussels and Washington in Europe was unquestioned. Yet over the last decade, the geopolitical situation has changed. The United States had already been hobbled by expensive foreign wars and the financial crisis before the election of Donald Trump as its president raised serious questions about Washington's commitment to its allies. In Europe, meanwhile, the consecutive shocks of the debt crisis, the refugee crisis, and Brexit have called the future of the EU itself into question. This came just as Russia, under the authoritarian government of President Vladimir Putin, was beginning to reassert itself as a regional power, seizing Crimea from Ukraine in 2014 and backing a secessionist insurgency in the country's east.

Huntington predicted in 1991 that a strong, nondemocratic Russia would pose problems for the liberal democracies of eastern Europe, and the rise of Putin's Russia has in fact undermined them. For eastern European leaders such as Orban, already fed up with liberalism, Putin's combination of authoritarian rule and anti-Western ideology has served as a model to emulate. For many Poles, the return of the Russian threat was one more argument to vote for an illiberal government that could protect the nation. In other eastern European countries, such as the Baltic states, Russia has simply acted as a spoiler by attempting to spread disinformation. Across the region, the return of geopolitical insecurity has contributed to the fading attractiveness of liberal democracy.

An Illiberal Europe?

Eastern European populism is a recent phenomenon, but it has deep roots in the region's politics and is unlikely to go away anytime soon. "The worrying thing about Orban's 'illiberal democracy,'" according to the Hungarian-born Austrian journalist Paul Lendvai, is that "its end cannot be foreseen." Indeed, illiberal democracy has become the new form of authoritarianism that Huntington warned about more than two decades ago. What makes it particularly dangerous is that it is an authoritarianism born within the framework of democracy itself.

The new populists are not fascists. They do not believe in the transformative power of violence, and they are not nearly as repressive as the fascists were. But they are indifferent to liberal checks and balances and do not see the need for constitutional constraints on the power of the majority—constraints that form a central part of EU law. The main challenge posed by eastern European populism is therefore not to the existence of democracy at the level of the nation but to the cohesion of the EU. As more countries in the region turn toward illiberalism, they will continue to come into conflict with Brussels and probe the limits of the EU's power, as Poland has already done with its judicial reforms. Eventually, the risk is that the EU could disintegrate, and Europe could become a continent divided and unfree.

Notes

1 This chapter was originally published in Foreign Affairs. The Editors gratefully acknowledge the permission of the author and Foreign Affairs to publish a slightly revised version in this volume.
2 For an English translation of Orbán's speech on illiberal democracy of July 26, 2014, see www.kormany.hu/en/the-prime-minister/the-prime-minister-s-speeches/prime-minister-viktor-orban-s-speech-at-the-25th-balvanyos-summer-free-university-and-student-camp.

Bibliography

Collett, Elizabeth. 2017. "Destination: Europe Managing the Migrant Crisis." *Foreign Affairs*, February 13. www.foreignaffairs.com/reviews/review-essay/2017-02-13/destination-europe.

Frum, David. 2017. "How to Build an Autocracy." *The Atlantic*, March 2017. www.theatlantic.com/magazine/archive/2017/03/how-to-build-an-autocracy/513872/?utm_source=atltw.

Huntington, Samuel P. 1991. "Democracy's Third Wave." *Journal of Democracy* 2(2): 12–34.

Li, Eric X. 2016. "Watching American Democracy in China: Liberals and Conservatives after Trump." *Foreign Affairs*, April 19. www.foreignaffairs.com/articles/china/2016-04-19/watching-american-democracy-china.

Rohac, Dominic. 2017. "Hungary Is Turning into Russia: On the CEU, Orban Mimics Putin." *Foreign Affairs*, April 12. www.foreignaffairs.com/articles/hungary/2017-04-12/hungary-turning-russia.

Zakaria, Fareed. 2016. "Populism on the March: Why the West Is in Trouble." *Foreign Affairs*, October 17. www.foreignaffairs.com/articles/united-states/2016-10-17/populism-march.

11

ILLIBERAL DEMOCRACY OR ELECTORAL AUTOCRACY

The Case of Turkey

Gülçin Balamir Coşkun and Aysuda Kölemen

Introduction

Liberal democracy, which has been the ideal and the norm in the Western world since World War II, spread to other parts of the globe with the third wave of democratization and the dissolution of the communist regimes in Eastern Europe (Huntington 1991). A serious challenge to the legitimacy of liberal democracy accompanied this last wave of expansion (Mounk 2018). A group of critics questioned the democratic legitimacy of the EU by pointing out a "democratic deficit" and a "bureaucratic despotism" in EU countries that result from an empowerment of the EU bureaucracy (see Wiesner in this volume). However, the perception of a democratic deficit has not remained limited to the EU. Technocratic structures of nation states have also come under attack for their inability to meet the needs of the public. This "undemocratic dilemma" (Mounk 2018) is one of the factors that contributed to the surge of a direct threat against liberal democracy, that is, illiberal democracy. Although the term became popular after a speech by Viktor Orbán (2014) discussed by both Marc Plattner and Ivan Krastev in this volume, Fareed Zakaria (1997) had coined it earlier for describing regimes in which popular participation is respected by holding regular elections, but civil liberties and freedoms are under attack. "Illiberal democracy" is a convenient conceptual tool for populist leaders to cast themselves as democratic, while dismantling liberal norms and institutions by breaking the rule of law as well as violating civil rights and freedoms in the name of "the people" under the guise of responding to the needs and concerns of the voters that gave them a mandate through elections (Mounk 2018).

This chapter aims to illustrate that the term illiberal democracy is a contradiction in terms that serves as little more than a rhetorical fig leaf for autocratizing regimes by examining the case of the AKP (Justice and Development Party) in Turkey. Liberal democracy is comprised of two pillars: constitutional liberalism and democratic procedure. Constitutional liberalism limits government authority and protects individual rights and liberties by instituting the separation of powers and the rule of law, while democracy is an "institutional arrangement for arriving at political decisions in which individuals acquire the power to decide by means of a competitive struggle for the people's vote" (Schumpeter 1975, 242). Although constitutional liberalism and democracy developed neither simultaneously nor harmoniously, they are inextricably intertwined because fair and free elections are a prerequisite for even the most rudimentary and procedural forms of democracy. Fair and free elections are only possible if the oppositional forces have equal rights to organize and a chance of winning office through elections as the incumbent (Przeworski et al. 1996, 50–51). This organizational capacity depends on the existence of an "autonomous public opinion," created and sustained by a "polycentric structuring of the media and their competitive interplay" (Sartori 1987, 98, 110) as well as on freedom of expression, freedom of access to information, freedom of association, and the protection of individual rights against arbitrary state intervention, all of which are fundamental elements of constitutional liberalism. Devoid of liberal rights and protections, a strong rule of law, and governmental accountability, elections become unfair and unfree, and majority rule, which is declared to be the sole measure of democracy by proponents of illiberal democracies, is undermined. Thus, "illiberal democracies are always in danger of degenerating into electoral dictatorships" (Mounk 2018, 100). Autocratizing regimes try to avoid a negative reaction from the international community by maintaining a democratic facade and instrumentalizing elections in a thinly veiled effort to legitimize their autocratic practices.

This chapter examines the degeneration of the fledgling Turkish democracy of the early 2000s into an electoral autocracy over the course of the AKP period. In the first section, we will provide a brief history of the emergence of the AKP. In the second section, we will review how the AKP imposed itself as the sole legitimate representative of the people by undermining checks and balances on the executive branch and weakening governmental accountability. We conclude that Turkey has devolved into an autocratic regime after 2007, and note that this authoritarian turn continues to be contested and mitigated by democratic forces in Turkish society.

The Rise and Transformation of the AKP

Turkey had never been a full democracy since its foundation in 1923. After the transition to multiparty system in 1950, the socially and religiously conservative and free market-oriented Democratic Party (DP) won the elections with a landslide over the CHP (Republican People's Party) that had ruled the country under a secular single party regime, of which the main ambitions were modernization, industrialization, secularization, and nation-building (to the detriment of religious and ethnic minorities) for almost three decades. However, after ten years in government, the DP was ousted by a military coup in May 27, 1960. Over the following decades, the military which saw itself as the true protector of the Republic against its enemies became an inextricable part of Turkish politics. The March 12, 1971 coup was followed by the September 12 coup in 1980 and the military established its permanent presence behind the seemingly democratic, electoral politics (Hale 1993; Gürsoy 2017). On February 28, 1997, the military forced the main partner of the governing coalition, the Islamist Welfare Party (RP), out of the government in what was called a "post-modern coup." Despite periods of military rule that brought grave human rights abuses and curtailment of democratic rights and freedoms, Turkish democracy managed to survive and flourish for brief periods until the next crisis arrived.

What precipitated the AKP's rise to power in 2002 was a series of crises between 1997 and 2001. Economic stability and democratic reforms appeared to mark the first term of the AKP between 2002 and 2007. However, after its decisive reelection victory in 2007, the AKP began to reveal an authoritarian streak that grew stronger at each turning point.

The Rise of the AKP to Power: An Era of Crises

Founded in 2001, the AKP was the latest incarnation in a series of Islamist political parties that emerged from the National Outlook (Milli Görüş) movement since the 1960s. Despite garnering 34% of the votes, the AKP gained nearly two-thirds of the parliamentary seats in 2002 as a result of the Turkish electoral system. Turkey had been ruled by coalition governments for over a decade and the AKP did not only form the first single party government in a long time but was also the first Islamist party to win a parliamentary majority in Turkish history (Sezer 2002).

The confluence of three major crises—political, economic, and natural—laid the groundwork for the disintegration of the fragmented center-right and the unexpected electoral success of the AKP in 2002: the 1997 coup against Islamists, the 1999 Izmit earthquake, and the 2001 economic crisis. The 1997 military coup against the Islamist-led government came first. The division between the secular center and the religious-conservative periphery had constituted one of the most fundamental dynamics since the foundation of the Turkish Republic (Sezer 2002, 15). The military had done little to disguise its distaste for political Islam and deemed it a grave threat to the secular republic. The peripheral religious-conservative majority had typically voted for center-right parties and Islamist parties remained a small but permanent actor in the political arena. The hostility and tension between the military and Islamists were heightened when the RP received the highest percentage of parliamentary seats and formed a coalition government with the center-right True Path Party (DYP) in 1996 (Aslan 2016).

On February 28, 1997, the military-controlled National Security Council issued a memorandum laying out a plan to fight Islamic reactionism that resulted in the dissolution of the coalition government led by the RP. In January 1998, the RP was banned by the Constitutional Court of Turkey (TCC) for engaging in anti-secular activities. Following the coup, Islamist activists and politicians, including Recep Tayyip Erdoğan, were sent to prison, many NGOs associated with political Islam were closed down, women with headscarves were banned from attending university, and the tarikahs (Islamic religious orders) were investigated. The Virtue Party (FP), which succeeded the RP, was also banned in 2001 (Aslan 2016).

The second crisis was the "failure of the Turkish government to deal effectively with the country's earthquake hazard" and "the inadequacy of the state's response" during the 1999 Izmit earthquake which resulted in 17,000 deaths and many more injuries according to official numbers (although unofficial estimates range between 35,000 and 50,000) as well as 75,000 collapsed and heavily damaged households and commercial buildings (Jacoby and Özerdem 2008, 298). The inadequate response to a disaster of this magnitude led to a precipitous decline of trust in the government. The ruling parties naturally bore the brunt of the anger of the electorate.

The third crisis was the 2001 economic collapse, which significantly impoverished the nation and led to increased individual and family stress (Aytaç and Rankin 2008). Many blamed the crisis on the unstable political environment caused by ever-changing coalitions. The coalition government led by the center-left Democratic Left Party (DSP) and its partners, the center-right Motherland Party (ANAP) and the Nationalist Action Party (MHP), started implementing an IMF restructuring program that required belt-tightening and led to further public discontent (Şenses 2003).

The Turning Points in the Transformation of the AKP

The newly established AKP inherited the political network and infrastructure of the FP, but positioned itself as a centrist, conservative-religious party to fill the vacuum left by the vanishing center parties of the crisis-laden late 1990s. Once in power, the AKP benefited from the economic stability that followed the IMF restructuring program the previous government had implemented and the global economic boom that developing economies enjoyed in the 2000s. Moreover, Erdogan promised and to a certain extent delivered democratic reforms to various ethnic, religious, and ideological groups that had suffered from the dominant Kemalist ideology and the military tutelage of the Republic. By challenging Kemalist authoritarian politics (Christofis 2018, 15), the AKP secured support not only from "devout Muslims" but also from liberals and Kurds who had long-standing grievances against Kemalism. The AKP promised them a public sphere in which they could participate with their ethnic, religious, and ideological identities. Simultaneously, the AKP reassured Turkey's Western allies and the global markets that had doubts about the Islamist roots of the party by adopting a democratic and pro-European international discourse. In this climate of economic stability and political democratization that many attributed to the political stability provided by a single party government (as opposed to the unstable coalition governments before), the AKP increased its vote share to 46.6% in 2007 and 49.8% in 2011.

However, soon after the 2007 elections, the policies and practices of the AKP began to look less and less democratic, and

> what seemed to be a promising reform movement that started during the early 2000s [...] has been replaced by a grim picture of illiberal political developments that are characterized by President Recep Tayyip Erdogan's power grab, loss of judicial independence, and electoral manipulations.
>
> *(Yeşilada 2016, 19)*

What defined the post-2007 AKP period was an escalating series of turning points that sent Turkey down the rabbit hole of autocratization. The first major turning point was a product of the increasing tension between the government and the Turkish military. In April 2007, the AKP nominated Abdullah Gül, an "Islamist" politician, whose wife wore a headscarf, for presidency. The AKP succeeded in electing Gül by simple majority in the third round of voting in parliament. The only opposition party in the parliament, the Republican People's Party (CHP), decided to boycott the first round and invalidate the voting because they argued that a quorum required two-thirds of all members of the parliament to be present for a presidential vote. After the first round, the CHP challenged the election in the TCC, arguing that the quorum had not been attained. In the meantime, the military issued a memorandum on its website stating that "it should not be forgotten that the Turkish armed forces are a side in this debate and a staunch defender of secularism" (BBC News 2007). On May 1, the TCC found the argument of the CHP valid and annulled the results of the presidential election, forcing Prime Minister Erdoğan to call for an early general election. When the AKP increased its votes, Erdoğan started presenting himself as the only representative of the people's will. The AKP overcame the quorum problem with the support of the MHP, which had returned to parliament, and elected Gül as the 11th president of Turkey. From this point onward, Erdoğan started arguing that he had the electoral mandate to fight military and judicial tutelage.

The AKP government capitalized on its fresh electoral success by implementing reforms that mitigated the role of the military in politics and by launching judiciary investigations (Ergenekon and Sledgehammer) against hundreds of active and retired military personnel in 2008 on charges of meddling in politics and conspiring to overthrow the elected government. Liberal intellectuals initially welcomed both the legal reforms and the operations against military officials even if they did not support the AKP because they believed that the AKP could end the military tutelage in Turkish politics that had plagued Turkish democracy since the first military intervention in 1960. However, these reforms and operations were turned into a witch hunt against secular opposition groups as well as critical groups to retaliate against the persecution that Islamists had suffered during the February 28 period and into an operation against the critics of the government to counter the challenge of their government during the presidential crisis (Rodrik 2011; Filkins 2013). The trial and imprisonment of Ahmet Şık is emblematic of this new phase of the Ergenekon trials. Şık, an anti-militarist journalist, was arrested and imprisoned from March 2011 to March 2012 for his investigative book on how the Gülen movement had infiltrated the state (Şık 2017). The attacks of the AKP on judicial autonomy started with these trials. Through its "strategic" alliance (Taş 2018, 397–8) or "obvious marriage of convenience" with the Gülen movement (an Islamic order that was actively involved in education, politics, and bureaucracy), the AKP began to exercise an unprecedented level of control over the judiciary (Şık 2017; DW 2018). The principles of fair trial and independent judiciary, which had never been strong in the first place, further eroded.

The Gezi protests constitute another turning point during the AKP rule. Up until the Gezi protests, the AKP referred to the constitutional referendum of 2010 and the third electoral victory in 2011 as conclusive evidence of popular support for its policies and practices. Erdoğan's discourse emphasized that they were acting for the people and in the name of the people. He targeted the Kemalist military and judiciary elites and accused his critics of collaborating with them or with foreign enemies. However, the Gezi protests revealed that contrary to what Erdoğan argued, Turkey had become an autocratic state in which civil rights and freedoms were under attack. Among other things, the Gezi occupation was a revolt against this authoritarianism (Tuğal 2013). During these protests, police violence was so harsh that seven protesters were killed and thousands of protestors were injured.

The surprising results of the 2015 general elections came with the promise of a new era in Turkish politics. The critics were voicing increasing dissatisfaction with the autocratic policies of the government on the eve of the elections. Under the leadership of its co-chair Selahattin Demirtaş, the Peoples' Democratic Party (HDP) reached beyond the traditional base of the pro-Kurdish political movement and "appealed to the Turkish secular middle class, which was strongly disappointed by the policies of the AKP government and opposed the introduction of a presidential system" (Grigoriadis 2016, 42). The HDP led a surprisingly successful campaign and support for Demirtaş surged outside the

Kurdish regions, too. On June 7, 2015, the party received 13.1% of the votes (up from around 6% that previous Kurdish parties normally received) and gained 80 seats (up from 40). More critically, the AKP lost its parliamentary majority in losing many seats to the HDP and was forced to engage in coalition negotiations for the first time since its establishment. However, in July 2015, multiple terrorist groups began to mount attacks, killing large numbers of civilians in cities across Turkey. Coalition talks failed and President Erdoğan called for new elections on November 1. Although the majority of terrorist attacks were linked to ISIS (Islamic State of Iraq and Syria) cells in Turkey, the AKP campaigned on an antiterrorism platform and succeeded in linking the terrorist attacks with the HDP in the minds of many voters. As a result of this strategy, the HDP lost votes and the AKP regained a parliamentary majority. Although the share of votes of the HDP dropped to 10.8% due to the climate of terror and conflict, it became clear that the HDP had become a permanent presence in the parliament. Soon after the November 1 elections, President Erdoğan called for lifting the parliamentary immunity of HDP deputies. After a temporary suspension of parliamentary immunity, 12 HDP parliamentarians, including the presidential candidate Demirtaş, were arrested.

The final and most drastic turning point that transformed post-2007 Turkey into an autocracy was the failed *coup d'état* in 2016 and the declaration of the state of emergency in its wake. Although the government alleged that the Islamist Gülen movement was behind the coup attempt, the AKP rejected proposals to open a parliamentary investigation about the coup, and President Erdoğan— calling the coup attempt "a blessing from God"—used the coup as an opportunity to crush the democratic opposition—particularly Kurdish and leftist movements—in its aftermath. The state of emergency lasted two years. During this period, 94 elected mayors in Kurdish cities were replaced with government-appointed trustees. Around 150 media outlets and 1,500 non-governmental organizations were closed down. More than 107,000 people were dismissed from public sector jobs, and more than 50,000 people were imprisoned pending trial (BBC News, 2018). The state of emergency was lifted after a referendum in 2017 that changed Turkey to a presidential system and gave the president vast powers with virtually no checks and balances from the judiciary and the legislative. There was no longer any need for the state of emergency because the state of emergency had been rendered permanent by the new constitution.

Incremental Autocratization

The AKP incrementally undermined all democratic forces and institutions that could check its expanding power and suppressed its opponents and critics. We review how the AKP attacked and undermined four crucial spheres of power in state and society that placed checks on executive authority: the media, the judiciary, civil society, and academia.

The Media

The AKP government used various methods for bringing the mainstream media under its full control: reconfiguration of media ownership, intimidation and criminalization of dissident journalists, broadcasting bans and financial sanctions, and closing down news agencies, TV stations, and radio channels.

Some big corporations, such as Doğan Group, Doğuş Media, Uzan Holding, and Çukurova Holding, dominated mainstream Turkish media in the pre-AKP period, while the Islamist newspapers and TV channels had limited reach. During the first term of the AKP (2002–7), especially Doğan Group tried to have good relations with the new government and benefited from this cooperation (Kaya and Çakmur 2010, 531). During the same period, some other media companies were placed under the control of the Savings Deposit Insurance Fund (TMSF) because of their debts (Waldman and Çalışkan 2019, 390), which facilitated the transfer of their broadcasting rights and assets to holdings more sympathetic to the AKP in the following years. As soon as the AKP started to monopolize the political power after 2007, it became easier for them to transform the media landscape. It acquired full control of mainstream media in three steps. First, Erdoğan directed his inner circle to buy or establish media conglomerates. One of Erdogan's close friends, Ethem Sancak, established Kanal 24 immediately before the 2007 elections. Next, the government took over the legal ownership of the second biggest media group comprising the newspaper Sabah and the leading TV channel ATV only to then transfer it—through a public tender—to the pro-government Çalık Holding, the CEO of which was Erdoğan's son-in-law Berat Albayrak. By 2008, the AKP had established its own "partisan media." The second step was the creation of Zirve Holding media company in 2013 by pooling money from various pro-AKP construction companies, which had won large state tenders during the AKP period. Çalık Holding then sold *Sabah* and *ATV* to this newly created pool company, transforming Turkish partisan media into what is now known as "the pool media" (Diken 2014). Following the 2007 electoral victory of the AKP, the clientelistic relationship between Doğan Media Group and the AKP suddenly broke down and its owner Aydın Doğan was designated enemy number one of the government (Waldman and Çalışkan 2019, 392). Fiscal authorities heavily fined Doğan Media Group for alleged tax irregularities. All Doğan companies were banned from state tender bids for one year. Company executives and Doğan family members were sued. In 2018, Aydın Doğan finally agreed to sell his media companies to the Demirören family, one of Erdoğan's associates. The sale included Hürriyet, one of the most prestigious mainstream newspapers, and Posta, the tabloid with the highest circulation, as well as two of Turkey's main entertainment and news channels, Kanal D and CNN Türk (RSF 2018). Today, almost 95% of the mainstream media in Turkey is under the direct control of the AKP government or, more precisely, President Erdoğan (IPI Report 2019).

The AKP government did not stop at controlling media corporations. It has also utilized various strategies to control individual journalists. One strategy has been to contact editors-in-chief of TV stations and newspapers and tell them what to cover and what to ignore in the news. These messages are accompanied by threats or promises of rewards. Another method of control has been to fire journalists who resist this censorship or force them to resign (Yeşil 2016, 93–94). The most extreme and internationally criticized measure against critical journalists has been criminalizing the journalists who resist censorship and continue to work in the "alternative" media by labeling them as terrorists who support "FETÖ" (the Fethullah Gülen Terrorist Organization), the PKK (Kurdish Workers' Party), or both, by bringing legal charges against, and by imprisoning them. Although the emergency decree laws have not introduced substantive changes to criminal law, the criminal prosecution of journalists and bloggers intensified considerably after the declaration of the state of emergency (CDL-AD 2017, 4). The penal code, criminal defamation laws, and antiterrorism legislation have been employed to jail large numbers of journalists and punish critical reporting. Judicial custody during trial has become a standard method of punishment. As of 2019, Turkey has the highest number of incarcerated journalists in the world (TGS 2019) and the annual report of Reporters without Borders places Turkey as 157th out of 180 ranked nations according to the World Press Freedom Index (RSF 2019).

Despite bringing all mainstream media under its control and persecuting dissident journalists, the AKP failed to create a monophonic media. Especially in the aftermath of major events that may spark criticism of the government, the governmental Radio and Television Supreme Council (RTÜK) routinely imposes publication and broadcasting bans. In addition, the RTÜK imposes financial penalties on those media the government does not control. Erdoğan's lawyers immediately filed a complaint with the RTÜK when the president was criticized on a program on Halk TV, a minor television channel owned by the main opposition party CHP. The complaint accused the critics of "targeting, insulting, and threatening Turkish President Erdoğan, in addition to calling for a military coup against the constitution." RTÜK fined Halk TV eighty thousand Turkish Liras (fifteen thousand US dollars), approximately 5% of their monthly advertisement revenue, and placed a five-day broadcasting ban on the TV show in question (IPA 2019).

After the 2016 attempted coup, which we discussed among the crucial turning points during the AKP period, the Turkish government declared a state of emergency and began to pass a large number of emergency decree laws on matters not related to the state of emergency. In this political atmosphere, the AKP intensified its attacks against all critical media outlets. Although the initial targets were newspapers, news agencies, and TV channels connected to Fethullah Gülen, after a brief period, the government started using the state of emergency as a pretext to shut down any media outlet that challenged the official line. The state of emergency was renewed at three-month intervals until

July 2018. During this period, 18 TV channels, 22 radio stations, 50 newspapers, and 20 magazines were shut down by way of decrees in law (nos. 668, 675, 677, and 683).

The Decree Law no. 680 introduced some permanent changes to the Law no. 612 on radio and television and gave broad authority to the Supreme Council over broadcasting bans and licenses. The Supreme Council could now reject applications for broadcasting licenses for reasons of national security and public order, provided that the national intelligence bodies have information that the applying media outlet executives or their partners had an affiliation or relations with a terrorist organization (Article 19 of the Decree Law) (CDL-AD 2017, 07: 6). Thus, those who did not support the government could easily be labeled terrorists and prevented from opening a television or radio channel.

In September 2019, the government extended the authority of the RTÜK to internet television outlets such as Netflix. The cumulative effect of these strategies—both intended and realized—was to suppress a "polycentric structuring of the media and their competitive interplay" in Turkey, thereby impeding the formation of "autonomous public opinion" (Sartori 1987, 98 and 110). It is not surprising to see the similarities between this effort and that of the Fidesz government in Hungary, which tries to "restrict by means of legislative measures the independence of the public bodies overseeing private and public media" (Polyák 2019, 283).

The Erosion of Judicial Independence: "Silivri Is Cold"

The AKP chipped away at judicial independence through three mechanisms: by passing constitutional amendments that increased the powers of the executive over the judiciary, by reorganizing the High Council of Judges and Prosecutors (HCJP), and by encouraging lower courts to defy orders of higher courts.

In the September 12, 2010 referendum, citizens of Turkey were asked to cast a single yes or no vote on a bundle comprising 25 constitutional amendments covering a wide range of issues such as the provision of special protections for women, children, and the elderly people, collective bargaining rights for public servants, the introduction of an ombudsman system, and changes to the appointment procedures for members of the TCC and the HCJP. Although the simultaneous voting for "several questions without any intrinsic link" was criticized by the Venice Commission, the reforms were largely welcomed by the European institutions and Turkish liberals (Özbudun 2014, 163). The opposition criticized the amendments concerning the TCC and the HCJP, and referred to the referendum as "the Prime Minister's court-packing plan" (Yeginsu 2010). They argued that the goal behind the new design of the TCC was to stump over the checks that the secular judiciary elites had set on the government (for detailed analysis and different points of view on the TCC decisions, see Arato 2016, 238–47 and Bâli 2013, 673–91).

The constitutional amendments that opened the path to court packing were hidden among the many democratic and progressive constitutional changes in the 2010 referendum. The democratic amendments enabled the AKP to garner support for the constitutional reform from liberal circles which were eager for amendments that would improve the 1982 constitution, which was the authoritarian and militaristic legacy of the junta period. The distaste for the highly undemocratic 1982 constitution led many liberal observers to optimistically downplay the degree to which the amendment on judicial appointments would allow the government to pack the courts. These amendments increased the number of permanent justices in the TCC from 11 to 17 and changed their appointment procedures. As predicted by the opponents of the constitutional referendum, these new arrangements provided the executive with the opportunity to reorganize the highest courts and establish tight control over them. Similar to other populist and authoritarian governments, such as those of Juan Perón in Argentina, Alberto Fujimori in Peru, or Hugo Chávez in Venezuela, the AKP attacked the higher courts to eliminate any remaining resistance against its will (Arato 2016, 249). Similarly, executives in Hungary and Poland have attacked constitutional courts to gain control over judges and restrict the powers of the court (Fleck 2018; Castillo-Ortiz 2019). As underlined by Pech and Scheppele (2017), these dramatic changes refer to an alarming process of "rule of law backsliding."

The second stage of the erosion of judicial independence took place in 2013 after the breakdown of the alliance between the AKP government and Gülen organization members after the scandals that came to light between December 17 and 25, 2013. In this series of scandals, four cabinet members, their relatives, and certain bureaucrats were accused of corruption and prosecuted by the judicial police. In response, the government immediately introduced changes to the "Regulation on the Judicial Police" on December 21, 2013 that made it obligatory for police forces involved in a criminal investigation to provide preliminary information to administrative authorities. They could thus no longer carry out investigations without the prior consent of the executive authority. Fifteen members of the HCJP issued a press release to protest the new regulatory rules leading to a swift reaction from Prime Minister Erdoğan. He openly declared that the lack of government oversight over the HCJP was "a mistake" (Hürriyet Daily News 2013). And shortly after this statement, the AKP government prepared a bill that radically altered the HCJP Law. The new HCJP Law (no. 6524) went into force in February 2014. A group of opposition MPs challenged the law in the Constitutional Court (TCC). However, the government did not wait for the decision of the court to implement the new law, according to which the Minister of Justice had the power to appoint and transfer judges and public prosecutors. He promptly replaced judges and public prosecutors involved in the corruption investigations against the government as well as HCJP members with pro-government people. On April 10, 2014, the TCC annulled some provisions of the law, including the Minister's appointment authority.

However, since the decisions of the court are not retroactive, the displaced judges and prosecutors did not have the right to return to their previous posts (Özbudun 2015, 47–48).

The new constitutional amendments in 2017 offered a permanent solution to the AKP's problems with the judiciary. The HCJP was rearranged and renamed to the Council of Judges and Prosecutors (CJP). This new council is composed of 13 members, 7 elected by the parliament and 6 appointed by the president, formalizing the influence of the executive on the CJP. The council is responsible for the election of the members of the Court of Cassation and the Turkish Council of State. Since these two bodies also play an important role in the composition of the TCC, the restructuring CJP further strengthened the influence of the President in the composition of the TCC (Haimerl 2017).

The degree to which the judicial branch has become an extension of the executive was revealed when lower courts defied higher court rulings to satisfy the wishes of the president. When the TCC ruled that the rights of the journalists Can Dündar and Erdem Gül had been violated and ordered their release in March 2016, President Erdoğan responded by declaring that he did not "recognize or respect this ruling" (Independent, 2016). On January 11, 2018, the TCC declared that the pre-trial detention of the journalists Mehmet Altan and Şahin Alpay was unconstitutional and ordered their release, but this time the courts of first instance refused to implement the TCC ruling for months, although they eventually released the journalists. This was nothing short of a "legalist rebellion against the Constitution and the TCC" (Çalı 2018). "Silivri must be cold now" is a popular meme on Turkish social media that has become emblematic of the utilization of the judiciary to silence criticism. The statement humorously implies that the speaker would like to criticize the government, but self-censors herself for fear of being imprisoned at Silivri Prison where many political prisoners remain incarcerated.

Civil Society in the Crosshairs

The Gezi protests were a turning point in the AKP's approach to all civil society movements and organizations. We will recount three cases in which the AKP government suppressed a diverse array of civil society groups that share one common trait: they were among the groups that carried "the protests forward at critical instances" during the Gezi protests because they were "rehearsed in their physical and theoretical confrontation with the police" (Nuhrat 2016). These groups are football fans, the Union of Chambers of Turkish Engineers and Architects (TMMOB), and the LGBTI+ community.

Tuastad provides examples from Jordan and Egypt to make the case that football has a "seismic" potential to affect political change (Tuastad 2014).

Given the outsized influence of football teams in Turkish society, football and politics have always been intertwined in the country. The AKP tried to have its political supporters elected as presidents of major sports clubs in Turkey. After a long struggle, the party managed to gain influence over the Football Federation. In typical clientelist fashion, the AKP directed funds to previously small, poor teams that Erdoğan had personal ties to: Kasımpaşa, the neighborhood Erdoğan grew up in; Rize, his parents' hometown; and Siirt, his wife's hometown (Kılıç 2006). The AKP also funneled a lot of money to the Istanbul Metropolitan Municipality team (ISM). In 2014, the city sold ISM to Başakşehir Spor (Başakşehir is a new neighborhood of Istanbul characterized by gated communities inhabited mostly by upper-middle-class AKP voters), which had been bought by AKP cronies. Başakşehir is one of the richest and most successful football teams in Turkey now. Much to Erdogan's chagrin, it does not have a fan base and is viscerally hated by anti-AKP football fans (Sözmen 2018).

Beşiktaş football team is the polar opposite of Başakşehir. It is a club with a long history, devout fans all over Turkey, and a very local core fan group. The club's core supporters are youths from the Beşiktaş district of Istanbul and they go by the name of Çarşı group, which refers to the marketplace (çarşı) that forms the center of Beşiktaş. Çarşı played a big and well-publicized role during the Gezi protests thanks to its "repertoire of resistance" (Turan and Özçetin 2019). In response, 35 leading Çarşı members who had played a prominent role during the Gezi protests were arrested and charged with a number of crimes, including attempting to overthrow the government, revealing how the fan group was viewed as a political threat (Eder and Öz 2017, 65). They were acquitted in 2015.

When fans of many teams continued Gezi-style protests in the tribunes after the Gezi protests themselves had ended, the AKP responded in two ways. First, a pro-AKP Beşiktaş fan group called 1453 (referring to the year in which the Ottomans took Istanbul from the Byzantines) sprang up to counter these protests. The group disappeared when Çarşı protests against AKP subsided. Second, the AKP brought the new *passolig* passes, which require fans to buy seasonal tickets instead of purchasing individual tickets for each match. The practice puts fans with low purchasing power in a difficult position and prevents spontaneous fan reactions. The introduction of *passolig* was partially motivated by a desire to prevent political protests at football matches (Türkiye Barolar Birliği 2014).

A second group that was targeted by the AKP after the Gezi protests was the TMMOB. An occupational association with a legally defined role, the TMMOB has always had a contentious relationship with governments that desired to sustain patron-client relationships through construction projects with no oversight or opposition. During the AKP period, the TMMOB successfully blocked many government-backed construction projects and resisted the urban transformation policy that defined the AKP era, but most importantly, the TMMOB and one of its prominent members, Mücella Yapıcı, played a front and center role in the Gezi protests. Erdoğan retaliated by physically, symbolically, and legally hollowing out the TMMOB (Akyarlı Güven 2013). The headquarters of the Chamber of Architects at Yıldız Park in Istanbul were requisitioned by the government and added to Erdoğan's presidential residence at the park on May 20, 2016, the anniversary of the Gezi events. Moreover, those members who resisted being thrown out of the building were charged with resistance to the police (T24 2016), but they were later acquitted. However, the real blow to the TMMOB was taking away most of its legal rights and rendering it toothless by changing the 70-year-old law regarding the rules and regulations that govern the Union (Radikal 2013). As of 2019, Yapıcı was on trial (along with some human rights activists and actors) for her role in the Gezi protests.

Gezi was also an unexpected turning point for the mainstreaming of the LGBTI+ movement in Turkey. LGBTI+ activists were front and center in the protests. They were also very well versed in how to deal with police brutality due to their long history of encounters with it. They did not act as individuals who also happened to be LGBTI+, but as LGBTI+ activists, and gained the sympathy of many protestors with their activist experience and their upbeat resistance style, chanting irreverent slogans such as "fags are here, where is Tayyip (Erdogan)?" (Karakayali and Yaka 2014). Right after the Gezi protests ended, the Pride month started. The pride parade had grown from a few dozen people to several thousand over two decades. The 2013 pride parade was the 11th in Istanbul in over 20 years, and its theme was resistance. Tens of thousands of people (and according to some estimates, over a hundred thousand) joined the pride parade to stand in solidarity with the LGBTI+ community as a result of the "intimate and affective ties that [had] emerged and grown between queer groups and other protestors" at the Gezi protests (Zengin 2013). It was an act of solidarity from fellow protestors. Izmir (the third largest city in Turkey) held its first pride parade in June 2013. The Istanbul Pride Parade drew even bigger crowds in 2014, befitting the theme of the year: contact. Other cities such as Antalya (a touristic city on the Mediterranean coast), Malatya (a relatively conservative city in eastern Turkey), and Samsun (an industrial city in the Black Sea region) held their first pride parades that same year.

The government reaction to LGBTI+ activities took a harsh turn after 2015. Istanbul Pride Parade was dispersed with water cannons by the police in 2015, and it was been banned after 2016. In 2017, during the state of emergency, Ankara governorship banned all LGBTI+ activities until further notice, citing societal sensitivities, public safety, protection of public health, and morality as reasons (HRW 2019) until a court lifted the ban on April 19, 2019. Izmir, however, continued to organize a pride week and a pride parade every year without intervention until 2019, when the governorship banned the activities of the seventh Izmir pride week. An administrative court stayed the execution of the ban, but the police nevertheless attacked the parade and arrested some activists. Pride weeks were also banned by governorships in Antalya and Mersin in 2019 (AMER 2019). However, the LGBTI+ activists continue to resist the bans by challenging them in the courts, while some activists in Istanbul defy these bans, clash with the police, and get arrested every year.

Academic Freedoms

Turkish higher education has never been a paragon of academic freedom, but under the AKP regime, existing academic freedoms were incrementally lost. The government opened new universities and staffed academia with its supporters, canceled rectorship elections, changed the disciplinary code, closed down universities, purged critical academics from academia, arrested and sued academics, and denied "problematic" academics promotion and research funding (HRFT 2019).

In the aftermath of the 1980 military coup, many leftist academics were purged from Turkish universities, while academic freedoms and autonomy were severely limited by the establishment of the Higher Education Council (HEC), a government institution that was tasked with monitoring all Turkish universities (Göcek 2016). Despite their lack of autonomy under the HEC, universities continued to provide space for dissent. By 2016, mainstream media and large sections of civil society had already been silenced by the autocratizing regime, but academics continued to publicly criticize the government. True to his *modus operandi*, Erdoğan turned a crisis into an opportunity and disposed of many of his critics in academia.

The AKP did not have the human resources to bring its own cadres into academia. One strategy was to lean on Fethullah Gülen's religious movement. After the 2016 coup attempt, the AKP government closed down 15 foundation universities for being affiliated with the Gülen movement, and dismissed over 6,000 academics from state universities (Kural and Adal 2018) most of whom were accused of being Gülenists. This massive purge revealed the extent to which Gülenists had taken a hold in Turkish academia. Former ÖSYM (Student Selection and Placement Center) president Ali Demir is on trial for stealing all exams between 2010 and 2015 for the Gülen movement during his tenure and Gülenists confessed in court that they stole exam questions from ÖSYM (Birgün 2020). ALES (Academic Personnel and Postgraduate Education Entrance Exam) is an ÖSYM exam that academics have to enter to be accepted into graduate programs and find employment. An investigation revealed that over 20,000 people had suspiciously received perfect and near-perfect scores in this exam, mostly in 2008 and 2009 (CNN Türk 2017). The second strategy of the government was to open new universities—which critics derisively labeled as nameplate universities—that offered little beyond a name, an address, and plenty of cadres to be filled with government supporters who had little merit

(Arap 2010, 23). The number of universities ballooned from 79 to close to 200 in the first 15 years after the AKP took control of the government. However, the AKP failed to establish a presence within the elite universities in metropolitan cities, which largely continued to be populated by secular, left, and liberal leaning academics who were less than sympathetic to the AKP regime.

Two events created the perfect opportunity for Erdogan to purge his most ardent critics from academia. The first event was the signing of a petition by a group called Academics for Peace that called on the government to stop massacring civilians in the conflict between the Turkish military and armed Kurdish groups after some Kurdish cities had declared autonomy. On January 12, 2016, after an ISIS attack that killed 13 German tourists in Istanbul, Erdogan declared that "whoever the members of terrorist organizations are, those who use their language are the same," referring to the 1,128 signatories of the Peace Petition (Cumhuriyet 2016) and called them "cruel and vile" in a speech he gave on January 15 (Sendika 2016). The prime minister and other government officials, the AKP media, and a mafia godfather were pointing their fingers at the peace academics, whose numbers had increased to over 2,000 after Erdogan's speech (a few days later, the petition was closed to signature). Erdoğan invited universities to take action against the signatories. Some of the petitioners received threats on their lives, their faces and names were published on government-backed media websites, some private universities fired their faculty members for signing the Peace Petition, and four signatories were arrested and kept in prison for months (HRFT 2019). However, faculty members in Turkish state universities could not be fired due to their protected status as state employees. Most of the peace academics refused to withdraw their signatures despite Prime Minister Davutoğlu's suggestion that they do so.

The second major turning point for academic freedoms was the July 15, 2016 coup attempt. On July 21, the government declared a state of emergency and proceeded to pass emergency decrees with the force of law. The first order of business was to close 15 universities that were under Gülenist control, and their students were distributed to universities from all over Turkey by another emergency decree (KHK 667). A total of 6,081 academics were dismissed from academia by decrees (TİHV 2019a). Although most of these academics were suspected to have ties with the Gülen movement, 406 of them were peace academics (BAK 2019). Some members of leftist unions who had always had a contentious relationship with the Gülenists were also dismissed. Most of the people who were removed from academia had not been formally investigated and no charge or evidence had been brought against them. Among other things, they lost their jobs and benefits, their pensions, their passports, and the right to travel abroad and work in the education sector (Öğreten 2020). Over 100,000 people were fired from state employment by emergency decrees, but academia suffered the largest proportional loss. Dismissal by decree was aptly labeled "civil death" (Newsweek 2018). In December 2017, the government started suing each signatory to the Peace Petition individually for disseminating terrorist propaganda through the media. As of September 9, 2019, 739 signatories had undergone trial and 204 of them had received prison sentences ranging from 15 to 36 months (BAK 2019). On July 27, 2019, the TCC reviewed the case of one of the signatories, and ruled that signing the petition was protected under the constitutional right to "freedom of expression" (Üstel et al. 2019). On September 6, 2019, lower courts started acquitting peace academics based on the TCC ruling.

With the Emergency Decree Law no. 676, the government abolished rectorship elections at universities. Currently, the president appoints all university rectors, and the rector does not have to be from the university to which she will be appointed. The government has the right to decide which universities will specialize in which fields, demolishing the last remnants of institutional autonomy. In the meanwhile, critical academics complain that TÜBİTAK (The Scientific and Technological Research Council of Turkey), the main Turkish research agency, engages in practices such as defunding critical academics and informally asking academics to cut ties with their black-listed colleagues if they desire to receive funding, while some chapters written by signatories are silently removed from newer editions (TİHV 2019b, 17). Dissenters are removed from editorial boards of academic journals. Many universities avoid holding events and issuing publications that may displease the government. A large number of persecuted Turkish academics moved to European countries after 2016 where they continue to work under precarious conditions and face an uncertain future (Baser et al. 2017, 26).

Conclusion

This brief account of the incremental autocratization process in Turkey aims to demonstrate why the label illiberal democracy is misleading. The Turkish regime is neither democratic nor competitive at this point. Without an independent media, reality bends to the shape of what the government desires it to be. A large section of society does not have access to alternative media outlets and knows only what the government allows the mainstream media to cover. Without an independent judiciary, the rule of law descends into judicial anarchy and courts become instruments of oppression and persecution. Without a free media and a functioning judiciary, civil society groups are atomized and crushed. Sources of dissent such as academia are hollowed out and subdued. Bureaucracy serves only partisan interests at the expense of the public. Political competitors that pose an actual threat to the authority or the reelection of the incumbent are silenced and, if need be, prosecuted and imprisoned. Local administrations that place checks on the central government are crushed.

It is not possible to hold fair and free elections in an environment in which information is not available and dissent is punished by the loss of livelihood and imprisonment. Although the loss of the Istanbul municipality to the CHP in the March 2019 elections may be seen as evidence of democratic competition, the real lesson that the Turkish public learned was that when all else fails, the AKP tries to cancel the elections, while appointing trustees in place of elected mayors in Kurdish cities. Ultimately, the AKP had to concede the election to the CHP after a second round because the public firmly stood behind the mayor-elect. After examining the evidence from 17 years of AKP rule, we contend that without an ecosystem of strong democratic institutions, democracy cannot survive with elections alone. However, a lesson that is equally—if not more—important is what autocratic governments have always understood all too well. Democratic resistance has the capacity to survive in the nooks and crannies as well as the periphery of government institutions and civil society. When the most visible and prominent democratic institutions fail, the job to resist the encroachment of autocracy may fall on the shoulders of football fans and research assistants. Ultimately, the most decisive democratic battles may be fought in parks, stadiums, and classrooms.

Bibliography

Akyarlı Güven, Ayşegül. 2013. "TMMOB'u Yalnızlaştıran Gece Yarısı Kanununun Hikayesi." WSJ June 10. https://www.wsj.com/articles/SB10001424127887324425 20457859742034292 8976

AMER. 2019. "Özel Bülten Türkiye'de Onur Yürüyüşü: Yasaklar ve Müdahaleler 2016–2017–2018–2019." Association for Monitoring Equal Rights. https://www.hyd.org.tr/attachments/article/541/Onur%20Y%C3%BCr%C3%BC%C5%-9Fleri%20%C3%96zel%20B%C3%BClten.pdf

Arap, Kavili S. 2010. "Türkiye Yeni Üniversitelerine Kavuşurken: Türkiye'de Yeni Üniversiteler ve Kuruluş Gerekçeleri." *Ankara Üniversitesi SBF Dergisi* 65(1): 10–25.

Arato, Andrew. 2016. *Post Sovereign Constitution Making.* Oxford: Oxford University Press.

Aslan, Ömer. 2016. "'Unarmed' We Intervene, Unnoticed We Remain: The Deviant Case of 'February 28th Coup' in Turkey." *British Journal of Middle Eastern Studies* 43(3): 360–77.

Aytaç, Işık A., and Bruce H. Rankin. 2008. "Unemployment, Economic Strain and Family Distress: The Impact of the 2001 Economic Crisis." *New Perspectives on Turkey* 38: 181–203.

BAK. 2019. "Rights Violations against Academics Peace Report." BAK. https://barisicinakademisyenler.net/node/314

Bâli, Aslı. 2013. "Courts and Constitutional Transition: Lessons from the Turkish Case." *I•CON* 11(3): 666–701.

Baser, Bahar, Samim Akgönül, and Ahmet Erdi Öztürk. 2017. ""Academics for Peace" in Turkey: A Case of Criminalising Dissent and Critical Thought via Counterterrorism Policy." *Critical Studies on Terrorism* 10(2): 274–96.

BBC News. 2007. "Army 'Concerned' by Turkey Vote." BBC News, April 28. http://news.bbc.co.uk/2/hi/europe/6602375.stm

BBC News. 2018. "Turkey Ends State of Emergency after Two Years." BBC News, July 18. https://www.bbc.com/news/world-europe-44881328

Birgün. 2020. "Ali Demir hakkında 18 yıl hapis istemi: ÖSYM soruları 'Sır Cihazı' ile çalınmış." Birgün January 2. www.birgun.net/haber/ali-demir-hakkinda-18-yil-hapis-istemi-osym-sorulari-sir-cihazi-ile-calinmis-282394

Çalı, Başak. 2018. "Will Legalism be the End of Constitutionalism in Turkey?" *VerfBlog*, January 22. https://verfassungsblog.de/will-legalism-be-the-end-of-constitutionalism-in-turkey

Castillo-Ortiz, Pablo. 2019. "The Illiberal Abuse of Constitutional Courts in Europe." *European Constitutional Law Review* 15: 48–72.

CDL-AD. 2017. *Venice Commission – Opinion on the Measures Provided in the Recent Emergency Decree Laws with Respect to Freedom of the Media.* Opinion No. 872 / 2016. https://www.venice.coe.int/webforms/documents/?pdf=CDL-AD(2017)007-e

Christofis, Nikos. 2018. "The AKP's 'Yeni Turkiye': Challenging the Kemalist Narrative?" *Mediterranean Quarterly* 29(3): 11–32.

CNN Türk.2017. "ALES'te 8 yıldaki 16 sınav şaibeli: 37 bin 'tavşan aday' dereceye girmiş." CNN Türk December 19. www.cnnturk.com/turkiye/aleste-8-yildaki-16-sinav-saibeli-37-bin-tavsan-aday-dereceye-girmis

Cumhuriyet. 2016. "İşid Bomba Patlattı, Erdoğan'ın Derdi Akademisyenler." Cumhuriyet January 12. www.cumhuriyet.com.tr/haber/siyaset/462500/isid-bomba-patlatti-erdoganin-derdi-akademisyenler.html

Diken. 2014. "9 Soruda Sabah-atv satışı." Diken, February 13. www.diken.com.tr/9-soruda-sabah-atv-satisi/

DW. 2018. "From Ally to Scapegoat: Fethullah Gulen, the Man behind the Myth." DW, April 6. www.dw.com/en/from-ally-to-scapegoat-fethullah-gulen-the-man-behind-the-myth/a-37055485

Eder, Mine, and Özlem Öz. 2017. "Spatialities of Contentious Politics: The Case of Istanbul's Beşiktaş Neighborhood, Çarşı Football Fandom and Gezi." *Political Geography* 61: 57–66.

Filkins, Dexter. 2013. "Show Trials on the Bosphorus." *The New Yorker.* August 13. www.newyorker.com/news/daily-comment/show-trials-on-the-bosphorus

Fleck, Zoltán. 2018. "Changes of the Judicial Structure in Hungary – Understanding the New Authoritarianism." *OER Osteuropa Recht* 64(4): 583–99.

Gocek, F.Müge 2016. "Why Turkey Wants to Silence Its Academics?" The Conversation July 27. http://theconversation.com/why-turkey-wants-to-silence-its-academics-62885

Grigoriadis, Ioannis N. 2016. "The Peoples' Democratic Party (HDP) and the 2015 Elections." *Turkish Studies* 17(1): 39–46.

Gürsoy, Yaprak. 2017. Between Military Rule and Democracy: Regime Consolidation in Greece, Turkey, and Beyond. Ann Arbor: University of Michigan Press.

Haimerl, Maria. 2017. "The Turkish Constitutional Court under the Amended Turkish Constitution." *VerfBlog.* January 27. https://verfassungsblog.de/the-turkish-constitutional-court-under-the-amended-turkish-constitution/

Hale, William. 1993. *Turkish Politics and the Military.* New York, NY: Routledge.

Haynes, Jeffrey. 2013. "Politics and Islam in Turkey: From Atatürk to AKP." In *Religious Actors in the Public Sphere: Means, Objectives and Effects*, edited by Jeffrey Haynes and Anja Hennig, 312–27. New York, NY: Routledge.

HRFT. 2019. "Academics for Peace: A Brief History." Human Rights Foundation of Turkey. www.tihvakademi.org/wp-content/uploads/2019/03/AcademicsforPeace-ABriefHistory.pdf

HRW. 2019. "Turkey: End Ankara Ban on LGBTI Events." Human Rights Watch. www.hrw.org/news/2019/02/14/turkey-end-ankara-ban-on-lgbti-events

Huntington, Samuel P. 1991. "Democracy's Third Wave." *Journal of Democracy* 2(2): 12–34.

Hürriyet Daily News. 2013 "Turkey Finishes 2013 with Corruption Row." Hürriyet Daily News December 31. https://www.hurriyetdailynews.com/ turkey-finishes-2013-with-corruption-row-60354

Independent. 2016. "Turkey's President Erdogan Rejects Court Ruling to Free Journalists." Independent, February 28. https://www.independent.co.uk/news/world/ europe/turkey-recep-tayyip-erdogan-rejects-court-ruling-to-free-journalists- can-dundar-and-erdem-gul-a6901726.html

IPA. 2019. "Turkey's TV Watchdog Imposes Broadcast Ban on FOX Prime, Public Arena." https://ipa.news/2018/12/28/turkeys-tv-watchdog-imposes-broadcast- ban-on-fox-prime-public-arena/

IPI Report. 2019. "Report on the December 2018 IPI Press Freedom Mission to Turkey." https://freeturkeyjournalists.ipi.media/wp-content/uploads/2019/02/ BOOKLET-VERSION_Turkey-Mission-Report-Dec-2018.pdf

Jakoby, Tim, and Alparslan Özerdem. 2008. "The Role of the State in the Turkish Earthquake." *Journal of International Development* 20: 297–310.

Karakayali, Serhat, and Özge Yaka. 2014. "The spirit of Gezi: The recomposition of political subjectivities in Turkey." *New Formations 83*: 117–38.

Kaya, Raşit, and Barış Çakmur. 2010. "Politics and the Mass Media in Turkey." *Turkish Studies* 11(4): 521–37.

KHK 667. www.resmigazete.gov.tr/eskiler/2016/07/20160723-8.htm

Kılıç, Ecevit. 2006. "Meşrutiyetten Bugüne Siyasetin Futbol Markajı." Bianet. April 29, 2006. https://bianet.org/kurdi/spor/78368-mesrutiyetten-bugune-siyasetin- futbol-markaji

Kural, Beyaz and Hikmet Adal. 2018. "Akademide İhraçlar 6 Bin 81'e Yükseldi." July 9, 2018. Bianet. http://bianet.org/bianet/ifade-ozgurlugu/198990-akademide- ihraclar-6-bin-81-e-yukseldi

Mounk, Yascha. 2018. "The Undemocratic Dilemma." *Journal of Democracy* 29(2): 98–112.

Newsweek. 2018. "Two Years after Overcoming Attempted Coup, Turkey Plagued by Widespread Arrests and Purges of Civil Servants." Newsweek July 15. https://www. newsweek.com/arrests-plague-turkey-two-years-after-coup-attempt-1024287

Nuhrat, Yagmur. 2016. The Violence Law and the Governmentalization of Football in Turkey. In *The Making of Neoliberal Turkey*, edited by Cenk Ozbay and et al., 83–96. New York, NY: Routledge.

Öğreten, Tunca. 2020. "KHK'lılar: Sosyal ölüme terk edildik." DW January 14. www.dw.com/tr/khkl%C4%B1lar-sosyal-%C3%B6l%C3%BCme-terk- edildik/a-52005145

Orbán, Viktor. 2014. "Prime Minister Viktor Orbán's Speech at the 25th Bálván- yos Summer Free University and Student Camp." www.kormany.hu/en/the- prime-minister/the-prime-minister-s-speeches/prime-minister-viktor-orban-s- speech-at-the-25th-balvanyos-summer-free-university-and-student-camp

Özbudun, Ergun. 2014. "AKP at the Crossroads: Erdoğan's Majoritarian Drift." *South European Society and Politics* 19(2): 155–67.

Özbudun, Ergun. 2015. "Turkey's Judiciary and the Drift Toward Competitive Au- thoritarianism." *The International Spectator* 50(2): 42–55.

Pech, Laurent, and Kim Lane Scheppele. 2017. "Illiberalism within: Rule of Law Back- sliding in the EU." *CYELS* 19: 3–47.

Polyák, Gábor. 2019. "Media in Hungary: Three Pillars of an Illiberal Democracy." In *Public Service Broadcasting and Media Systems in Troubled European Democracies*, edited by E. Połońska and C. Beckett, 279–303. London: Palgrave Macmillan.

Przeworski, Adam, Michael Alvarez, José A. Cheibub, and Fernando Limongi. 1996. "What Makes Democracies Endure?" *Journal of Democracy* 7(1): 39–56.

Radikal. 2013. "TMMOB gece yarısı bitirildi." July 10. www.radikal.com.tr/turkiye/tmmob-geceyarisi-bitirildi-1141155/

Rodrik, Dani. 2011. "Ergenekon and Sledgehammer: Building or Undermining the Rule of Law." *Turkish Political Quarterly* 10(1): 99–109.

RSF. 2018. "Doğan Media Group Sale Completes Government Control of Turkish Media." https://rsf.org/en/news/dogan-media-group-sale-completes-government-control-turkish-media

RSF. 2019. "2019 World Press Freedom Index." RSF. https://rsf.org/en/ranking

Sartori, Giovanni. 1987. *The Theory of Democracy Revisited. I. The Contemporary Debate.* Chatham: Chatham House Publishers.

Schumpeter, Joseph. 1975 [1942]. *Capitalism, Socialism, and Democracy.* New York, NY: Harper.

Sendika. 2016. "Erdoğan'dan akademisyenlere: 'Bunlar zalimdir, alçaktır.'" Sendika63.org January 15. https://sendika63.org/2016/01/erdogandan-akademisyenlere-bunlar-zalimdir-alcaktir-322453/

Şenses, Fikret. 2003. "Economic Crisis as an Instigator of Distributional Conflict: The Turkish Case in 2001." *Turkish Studies* 4(2): 92–119.

Sezer, Duygu Bazoglu. 2002. "The Electoral Victory of Reformist Islamists in Secular Turkey." *The International Spectator* 37(4): 7–19.

Şık, Ahmet. 2017. *İmamın Ordusu.* İstanbul: Kırmızı Kedi.

Sözmen, Mithat F. 2018. "'Başkan'ın Takımı' Başakşehir ve Hedefleri." Evrensel. April 18. www.evrensel.net/yazi/81289/baskanin-takimi-basaksehir-ve-hedefleri

Taş, Hakkı 2018. "A History of Turkey's AKP-Gülen Conflict." *Mediterranean Politics* 23(3): 395–402.

TGS. 2019. "126 Medya çalışanı ve gazeteci cezaevinde." https://tgs.org.tr/cezaevindeki-gazeteciler/

TİHV. 2019a. Akademisyen İhraçları: Hak İhlalleri, Kayıplar, Travma ve Güçlenme Süreçleri. İzmir: TİHV Akademi. https://tihvakademi.org/wp-content/uploads/2020/02/akademisyenihraclariy.pdf

TİHV. 2019b. *Barış İçin Akademisyenler Vakasının Kısa Tarihi.* İzmir: TİHV Akademi. https://www.tihvakademi.org/wp-content/uploads/2019/03/Barisicinakademisyenlervakasi.pdf

Tuastad, Dag. 2014. "From Football Riot to Revolution. The Political Role of Football in the Arab World." *Soccer & Society* 15(3): 376–88.

Tuğal, Cihan. 2013 ""Resistance Everywhere": The Gezi Revolt in Global Perspective." *New Perspectives on Turkey* 49: 157–72.

Turan, Ömer and Burak Özçetin. 2019. "Football Fans and Contentious Politics: The Role of Çarşı in the Gezi Park Protests." *International Review for the Sociology of Sport* 54(2): 199–217.

Türkiye Barolar Birliği. 2014. "Gezi Raporu." Ankara: Türkiye Barolar Birliği Yayınları. http://tbbyayinlari.barobirlik.org.tr/TBBBooks/518.pdf

T24. 2016. "Tam liste: 15 Temmuz'dan sonra kaç KHK çıkarıldı, kaç kurum kapatıldı, hangi kurumdan toplam kaç kişi ihraç edildi?" https://t24.com.tr/haber/

tam-liste-15-temmuzdan-sonra-kac-khk-cikarildi-kac-kurum-kapatildi-hangi-kurumdan-toplam-kac-kisi-ihrac-edildi,374482

Üstel vd. 2019. Zübeyde Füsun Üstel ve Diğerleri Başvurusu Anayasa Mahkemesi Kararı. https://kararlarbilgibankasi.anayasa.gov.tr/BB/2018/17635

Waldman, Simon A. and Emre Caliskan. 2019. "Power, Patronage, and Press Freedom: The Political Economy of Turkey's Media." In *Public Service Broadcasting and Media Systems in Troubled European Democracies*, edited by E. Połońska and C. Beckett, 283–408. London: Palgrave Macmillan.

Yeginsu, Can. 2010. "Turkey Packs the Court." *The New York Review of Books*, September 22. www.nybooks.com/daily/2010/09/22/turkey-packs-court/

Yeşil, Bilge. 2016. *Media in New Turkey: The Origins of an Authoritarian Neoliberal State.* Urbana: University of Illinois Press.

Yeşilada, Birol A. 2016. "The Future of Erdoğan and the AKP." *Turkish Studies* 17(1): 19–30.

Zakaria, Farid. 1997. "The Rise of Illiberal Democracy." *Foreign Affairs* 77(6): 22–43.

Zengin, Aslı. 2013. "What Is Queer about Gezi." *Fieldsights—Hot Spots, Cultural Anthropology* website. https://culanth.org/fieldsights/what-is-queer-about-gezi

12

INDIA'S UNOFFICIAL EMERGENCY

Nandini Sundar

Introduction

On August 5, 2019, India's ruling Bharatiya Janata Party (BJP) regime tabled a bill in Parliament fundamentally changing the Constitution and Indian politics. Article 370, the clause related to the former kingdom of Jammu and Kashmir (J & K) that was incorporated into the Indian Constitution as a condition of the kingdom's accession, was virtually abolished, and the former state of J & K was bifurcated into two Union Territories (UTs), which have fewer powers than a State within the Indian union. Article 35A which disallowed outsiders from buying land in the state was abolished, potentially opening the state to land grabs on a large scale. Misogynist and racist members of the ruling party followed this up by claiming that it also made available "fair Kashmiri girls" for marriage to outsiders (Times of India, ANI, 2019).

Even as the government has consistently claimed that Kashmiris are happy with the changes, which were for their own good (Times of India, PTI, 2019), in anticipation of resistance, 40,000 extra troops were moved into the state, adding to the existing roughly eight hundred thousand; over 4,000 people were arrested under the Public Safety Act, including all the major political leaders (AFP 2019); phone and internet lines shut down; and the Kashmir Valley was placed under an indefinite curfew. Even on the eve of the announcement, the Governor denied any plans to change the Constitution or divide the state. The Home Minister also lied in Parliament that former Chief Minister of J & K and now Member of Parliament, Farooq Abdullah, was 'enjoying himself at home,' when he was actually under house arrest.

An already pliant media went overboard with triumphalism, with headlines like 'historic moment,' 'geography being redrawn,' 'surgical strike,' etc., both reflecting and mobilizing popular support for the change (on the variance between domestic and international coverage, see John and Grewal 2019). Worse, opposition Members of Parliament, including those from regional parties which stand to lose the most from this blatant violation of federalism, supported the downgrading of Kashmir, with the result that the bill was passed by a majority in both houses of parliament within the day. When asked to intervene to remove the communications blackout, free opposition leaders, and address the constitutionality of the changes to Article 370, India's Supreme Court deferred to the superior wisdom of the executive, postponing a hearing of the petitions. On January 10, 2020, over 150 days after the internet ban, the Supreme Court ruled that banning access to the internet was a violation of the fundamental rights of expression and speech, but instead of immediately ordering a lifting of the restrictions, it referred the issue back to the government for review. Public anger hardened into non-violent civil disobedience, but as far as the wider nation goes, the people are totally invisible.

In his discussion of "democratic recession," Larry Diamond (2015, 144) argues that one major methodological problem in deciding whether a country is or is no longer a democracy is fixing a date for the collapse. But in India, one might well point to August 5, 2019, though as with all such phenomena, the degradation into a non-democracy has been a long time coming. With the media, parliament, and the courts abdicating their responsibilities to maintain a system of checks and balances and ensure the rights of minorities, and the public overlooking the lies of the government, all that appears to remain of democracy in India is that the government is chosen on the basis of an electoral majority or what one might call mere 'electoralism' (for the term, see Richards 1999).

Defining the Politics of Contemporary India

There are many terms being proposed to describe the phenomenon creeping across the world—illiberal democracy (Zakaria 1997; Diamond 2015; Hansen 2019); competitive authoritarianism (Levitsky and Way 2002); ethnic democracy (as applied to Israel and India, see Smooha 2002; Jaffrelot 2019); authoritarian populism (see Hall 1979; Brown et al. 2018; Morelock 2018); ur-fascism or proto-fascism (see Eco 1995; Ahmad 2017; Stanley 2018). In India, several edited volumes have attempted to capture this visibly new slide in democratic politics (see essays in Chatterji et al. 2019; Hariharan and Yusufji 2019; Jayal 2019; Nilsen et al. 2019).

Defining democracy is, of course, key to much of this debate. Zakaria (1997), for instance, argues that democracy which involves a form of government chosen by the majority should not be confused with constitutional liberalism which involves separation of powers. The term 'illiberal democracy' thus denotes regimes which combine electoral democracy with illiberal features such as human rights abuses, executive authoritarianism, weak separation of powers, etc. Others would argue that freedom of speech, separation of powers, rule of law, minority protections, and participation in governance are intrinsic to democracy, and that democracy is a basket concept rather than a single concept denominator. In this section, I select three terms—illiberal democracy, authoritarian populism, and fascism, and discuss their applicability to the Indian context. I argue that in the game of labeling, all regimes till 2014 would count as regular 'illiberal democracies'; the 'Emergency' (1975–77) would qualify as a period of 'authoritarian populism,' while the BJP under Modi (2014 onward) is well on the road to a form of fascism.

It is important to mention the Emergency because the only struggle that the Rashtriya Swayamsevak Sangh (RSS), the ideological parent of the BJP, a deeply chauvinist and exclusionary Hindu majoritarian organization, has ever waged since its inception in 1924 has been against the Emergency, and it constantly uses this to claim how democratic it is by contrast. The RSS was not involved in India's freedom struggle from the British. Under the Emergency (1975–77), fundamental rights and elections were formally suspended, and various independent institutions like the media and judiciary suborned (see Prakash 2019). However, the Emergency was mostly a top-down process. The Congress did not have the same reach into society as the RSS currently does, and while the Prime Minister, Indira Gandhi, was personally popular even among those affected by her policies of sterilization and displacement (Tarlo 2003), her government did not create the kind of social divisions one now sees, and the fundamental challenges to the constitutional idea of a secular, diverse India. In terms of its authoritarianism, the current period is very similar to the Emergency but the fact that it is not officially declared and rests on widespread consent in society makes it perhaps even more dangerous.

Illiberal Democracy?

India has always been an illiberal democracy, at least for significant sections of its citizens, though the sheer size and diversity of the country has precluded its being labeled as one. Even as elections take place with regularity and there is considerable investment in representation by political parties, this is accompanied by high levels of violence against religious and caste minorities and a shaky rule of law.[1]

Large parts of the country have been militarized. For decades, geographical peripheries like the Northeast and Kashmir have been under 'emergency' laws like the Armed Forces Special Powers Act (AFSPA), which empowers the army to shoot to kill on mere suspicion (Baruah 2014). A wave of repression in the 1970s did not fully succeed in wiping out the Naxalite or armed Maoist guerilla movement, representing some of India's poorest peasants. The movement resurfaced again in the early 2000s. Since 2005, several hundred thousand paramilitary armed forces have been poured into central India to fight Maoist guerillas, resulting in thousands of killings, rapes, and large numbers of villages being burnt (Sundar 2019). Almost none of the civilian victims of counter insurgency have got judicial redress.

Organized pogroms of minorities in which members of the ruling party or administration have played a leading role or at least stood by in complicity include the massacre of Sikhs (Delhi 1984), Muslims (Gujarat 2002), and Christians (Kandhamal, Odisha, 2008), to name just a few. Every day, extrajudicial killings, custodial deaths and disappearances by the police and armed forces, especially but not only in conflict areas (see Hoenig and Singh 2014), violent clashes over land acquisition for industry (see Levien 2015), and atrocities against women, lower castes, and minorities, add to the insecurity of ordinary citizens.

After the BJP took power in 2014, a series of mob lynchings, mostly of Muslims accused of cow-smuggling, but also of scheduled castes and scheduled tribes, have taken place. In the majority of cases, the vigilantes have been fronts of the RSS, but the desire and ability to kill has percolated more widely into society, with people also being lynched on suspicion of theft and child stealing. The attacks have been videographed and circulated, in most cases by the perpetrators themselves, confident in the impunity they enjoy (The Quint 2019). As against the artists, writers, film-makers, and others who protested against the lynchings by returning their state awards, the RSS/BJP has propped up counter movements of pro-government personalities to claim that the critics were 'anti-national.' Hindutva (a term used for Hindu chauvinism) groups have killed rationalist intellectuals who they disagreed with, while the application of 'sedition' charges to dissenters is increasingly widespread (see essays in Hariharan and Yusufji 2019; Tiwary 2019). In July 2019, the BJP enacted a draconian amendment to the Unlawful Activities Prevention Act (UAPA) which permits the government to declare individuals to be terrorists, in addition to organizations, a provision that is widely expected to be used against critics of the government.

Authoritarian Populism?

Much of the analysis explaining the 2014 and 2019 victories of the BJP has focused on the person of Prime Minister, Narendra Modi, whose rhetorical talents and personal charisma, albeit heavily mediated (Chakravarty and Roy 2015), have undoubtedly played a major role in the BJP's victories. Modi's relentless campaigning in both state and federal elections, his weekly monologues aired on the radio, the ubiquity of his images in the public sphere, the expenditure on advertisements promoting the achievements of the government, and choreographed events with world leaders and non-resident Indians have all served to identify the government with his personality. Carefully cultivated myths about the way in which he overcame a difficult past to become a selfless politician help Modi to portray himself as a man of the people against an entrenched dynastic political elite (on Modi's populist connect, see Ghassem-Fachandi 2019; on the 2014 campaign, see Price 2015; Sardesai 2015; for an analysis of the 2019 results, see Hindu-Lokniti-CSDS 2019). It is important to note that this communication overkill is entirely one-way—Modi has not addressed a single press conference since he took power in 2014.

Similarities in style with other right-wing, majoritarian leaders like Trump, Erdogan, Orban, or Bolsanaro have led to scholars using the term 'authoritarian populist' to describe this type of regime. As Morelock defines it,

> 'authoritarian populism' refers to the pitting of 'the people' against 'elites' in order to have the power to drive out, wipe out, or otherwise dominate Others who are not 'the people.' Generally, this involves social movements fuelled by prejudice and led by charismatic leaders that seek to increase governmental force to combat difference.
>
> *(Morelock 2018, xiv)*

The term, as initially defined by Hall (2017 [1979], 174), referred to "an exceptional form of the capitalist state—which, unlike classical fascism, has retained most (though not all) of the formal representative institutions in place, and which at the same time has been able to construct around itself an active popular consent" (Hall 2017 [1979], 174). The ability to transmit messages through the personality of a charismatic leader in a manner which unifies contradictory discourses (in Modi's case, being both pro-corporates and pro-poor) and makes people complicit in the destruction of their freedoms and economic well-being in the name of a greater, usually neo-liberal goal certainly captures much of what is going on in India today. The best example perhaps is the acquiescence of the public at large to the havoc caused by demonetization or a decree in November 2016 rendering 87% of all currency in the country invalid. This decision which seems to have been taken by Modi with little consultation with economic experts or even his own cabinet caused enormous hardship, with some immediate deaths, small businesses closing, and the loss of some five million jobs. Demonetization brought little of the promised benefits like ending black money or corruption as nearly all the money came back into the banks (Kumar, 2017, Azad et al. 2019). Yet demonetization paradoxically enhanced Modi's reputation as a strong leader willing to take on the big corrupt guys.

Proto-fascism

A focus on authoritarian populism, while capturing several elements of the Modi regime, leads one to obscure the cadre base of the RSS, and its long-term fascistic ideology as well as organizational links (Casolari 2000). Golwalkar, one of the RSS's founding fathers, famously advocated the emulation of Hitler's final solution to deal with India's non-Hindu minorities.[2] The RSS describes itself as a "movement for the assertion of Bharat's national identity" which they equate with Hindu identity. Its main goal has been to "organize Hindus" and "to restore the Hindu psyche to its pristine form" after centuries of "alien rule" (*rss.org*). The RSS sees Muslims and Christians as outsiders who must be taught their place in a Hindu nation; they yearn for the recognition of the glories of ancient ("Hindu") India, and organize citizens on militaristic lines to achieve these goals (on RSS ideology, see Sharma 2007, Noorani 2019).

Starting from its foundation in 1925, the formerly secretive Sangh has proliferated into hundreds of fronts which work with different sections—students, soldiers, women, workers, peasants, scheduled castes and scheduled tribes, etc. The RSS claims to have nearly 700,000 members and some 57,000 shakhas or cells which hold daily meetings (see rss.org). The ruling BJP is merely the political front of the RSS, and currently all leading institutional figures are members of the RSS, including the President, Prime Minister, the Governors of States, Vice Chancellors of universities, and the heads of various research institutions, among others.

Unlike Trump or Bolsanaro, Narendra Modi is a long-term *pracharak*, or evangelist of the RSS, and acts not as a single individual but as the most effective electoral instrument that the RSS currently possesses. As Pralay Kanungo, a long-term observer of the Sangh, has noted, "while Modi's undisputed writ runs through major areas like the economy, commerce, foreign affairs and security, the RSS gets a free hand in determining the social, cultural and educational agenda; besides, the RSS chief extends his role as the 'philosopher and guide' beyond the RSS by legitimating and expanding Hindutva in a larger public sphere" (Kanungo 2019, 134). In its second term, the Modi government has come out openly to prioritize the RSS's long-standing themes—the building of a Ram temple at Ayodhya, the abolition of Article 370, 'love jehad' (preventing marriages across religions), population control (a coded term for controlling Muslim fertility), land jehad (taking over Muslim mosques while accusing them of encroaching on public space, ignoring similar Hindu encroachments), and *ghar wapsi* or reconversions (targeting Christian converts).

The cadre base is one factor which makes the Modi regime unique among the current crop of right-wing governments. The combination of a state monopoly over the police and army meant to enforce law and order and state-sponsored vigilantism, which I have previously described as a "public private partnership in the industry of insecurity" (Sundar 2013), is now a pronounced feature of governance, and extends beyond authoritarian populism to a form of fascistic politics (see also Banaji 2017 on state support to stormtroopers as a key symptom of fascism).

While the jury on what counts as fascism is still out (see Payne 1980; Jacoby 2016) with several scholars wishing to restrict fascism to a particular inter-World

War European phenomenon, there are certain features which bear a close family resemblance to fascist politics. Organizational forms include a mass mobilizing party with a cult leader, support by the most powerful forms of capital, and the role of organized propaganda in purveying half-truths and distortions. Culturally, we see anti-intellectualism, the creation of an internal enemy, resentment by the hitherto dominant transformed into claimed victimhood, the focus on a mythic past, and the continuous shifting of focus indentifying plots against the nation and its leader (see Eco 1995; Banaji, 2017; Stanley 2018).

In its emphasis on military training through the *shakhas* or cells it runs; emphasis on Muslims as the enemy within; denunciation of all critics as antinational; attacks on free speech and critical thought in universities; its reference to plots to destabilize the nation;[3] its justification of upper-caste Hindu resentment against affirmative action for scheduled castes and tribes, which then get embodied in policies like affirmative action for poor upper-castes; the arrests of people for social media posts critical of the government; the capture of the media to spread hate against minorities and blank out criticism of the government's policies; the relentless trolling by Modi supporters of critics; and the legal impunity provided to right-wing terror accused and vigilantes—the Modi government has employed all the elements of fascist politics. The entrenchment of bitter resentment against minorities and dissenters as the primary emotion of the Hindu majority is a product of and further enables the government's fascist agenda.

The Immediate Context for Electoral Wins

Even while trying to explain Modi's unprecedented popularity and the spread of the RSS, it is important to note that the BJP has still not won a majority of the popular vote. In 2014, the BJP's vote share was 31% which went up to nearly 37.4% in 2019, with the NDA (National Democratic Alliance, the coalition of which the BJP is the leading member) getting 38.5% in 2014 and 45% in 2019. Further, on both occasions, the opposition was in considerable disarray.

In 2004, the UPA (United Progressive Alliance, of which the Indian National Congress is the leading member) government came in on a compassion and change platform. The campaign run by the then BJP government (1999–2004), 'India Shining,' flopped because, in fact, the economy was not shining at all. The anti-minority venom that became daily feed under the BJP (with the 'moderate' Prime Minister Vajpayee declaring at one election rally that they did not need Muslim votes) gave way to a conversation on economic growth. For a few years, the government appeared to want to steer a middle path between a pro-business 'reform' agenda and an acknowledgment that India remained, largely, a poor, peasant country, even if urbanization and the knowledge economy were claimed to be the face of the future. The 'social agenda' of the National Advisory Council which was reflected in landmark legislation like the Right to Information Act 2005, the National Rural Employment Guarantee Act 2005, the Scheduled Tribes and other Traditional Forest Dwellers (Recognition of Forest Rights) Act 2006, and the Right to Education Act 2009 coexisted with the Special Economic Zones Act 2005, which involved the acquisition of huge tracts of agricultural land, significant tax concessions to corporate houses, and a space where regular labor laws did not apply. "Growth," it was argued, was what enabled social welfare programs like the rural employment guarantee act, though even a cursory attention to the struggles over these acts would show that they owed less to those in power and more to the persistence of social movements. Similarly, expanded opportunities for affirmative action for 'other backward castes' (OBCs) in education, and the setting up of a Commission under a retired Chief Justice of the High Court (the Sachar Commission) which showed how badly Muslims were doing on every indicator (education, employment, etc.) produced the sense of a government which cared about disadvantage.

In the second term of the UPA, however, 2009–14, that narrative of 'balance' began crumbling, and even though the government amended the Land Acquisition Act in 2013 to include social audits, consent, and rehabilitation, frequent land clashes had already begun to generate disaffection. On the other side, business complained of policy paralysis. What really did the UPA government in, however, were the allegations of corruption and crony capitalism.[4] The India Against Corruption movement, some of whose members later formed the Aam Aadmi Party, became the most visible symbol of public disgust with this. However, it was the BJP which successfully capitalized on this, with Modi promising to end corruption, bring development (*vikas*) and good days (*ache din*), propagating the alleged successes of his tenure as Chief Minister of Gujarat in attracting industry, building roads, etc. This was showcased as the 'Gujarat Model.'

In short, lower growth rates, growing inequality, corruption allegations, and a general sense of ennui with Congress leadership led the public to want the aspirational politics that Modi held out. There were two other elements, however, that actually managed the BJP's electoral victory: first, money and second, hands-on electoral management relying on data analysis (see Jha 2017).

In 2014, the BJP spent almost as much on media advertising alone as Obama spent under all heads in the 2012 presidential elections (Varadarajan 2014). Once in power, the BJP passed an electoral bond scheme, which enabled donors to buy electoral bonds anonymously—with the identity of the donors known only to the government. Inevitably, 95% of the funding from the electoral bonds went to the BJP (Vishnoi, 2019, Wire Staff 2019). This, among other things like the government's continuing power to tweak policy in favor of certain corporates, and the ability to investigate recalcitrant businesses or political opponents for tax evasion,[5] ensured that the BJP has managed to become the richest party in India, outspending its rivals by a huge margin. In the 2019 elections, on which 8.65 billion USD was spent, according to a report by the

Centre for Media Studies as reported in Scroll, the BJP spent Rs 27,000 crores or nearly 45% of the total election spending:

> (a)round Rs 12,000 crore to Rs 15,000 crore was distributed directly to voters, while Rs 20,000 crore to Rs 25,000 crore was spent on publicity. Logistics accounted for about Rs 5,000 crore, formal expenditure was between Rs 10,000 crore and Rs 12,000 crore, while miscellaneous expenses were about Rs 3,000 crore to Rs 6,000 crore.
>
> *(Scroll 2019)*

By 2019, it appears that 'democratic recession' (Diamond 2015) has been accompanied by an economic recession in the Modi regime (see Azad et al. 2019). But expectations that the loss of jobs, growing rural distress, or a downturn in investments, would lead to a disenchantment with the Modi regime have been proven wrong. With the help of a punitive air strike on Pakistan in February 2019, cheerleading media, unprecedented funds, and subversion of all independent institutions, the BJP came back to power in 2019. The BJP's skillfully marketed welfare schemes like providing gas cylinders may also have had some impact (Atri and Jain 2019). Overall, however, it was clearly a vote for a strong leader, muscular nationalism, and Hindutva. The singular mark of fascism is how people have subordinated their own personal economic issues to vote in the interests of the 'nation'; and how the normal indifference to the problems of people from other communities, regions, religions, classes, and castes has given way to active hatred for Muslims in particular, and disadvantaged groups in general (though the contours of the majority keep changing with even other oppressed groups like scheduled castes and tribes taking part in anti-Muslim pogroms or lynchings).

Institutional Subversion

In addition to cadre-based mobilization, state-supported vigilantism, and the diffusion of hate in society, two other features of the current BJP regime stand out: first, the use of legal processes and state institutions to frame opponents and acquit sympathizers, including those accused of terror; second, institutional capture—almost every independent regulatory institution which is intended to provide a system of checks and balances has been subverted. This has, of course, been in the making for a while, especially when it comes to 'national security' where the independent institutions of democracy have been enfeebled over time.

The list of institutions which have suffered a loss of autonomy since 2014 is fairly exhaustive. Two governors and one deputy governor of the Reserve Bank of India resigned, indicating governmental interference (Ghosh and Gopakumar 2019); an inconvenient director of the Central Bureau of Investigation, India's premier investigative agency into corruption and major criminal cases, was divested of his job overnight (Venu 2019); Army chief Bipin Rawat was promoted over two other officers, violating the principle of seniority the Army previously followed (India Today 2017); two members of the National Statistical Commission quit over a delay in releasing employment statistics (Kumar 2019); the Election Commission which was hitherto a model for the independent conduct of elections was seen as blatantly partisan in 2019, in the way it fixed the election schedule to favor the BJP and did not censure Modi's hate speeches, and refused to respond to concerns over the electronic voting machines (Mishra, 2019). Universities have come under severe stress with interference in appointments, right-wing attempts to control the syllabi, and physical attacks by the ABVP, the BJP student wing, on seminars and extra-curricular events which challenge the government narrative (see Sundar 2018, essays in Apoorvanand ed. 2018). The majority of the mainstream print and television media has been silenced, bought over, with pressure being brought to bear on corporate owners. They become willing purveyors of genocidal lies (see Varadarajan 2019). Since its electoral victory in 2019, the BJP has also inducted several MLAs from opposition parties, breaking these parties, and subverting the principle of electoral representation. While the BJP publicly claims that this is because of the superiority of its nationalist ideology, the war chest it has amassed surely has something to do with the switch.

The promotions of judges who have ruled against the BJP have been put on hold, while an unprecedented press conference held by four Supreme Court judges questioning the manner in which cases were being allotted to benches indicated governmental subversion in the higher judiciary too (see Khosla 2019).

In major criminal cases involving Hindutva politicians or officials, the investigative agencies appeared to have purposefully botched the investigations or not appealed (see, for example, Apoorvanand 2019). BJP MP Sadhvi Pragya who is on trial for a 2008 bomb blast in Malegaon where ten people were killed, and 82 injured, was put up by the BJP as a candidate in 2019 to show that 'Hindu terror' does not count as terror in their books. Millions of people in Assam are in danger of being put indefinitely into detention camps on the grounds that they are foreigners, and the process is likely to be extended to the whole country. Disturbingly, this entire process of denying fundamental rights is taking place under the supervision of the Supreme Court.

Conclusion

The BJP's electoral victory in 2014 was closely bound up with the state of India's faltering economy with its growing inequality but rising expectations. Despite its claims to be for "minimum government and maximum governance," and its election-time contempt for welfare policies and subsidies for the poor, the BJP has continued to broadly follow the same neo-liberal policies as the Congress (pro-corporate policies on land and environmental clearances coupled with some welfare schemes), leading Arun Shourie, a leading journalist and former BJP member to describe the BJP regime as 'Congress plus cow.' However, where it has departed radically from earlier regimes is its willingness to abandon basic principles of the Constitution, its openly majoritarian agenda (the Congress was mostly opportunist in this regard), and its redrawing of the lines of political as well as social propriety. Major institutions have been suborned such as the army, judiciary, and media; inclusiveness has given way to a strident Hindu nationalism and indifference and hatred have become the ruling emotions. It is not clear whether and when India will recover from this to become a regular democracy.

Notes

1 Frequent victims of violence include religious minorities, indigenous people, or what are officially called Scheduled Tribes, former untouchables or Scheduled Castes. The term Scheduled comes from lists or Schedules drawn up by the Government for the purposes of affirmative action.
2 "To keep up the purity of the Race and its culture, Germany shocked the world by her purging the country of the Semitic Races—the Jews. Race pride at its highest has been manifested here. Germany has also shown how well nigh impossible it is for Races and cultures, having differences going to the root, to be assimiliated into one united whole, a good lesson for us in Hindusthan to learn and profit by" (Golwalkar 1939, 35).
3 In 2018, several well-known civil liberties activists were arrested on accusations that they were out to kill Modi in what is known as the Bhima-Koregaon case.
4 The more prominent 'scams' include the allocation of mobile telephone spectrum to cherry-picked companies for an estimated loss of $40 billion to the treasury (the 2G spectrum scam), overpriced contracts for the Commonwealth games favoring associates of the chairman of the organizing committee, the illegal diversion of government land to the Karnataka Chief Minister's sons, which was then resold for a huge profit, the Adarsh housing society scam in Mumbai in which flats meant for war widows were given to influential politicians and senior members of the armed forces; the 'Coalgate scam' in which leases for coal mining were handed out practically free to favored companies by governments of both parties acting at both state and central level, and the allegations against the son-in-law of Congress Chief, Robert Vadra, for collusion with a big real estate company.
5 Bhattacharya and Guha Thakurta (2019) note that while India's position has come down in the Economist's crony capital index, the contours have perhaps changed rather than disappeared, and media silencing may in fact be keeping scandals from being investigated. Certainly, the Rafael aircraft deal with France in which Anil Ambani's group was awarded offset contracts without any prior experience and which is the subject of ongoing litigation before the Supreme Court would seem to indicate so.

Bibliography

AFP. 2019. "At Least 4000 Detained in Kashmir Since August 5: Govt." Deccan Herald. www.deccanherald.com/national/north-and-central/at-least-4000-detained-in-kashmir-since-aug-5-govt-755231.html
Ahmad, Aijaz. 2017. "India: Liberal Democracy and the Extreme Right." Verso. www.versobooks.com/blogs/3144-india-liberal-democracy-and-the-extreme-right
Apoorvanand (ed.). 2018. *The Idea of a University.* Delhi: Context.

Apoorvanand. 2019. "The Samjhauta Acquittals: Hindu Terror Goes Unpunished in India." Al Jazeera, March 28. www.aljazeera.com/indepth/opinion/samjhauta-acquittals-hindu-terror-unpunished-india-190327111755815.html

Attri, Vibha, and Anurag Jain. 2019. "Post Poll Survey: When Schemes Translate into Votes." *The Hindu*, May 27. www.thehindu.com/elections/lok-sabha-2019/when-schemes-translate-into-votes/article27256139.ece

Azad, Rohit, Shouvik Chakraborty, Srinivasan Ramani, and Dipa Sinha. 2019. *A Quantum Leap in the Wrong Direction*. New Delhi: Orient Blackswan.

Banaji, Jairus. 2017. The Political Culture of Fascism. Historical Materialism, www.historicalmaterialism.org/blog/political-culture-fascism, accessed 26 January 2020.

Baruah, Sanjib. 2014. "Routine Emergencies: India's Armed Forces Special Powers Act." In *Civil Wars in South Asia*, edited by Aparna Sundar and Nandini Sundar, 189–211. New Delhi: Sage Publications.

Bhattacharya, A.K, and Paranjoy Guha Thakurta. 2019. "The Contours of Crony Capitalism in the Modi Raj." In *Majoritarian State: How Hindu Nationalism is Changing India*, edited by Angana P. Chatterji, Thomas Blom Hansen and Christophe Jaffrelot, 41–68. London: Hurst and Company.

Brown, Wendy, Peter Gordon, and Max Pensky. 2018. *Authoritarianism. Three Enquiries in Critical Theory*. Chicago, IL: University of Chicago Press.

Casolari, Marzia. 2000. "Hindutva's Foreign Tie-up in the 1930s: Archival Evidence." *Economic and Political Weekly*, January 22, 2000, 218–28.

Chakravarty, Paula, and Srirupa Roy 2015. "Mr. Modi Goes to Delhi: Mediated Populism and the 2014 General Elections." *Television and New Media* 16(4): 1–12.

Chatterji, Angana P., Thomas Blom Hansen and Christophe Jaffrelot. 2019. *Majoritarian State: How Hindu Nationalism is Changing India*. London: Hurst and Company.

Diamond, Larry. 2015. "Facing Up to the Democratic Recession." *Journal of Democracy* 26(1): 141–55.

Eco, Umberto. 1995. "Ur Fascism." *The New York Review of Books*, June 22, 1995, www.nybooks.com/articles/1856.

Ghassem-Fachandi, Parvis. 2019. "Reflections in the Crowd: Delegation, Verisimilitude, and the Modi Mask." In *Majoritarian State: How Hindu Nationalism is Changing India*, edited by Angana P. Chatterji, Thomas Blom Hansen and Christophe Jaffrelot, 83–100. London: Hurst and Company.

Ghosh, Shayan and Gopika Gopakumar. 2019. "Viral Acharya's Exit Raises Fresh Questions over RBI's Independence." *Livemint*. www.livemint.com/industry/banking/viral-acharya-s-exit-raises-fresh-questions-over-rbi-s-independence-1561344511637.html.

Golwalkar, M.S. 1939. *We or Our Nationhood Defined*. Nagpur: Bharat Prakashan.

Hall, Stuart. 2017 [1979]. "The Great Moving Right Show." In *Stuart Hall: Selected Political Writings*, edited by Sally Davison, David Featherstone, Michael Rustin and Bill Schwarz, 172–86. Durham, NC: Duke University Press.

Hansen, Thomas Blom. 2019. Democracy against the Law: Reflections on India's Illiberal Democracy. In *Majoritarian State: How Hindu Nationalism is Changing India*, edited by Angana P. Chatterji, Thomas Blom Hansen and Christophe Jaffrelot, 19–40. London: Hurst and Company.

Hariharan, Githa, and Salim Yusufji. 2019. *Battling for India: A Citizen's Reader*. New Delhi: Speaking Tiger.

Hindu, The. 2019. "CSDS Lokniti Post Poll Survey." *The Hindu*, May 27. www.thehindu.com/specials/the-hindu-csds-lokniti-post-poll-survey/article27259339.ece.

Hoenig, Patrick, and Navsharan Singh 2014. *Landscapes of Fear: Understanding Impunity in India*. New Delhi: Zubaan

India Today. 2017. "Army Chief Bipin Rawat's Chemistry with Controversy." *India Today*, June 12. www.indiatoday.in/fyi/story/bipin-rawat-army-chief-kashmir-stone-pelting-indian-army-controversy-982328-2017-06-12.

Jacoby, Tim. 2016. "Global Fascism: Geography, Timing, Support and Strategy." *Journal of Global History* 2016(11): 451–72.

Jaffrelot, Christophe. 2019. "A De Facto Ethnic Democracy? Obliterating and Targeting the Other, Hindu Vigilantes and the Ethno-State." In *Majoritarian State: How Hindu Nationalism is Changing India*, edited by Angana P. Chatterji, Thomas Blom Hansen and Christophe Jaffrelot, pp. 41–68. London: Hurst and Company.

Jayal, Niraja Gopal (ed.). 2019. *Re-forming India: The Nation Today*. New Delhi: PenguinViking.

Jha, Prashant. 2017. *How the BJP Wins: Inside India's Greatest Electoral Machine*. New Delhi: Juggernaut Press.

John, Rachel, and Kairvy Grewal. 2019. "How Foreign Media Has Covered Kashmir Crises – and Run Foul of the Modi Government." *The Print*, September 3. https://theprint.in/india/how-foreign-media-has-covered-kashmir-crisis-and-run-foul-of-modi-govt/285602/

Kanungo, Pralay. 2019. "Sangh and Sarkar: The RSS Power Centre Shifts from Nagpur to New Delhi." In *Majoritarian State: How Hindu Nationalism is Changing India*, edited by Angana P. Chatterji, Thomas Blom Hansen and Christophe Jaffrelot, 151–76. London: Hurst and Company.

Khosla, Madhav. 2019. "Judicial Accountability and Independence." In *Re-forming India: The Nation Today*, edited by Niraja Gopal Jayal, 287–97. New Delhi: Penguin Books.

Kumar, Arun. 2017. *Demonetisation and the Black Economy*. New Delhi: Penguin Books.

Kumar, Manoj. 2019. "Members of National Statistical Commission Quit over Jobs Data Dispute." Reuters, January 30. https://in.reuters.com/article/india-economy-statistics/members-of-national-statistical-commission-quit-over-jobs-data-dispute-idINKCN1PO211

Levien, Michael. 2015. "Six Theses on India's Land Question. From Primitive Accumulation to Regimes of Dispossession." *Economic and Political Weekly* 50(22), May 30: 146–57.

Levitsky, Steven, and Lucan A. Way. 2002. "The Rise of Competitive Authoritarianism." *Journal of Democracy* 13(2): 51–65.

Mishra, Satish 2019. "Election Commission of India and 2019 Lok Sabha Polls." Orfonline. www.orfonline.org/expert-speak/election-commission-of-india-and-2019-lok-sabha-polls-51172/.

Morelock, J. 2018. "Introduction: The Frankfurt School and Authoritarian Populism – A Historical Outline." In *Critical Theory and Authoritarian Populism*, edited by J. Morelock, xiii–xxxviii. London: University of Westminster Press.

Nilsen, Alf Gunvald, Nielsen, Kenneth Bo, and Anand Vaidya (ed.). 2019. *Indian Democracy*. London: Pluto Press.

Noorani A.G. 2019. *The RSS: A Menace to India*. New Delhi: Leftword.

Payne, Stanley. 1980. *Fascism: Comparison and Definition*. Madison: The University of Wisconsin Press.

Prakash, Gyan. 2019. *Emergency Chronicles: Indira Gandhi and Democracy's Turning Point*. Princeton, NJ: Princeton University Press.

Price, Lance. 2015. *The Modi Effect: Inside Narendra Modi's Campaign to Transform India.* London: Hodder & Stoughton.

Richards, David L. 1999. "Perilous Proxy: Human Rights and the Presence of National Elections." *Social Science Quarterly* 80(4): 648–65.

Sardesai, Rajdeep. 2015. *2014: The Election That Changed India.* New Delhi: Viking.

Scroll Staff. 2019. "BJP Spent Nearly 45% – or Rs 27,000 Crore – of Total Expenditure for 2019 Lok Sabha Polls." June 4. https://scroll.in/latest/925882/bjp-spent-nearly-45-or-rs-27000-crore-of-total-expenditure-for-2019-lok-sabha-polls-report

Sharma, Jyotirmaya. 2007. *Terrifying Vision: M.S. Golwalkar, the RSS and India.* New Delhi: Penguin/Viking.

Smooha, Sammy. 2002. "The Model of Ethnic Democracy: Israel as a Jewish and Democratic State." *Nations and Nationalism* 8(4): 475–503.

Stanley, Jason. 2018. *How Fascism Works: The Politics of Us and Them.* New York: Random House.

Sundar, Nandini. 2013." Public-Private Partnerships in the Industry of Insecurity." In *Rhetorics of Security*, edited by Zeynep Gambetti and Marcial Godoy-Anativia, 153–74. New York, NY: New York University Press.

Sundar, Nandini. 2018. "Academic Freedom and Indian Universities." *Economic & Political Weekly* LIII(24) June 16: 48.

Sundar, Nandini. 2019. *The Burning Forest: India's War against the Maoists.* London: Verso Press.

Tarlo, Emma. 2003. *Unsettling Memories: Narratives of the Emergency in Delhi.* Berkeley: University of California Press.

The Quint. "2019 Hunted: India's Lynch Files." The Quint. www.thequint.com/quintlab/lynching-in-india/.

Times of India/ANI. 2019. "Now We Can Bring Girls from Kashmir, Says Manohar Lal Khattar." *Times of India*, August 10. https://timesofindia.indiatimes.com/city/gurgaon/now-we-can-bring-girls-from-kashmir-says-manohar-lal-khattar/articleshow/70616131.cms.

Times of India/PTI. 2019. "Kashmir Situation Normal. People Happy with Article 370 Abrogation: Prakash Javdekar." *Times of India*, October 6. https://timesofindia.indiatimes.com/india/kashmir-situation-normal-people-happy-with-article-370-abrogation-prakash-javadekar/articleshow/71464893.cms

Tiwary, Deeptiman. 2019. "Sedition Cases Reality Check: Only Two Convictions in Three Years." *Indian Express*, January 18. https://indianexpress.com/article/india/sedition-case-punishment-convictions-kanhaiya-kumar-jnu-5543891/

Varadarajan, Siddharth 2014. "The Best Democracy That Money Can Buy." *Economic Times*, April 30.

Varadarajan, Siddharth. 2019. "The State and/or the Media in Modi's India." In *India's Democracy*, edited by Alf Nilsen, Kenneth Nielsen, and Anand Vaidya, 58–71. London: Pluto Press 2019.

Venu, M.K. 2019. "Modi-Led Panel's Decision to Remove Alok Verma as CBI Chief Is Fundamentally Flawed." The Wire, January 11. https://thewire.in/government/narendra-modi-alok-verma-cbi.

Vishnoi, Anubhuti 2019. "Electoral Bonds: Ruling BJP Bags 95% of the Funds." *Economic Times*. https://economictimes.indiatimes.com/news/politics-and-nation/electoral-bonds-ruling-bjp-bags-95-of-funds/articleshow/66858037.cms?from=mdr.

Wire Staff. 2019. "In 2019, Is the BJP Riding a Modi Wave or a Money Wave." May 6.

Zakaria, Farid. 1997. "The Rise of Illiberal Democracy." *Foreign Affairs* 77(6): 22–43.

13

JAPAN

Land of the Rising Right

Kristin Surak

Introduction[1]

On May 1, 2019, Japan welcomed a new emperor. The aging Akihito allowed his 59-year-old son, Naruhito, to take over a lineage reputed to be the oldest unbroken line of royals in the world. In comparison to its European counterparts, Japan's imperial family is at once more unassuming and more withdrawn from the people it represents. Nowhere are the extramarital affairs, drug scandals, offensive statements, and awkward sexual proclivities that feed the media machine around the Windsors. The top gossip in recent years has been a potential marriage between a royal granddaughter and a law school student with a (gasp) indebted mother. The in-coming monarch yields little additional fodder. He is a royal with a reputation for steadfast competence, international curiosity, and the incongruous desire to never really stand out. His two-year stint at Oxford University resulted in a book on waterways bracingly titled *The Thames and I*. He even switched from the violin to the viola, explaining that the larger instrument, which typically supplies a supporting role rather than the melody, is more appropriate for his tastes.

May 1 marked the beginning of a new era, and quite literally: the imperial calendar, used in much bureaucratic and official business, changed from the 31st year of Heisei to the 1st year of Reiwa.

At the same point a generation ago, the future of Japan could not have looked brighter. When Emperor Akihito began his reign in 1989, the economy was the second largest in the world. Nominal per capita GDP outstretched that of the US by a margin. The country was producing the most cutting-edge consumer technology of the day, including Nintendo entertainment systems, Sanyo stereos, Canon cameras, and Panasonic VCRs. Pundits predicted, and sometimes feared, a new Japan-led era of global growth (Vogel 1979). Within months, however, the stock market crashed, the economy flatlined, and the country never recovered. Though Japan remains economically more powerful than any country in Europe, it is now easy to forget that fact in the shadow of its much larger neighbor, China, which is a reason for pause. Indeed, many of the issues that Japan faces are not so different to those of another set of islands, off the coast a more powerful EU (even if the aging British monarch has proved far more tenacious).

Abenomics and Japan's Low-yield Economy

Japan is a sobering test case of just how obstinate a low-yield economy can be. The GDP has barely budged over the past 30 years and economic growth rarely breaks 2%. Initially, the government attempted to end the malaise through deregulation, particularly of the labor market. In the country once known for lifetime employment, 40% of the labor force now works on temporary contracts. With job security a thing of the past for many, so are the generous pensions, health coverage, and unemployment insurance that came with life-time employment. The precarious future has driven marriage and fertility rates to record lows. One in three people in their twenties expects to work until they die.

Guiding Japan through these challenges is Prime Minister Shinzo Abe. A strategic conservative, he is the jammy heir to two powerful political dynasties: his father was a minister, his paternal grandfather an MP, and his great-uncle was one of the longest-serving prime ministers. But the most conspicuous or-nament in the family tree is his maternal grandfather, Nobusuke Kishi, who ran the brutal conscript labor system in Japanese-occupied Manchuria (Driscoll 2010). Held for war crimes, he was released before trial and eventually became prime minister, calling—unsuccessfully—for the revision of the Constitution and the expansion of Japanese military capabilities. However, the hound-faced Abe lacks the social skills of his extrovert grandfather, whom he lauds in speeches. Indeed, when he took power in 2013, few expected him to last long or accomplish much. They had seen him in the role before, in 2006, but he held on for less than a year before resigning in the face of gaffes, money scandals, and parliamentary losses. His second go, however, could hardly be more different in perseverance, with Abe set to become the country's longest-serving prime minister (on Abe's family past, see Hayashi 2014).

Distinguishing his first stint from his second is 'Abenomics,' a powerful economic salvo that was to jolt the Japanese economy back to life. The com-bination of monetary easing, fiscal stimulus, and structural reform aimed to lift inflation to 2% and produce a virtuous cycle of business expansion and consumer spending. But instead, the economy rebounded like a dropped dead cat: a small bounce, then nothing. The effect on the national debt has been far greater. It now stands at an eye-watering 250% of GDP (Pilling). (By contrast, even Greece at the height of its economic crisis in 2012–13 never broke 180%.) A long-planned sales tax hike, meant to pay for the mammoth borrowing, is likely to be delayed yet again as economists fear that it will drag the fragile economy back into recession. As in the UK, economic stagnation has not been accompanied by mass unemployment—just mass under-employment, if measured by the amount of money people have to live on. Though over 97% of people who want jobs are working, inequality has grown substantially, with Japan now one of the most unequal countries in the OECD (OECD 2019). Compared to Europe, only in Lithuania and Latvia is the poverty rate higher. More than 1.5 million Japanese households survive on welfare. And the future is not promising: one in six Japanese children lives in poverty (Foreign Press Center Japan 2017).

Still the meager economic growth is remarkable when one considers the shrinking population, which has been on the decline since 2008. The fertility rates in both Japan and the UK—1.45 and 1.80, respectively—are below replacement levels of 2.1%. But in the British case, immigration helps maintain the population growth at a mild 0.6%, due to both the influx of people and their higher average birth rates If Brexit removes this strut, policy makers might turn to Japan to gauge the effects. From the point of view of economic growth and social provision, it's not a very attractive prospect. Japan is losing more than 400,000 people per year, and the rate is accelerating as the baby boomers wane. Bureaucrats hope to sustain the total population at 100 million, a fifth smaller than its present size (Tsuya 2015). But no one knows how this will work—or how the pension and public health care systems will be kept afloat—without significant immigration. Even as the government looks into robotics to plug some of the gaps, it is clear that in many industries, such as elderly care, there are limits to how far machines can substitute for human services. Plus, robots do not pay taxes or pension contributions (Pilling 2014).

Nativists in the West may hail Japan, with its foreign population of around 2%, as a model to follow. But on the edge of the Pacific, even arch-conservatives realize that the system is untenable. Prime Minister Shinzo Abe, known more for his chauvinism than multiculturalism, has been expanding migration channels, rather than closing them down. In the past year, the government was gratified to see foreign workers increase by nearly 15% to 1.5 million, a total that has tripled over the past decade (Ministry of Justice, Immigration Control Report 2018). It is not only innocuous programs to attract highly skilled workers that are driving this growth; the government now courts low- and medium-skilled foreign workers to fill labor gaps in agriculture, construction, manufacturing, and care work. It's even opened the way for settlement and family reunion, options previously unavailable to low-paid workers meant to leave once their labor was unwanted (Endoh 2019). The conservative state is still hesitant to call the mix anything like "immigration," and Japan is hardly a choice destination of migrants (it ranks below Estonia and Taiwan on its ability to attract and develop talent; see IMD World Competitiveness Center). But the Minister of Justice has described the new system as a way to accept foreign workers to fill labor shortages, and the government expects that it will attract an additional 345,000 foreign workers over the next five years.

A Nationalist Reawakening

In the wake of the Allied victory in World War II, the American occupying army ensured that economic ties with a communist China were not revived and that Japan's economic lot was thrown in with the capitalist West. Its Prime Minister at the time, Yoshida Shigeru, gave his name to the system under which Japan would hand over responsibility for its defense and foreign policy to the Americans, while focusing its efforts on economic growth (Dower 2000). And with remarkable success. In the space of a decade, Japan's GDP doubled. In return, Japan relinquished large swaths of the country to the American military. The greatest surrender is in Okinawa, where US bases cover over 15% of the main island—and where locals have most fervently resisted the foreign presence, both at the ballot box and through spectacular demonstrations. Yet, Tokyo has turned a deaf ear to the protests of the Okinawan people, many of whom are of aboriginal Ryūkyū extraction, who themselves were colonized by Japan in the 19th century (McCormack and Norimatsu 2012). Still today, around two-dozen bases and 50,000 US soldiers remain in the state that is also host to America's Seventh Fleet, the largest abroad. It pays for this, too: Japan shoulders three-quarters of the cost for America to extend its military reach deep into Asia. If the UK has a "special relationship" with the US, it is not alone.

With few exceptions, Japan has toed the line when it comes to American demands. It's easy to see what is forthcoming in Japanese military developments by reading reports drawn up by the Harvard political scientist and influential foreign policy mandarin, Joseph Nye, and his associates in Washington (Armitage and Nye 2012). These have called for legalizing "collective security" or collective self-defense, revising the Japanese Constitution, increasing military spending, allowing Japanese forces to be regularly dispatched overseas, and integrating Japanese military systems into the US ones.

The same pliability holds for the economy, despite Japan's reputation for hardball. When Americans began buying up Japanese consumer products in the 1980s, the Japanese simply lent the dollars back by purchasing US debt—a tactic that China has learned from. And perhaps too well. In 2010, China overtook its neighbor to become world's second largest economy, a tango turn that has been complicated for Japan. Though China is the country's largest trading partner, the island nation still cleaves close to the US (McCormack 2007). After

Trump was elected, Abe raced to New York to become the first foreign leader to meet the president-to-be. But since then, he has found that the Americans are not as reliable as they once were. The US jumped ship on his treasured Trans-Pacific Partnership (the "everyone but China club"); Japan has been shut out of meetings with North Korea, much to Abe's chagrin; and the most recent round of trade negotiations with America has proceeded only haltingly. If nationalist resurgence has rendered rapprochement with China, South Korea, and Taiwan tricky, some in Japan wonder if tagging along with the US is worth the cost of turning away from the country's economically important and geopolitically powerful neighbors.

The hype around Abenomics has distracted attention from the Prime Minister's more ominous policy successes (for a substantial overview, see Nakano 2016). Within a year of election, Abe side-stepped debate to pass a State Secrecy Law that greatly expands the government's remit for designating information a state secret. Now even environmental and health information can be rendered virtually inaccessible to the public. Pundits were quick to dub it an anti-whistle blower law for the steep prison penalties it levies on leakers and reporters (Repeta 2013). But the media seems unlikely to present much of a threat. Within days of taking office, Abe installed at the helm of the national broadcasting agency one of his hard-right cronies, who immediately confirmed that the most-watched television network would remain complacent: "If the government says right, we won't say left," he declared (Uemura 2016). The following year saw the ouster—or surrender—of several of the top journalists and news hosts in the country. Meanwhile, the UN and Reporters Without Borders have expressed concerns about the erosion of freedom of the press.

By 2014, Abe had moved on to the military. Though Article 9 of the Constitution forbids Japan from waging war, he decided to reinterpret the foundational law to allow it to take up arms for its allies. His explanation was weak: it would enable Japan to come to the aid of America—a difficult situation to imagine, given that the US military is greater than that of the next seven countries combined. Over 200 legal scholars declared the interpretation unconstitutional. Still more worrying were the tactics Abe used to get it through. Rather than letting the Supreme Court adjudicate how the Constitution should be read, the Prime Minister's office made the call, in an egregious example of executive overreach.

"Reiwa": Nationalist Agenda-setting and "Normalizing" Japan

Most recently, Abe employed his hallmark legislative style—ramming through Acts by short-circuiting debate and votes—to pass a new Anti-Terrorism Bill. He pitched the law, which criminalizes over 250 actions, as necessary to protect the country during the upcoming Olympics. The Japan Federation of Bar Associations has noted that many of the forbidden deeds—like sit-in protests or copying music—do not have the remotest connection to terrorism, merely offering pretexts to squelch grassroots political movements.

But these are mere side stories to Abe's main agenda, which is to "normalize Japan"—shorthand for revising the Constitution and creating a standing army. The Japanese Constitution, written largely by American occupiers, has been a bugbear of the political right since inception. Abe's own Liberal Democratic Party (LDP) has hoped to replace it for more than 60 years. But no Prime Minister has come as close as Abe to achieving this. The reform he seeks is no light overhaul. LDP proposals call for rewriting nearly all of the 103 articles, weakening the protection of individual rights, strengthening the preeminent importance of public order, qualifying basic freedoms, and underscoring the centrality of the emperor to the nation. Central to this endeavor is the revision of Article 9, which bans Japan from maintaining an army. The government spends around 1% of its budget on its "self-defense forces," but the country's economic size means that these still constitute the eighth largest military in the world. Still, the difference between a *de facto* and a *de jure* army leaves its once-colonized neighbors—China and the Koreas—on edge. The Americans, by contrast, are in full support. They have worked for years to ensure that the Japanese forces are "interoperable" with US counterparts, rendering them an extension of the range of the Pentagon. For Washington, a well-armed Japan is both cheaper and more expedient, especially as Beijing expands its reach into the Pacific.

Variations on a Global Theme?

Abe's strong-man approach to rule might be seen as part of a broader global trend. But unlike the waves of supporters who showed up at the polls for Bolsonaro, Trump, Modi, and Duterte, voter turnout in Japan has plummeted. If there are any lessons for Britain's Labour Party, they are not from the Democratic Party of Japan, the main counterbalance to the conservative LDP over the past two decades. In the last election, this Blairite formation hoped to take down Abe by throwing in its lot with a break-away center-right group. Each collected just 10% of the available seats, against the LDP's thumping 60%. The poverty of viable options at election time has meant that nearly half of the population—and 70% of the voting-age youth—no longer bother to cast a ballot.

Into this space of political inaction has stepped the Nippon Kaigi—"The Japan Conference." The stated aim of this right-wing organization is to "build a nation with pride" (Tawara 2017). Its goals are not just nationalist but neo-imperial, inspired by a selective memory of Japanese "greatness" at the height of colonial expansion. The group seeks a new Constitution recalling that of the Meiji Era, when the Japanese were duty-bearing subjects rather than rights-bearing citizens. It hopes to return the emperor to the center of political power, in a throwback to the rhetoric and image-system used to rally the populace during World War II. Traditional family values—women in the kitchen, off the throne, and under their husband's family name—form another area they want to strengthen. The Conference claims nearly 40,000 members, but more important is who they are. Its reach into political offices and Shinto religious organizations is long: around 60% of parliamentarians are members of the Nippon Kaigi, which uses its networks to rally voters to the polls. So far, the group's biggest success has been in schools. It's led the suppression of "masochistic" views of history, as well as "excessive" focus on human rights, and has pressured governments and school boards to revise curricula accordingly (on the Nippon Kaigi, see: Mizohata 2016; Tawara 2016).

Current calls for greater pride and sovereignty in Japan are as inconsistent a mash-up of imperial imaginings, if not hallucinations, as they are in the UK. It's little wonder, then, that the name for the new imperial era selected by the Abe government has unsettling overtones. Emperor Naruhito's reign will be called "Reiwa." The term, taken from classical poetry, means "auspicious harmony." In the official translation, it's rendered "beautiful harmony"—a choice that recalls Abe's own multiple appeals to create a "beautiful Japan" (Abe 2007). By itself, the character for "rei" also means "command" or "order." In everyday speech, the semantic overlap may be innocuous—few English-speakers pause to reflect on the common Greek origin of "hospitality" and "hostility," or that the root of "pharmacy"—*pharmakon*—contains both "remedy" and "poison" among its meanings (Derrida 1981).

How the reign-name will be understood depends a lot on how Naruhito defines his role—a job not as easy as one might think. The separation of the monarch from any political issues is so complete that when Emperor Akihito floated the possibility of stepping down, commentators debated whether he had exceeded his station. Nonetheless, the retiring royal carved out a role for himself by supporting social welfare causes. In contrast to his distant father, he went out to the streets to offer solace and consolation to the underprivileged, disaster victims and others in need. His actions were so unexpected that even the most mundane gestures—squatting to talk to an old woman sitting on the floor of an evacuation center—grabbed headlines. Outside the country (and to the chagrin of ultra-nationalists), he made a point of recognizing Japanese wartime aggression with a remorse that rang truer than Abe's pro forma apologies (on Emperor Akihito, see Breen 2019). It remains to be seen what path his son will take amid a landscape of continuing economic stagnation and escalating nationalism.

Note

1 This chapter was originally published in the New Statesman. The editors gratefully acknowledge the permission of the author and the New Statesman to publish a slightly revised version in this volume.

Bibliography

Abe, Shinzo. 2007. *Towards a Beautiful Country: My Vision for Japan*. New York, NY: Vertical, Inc.

Armitage, Richard L., and Joseph S. Nye. 2012. *The U.S.-Japan Alliance: Anchoring Stability in Asia*. Washington, DC: Center for Strategic and International Studies. https://csis-prod.s3.amazonaws.com/s3fs-public/legacy_files/files/publication/120810_Armitage_USJapanAlliance_Web.pdf

Breen, John. 2019. "Abdication, Succession, and Japan's Imperial Future: An Emperor's Dilemma." *Asia-Pacific Journal: Japan Focus* 17(9.3): 1–15.

Derrida, Jacques. 1981. "Plato's Pharmacy." In *Dissemination*, translated by Barbara Johnson, 63–171. Chicago, IL: University of Chicago Press.

Dower, John. 2000. *Embracing Defeat*. New York, NY: W.W. Norton and Company.

Driscoll, Mark. 2010. *Absolute Erotic, Absolute Grotesque: The Living, Dead, and Undead in Japan's Imperialism, 1895–1945*. Durham, NC: Duke University Press.

Endoh, Toake. 2019. "The Politics of Japan's Immigration and Alien Residence Control." *Asian and Pacific Migration Journal* 28(3): 324–52.

Foreign Press Center Japan. 2017. *Child Poverty: Problems and Initiatives*. https://fpcj.jp/wp/wp-content/uploads/2017/05/99d7fdc56c9ee4ad9b4558c0d412659f.pdf

Hayashi, Yuka. 2014. "For Japan's Shinzo Abe, Unfinished Family Business." *The Wall Street Journal*. December 11.

McCormack, Gavin. 2007. *Client State: Japan in the American Embrace*. London: Verso.

McCormack, Gavin and Satoko Oka Norimatsu. 2012. *Resistant Islands: Okinawa Confronts Japan and the United States*. Lanham, MD: Rowman & Littlefield.

Ministry of Justice. 2018. *Immigration Control Report*. Immigration Bureau, Japan. Tokyo: Ministry of Justice.

Mizohata, Sachie. 2016. "Nippon Kaigi: Empire, Contradiction, and Japan's Future." *Asia-Pacific Journal: Japan Focus* 14(21.4): 1–21.

Mortimer, Caroline. 2017. "UK Birth Rate: Number of Children being Born in Britain Hits 10-year Low." *Independent*, November 20. www.independent.co.uk/news/uk/home-news/uk-birth-rate-latest-number-babies-born-lowest-decade-a8066101.html

Nakano, Koichi (ed.). 2016. *Tettei Kenshō: Abe Seiji*. Tokyo: Iwanami Press.

OECD. 2019. Income Inequality (indicator). doi: 10.1787/459aa7f1-en

Pilling, David. 2014. *Bending Adversity: Japan and the Art of Survival*. New York, NY: Penguin Books.

Repeta, Lawrence. 2013. "A New State Secrecy Law for Japan?" *The Asia-Pacific Journal: Japan Focus* 42(1): 1–10.

Tawara, Yoshifumi. 2016. *Nippon Kaigi no Zenbō: Shirarezaru Kyodai Soshiki no Jittai*. Tokyo: Kadensha.

Tawara, Yoshifumi. 2017. "What Is the Aim of Nippon Kaigi, the Ultra-Right Organization That Supports Japan's Abe Administration?" *The Asia-Pacific Journal: Japan Focus* 15(21), Article ID 5081. https://apjjf.org/2017/21/Tawara.html

Tsuya, Noriko O. 2015. "Below-Replacement Fertility in Japan: Patterns, Factors, and Policy Implications." In *Low and Lower Fertility: Variations across Developed Countries*, edited by Ronald R. Rindfuss and Minja Kim Choe, 87–106. Berlin: Springer.

Uemura, Tatsuo. 2016. "Is NHK Worth Its Subscription Fees as Japan's Public Property?" *Japan News*, November 16. https://yab.yomiuri.co.jp/adv/wol/dy/opinion/society_161121.html

Vogel, Ezra. 1979. *Japan as Number One: Lessons for America*. Cambridge, MA: Harvard University Press.

14

"IT'S ALL CORRUPT"

The Roots of Bolsonarism in Brazil

Esther Solano

Introduction

The Bolsonarist tsunami ran over Brazilian politics with unexpected force. Jair Bolsonaro won the elections, despite having only managed eight seconds of television campaigning. He managed to earn the Social Liberal Party (PSL), until then an insignificant player in Brazilian electoral politics, 52 deputies. This defied the classic analyses of political science, which assumed, categorically, that without enough time for TV campaigning, and without a significant political party, there was no chance of the candidate reaching the Presidency. As if that were not enough, some of the new state and federal congressmen of the PSL had massive voter support, like Eduardo Bolsonaro, Jair's son, who received the highest vote total of anyone running for the Federal Congress in History.

What can explain this unprecedented and unpredictable success? Jair Bolsonaro built his popular legitimacy on elements that had strongly consolidated within society and the electorate in Brazil since the impeachment process in 2015 and 2016. The elements include anti-system rhetoric; anti-partisanship; anti-petism, i.e. opposition to the Workers' Party (PT); anti-leftism; conservative ideology; neoliberalism; and support from evangelical and militarist political bases (Solano 2019). Bolsonarism and its electoral success is not a phenomenon restricted to an individual; rather, it is an ideological matrix with strong social roots. This chapter seeks to characterize the elements that brought electoral success to Bolsonarism and which made it plausible for Bolsonaro to present himself as the only candidate with workable solutions for the economic, political, and moral crises of Brazil today.

Bolsonaro and the Economic Crisis: More Neoliberalism for the Neoliberal Crisis

At the heart of the current crisis of representative democracy is the crisis of neoliberalism itself that has brought a new political form to life: post-democracy. Crouch (2004) defines post-democracy as a political system with a democratic facade, beneath which the system is totally captured by neoliberal logic. Democracy is being replaced by *corporocracy*, becoming an accessory to market logic, which comes to rest at the very heart of the system of political representation. Decision-making power is removed from the electorate and placed in the orbit of large companies and political oligarchies. In this system, neoliberalism is the center and nucleus of everything. Everything belongs to it and nothing out of it survives. The conditions of existences and subjectivities are built within, and only within, the logic of neoliberal rationality (Laval and Dardot 2016). Brazil presents a striking example of this situation of economic capture of the democratic representation: among 513 members of Federal Congress elected in 2018, 248 declared to the Electoral Justice to have a fortune over R$ 1 million in a country where the average monthly income is R$ 928 according to the Brazilian Institute of Geography and Statistics (IBGE).

Flexibility, hyper-productivism, *home-office*, and young people who lack horizons for personal and career development, precariousness, accelerated vulnerability, millions of disposable people in chronic unemployment situation, and impoverished middle class *are* the result of this new labor morphology. According to the data from the IBGE, in 2018, the number of Brazilian informal workers was 38.3 million (41.3%); in 2019, unemployment reached 13.2 million and 3.8 million Brazilian workers list applications such as Rappi, Uber, UberEats, or iFood as their main source of income. In this scenario of increasing informality in the labor market, constantly increasing precarity is the reality for most workers. According to a survey by the Institute Locomotiva in 2018, 56% of formal workers in Brazil said that they were dissatisfied with their working conditions.

Achille Mbembe (2014) describes this process as the universalization of the black condition, which causes permanent existential uncertainty in the worker, who feels increasingly insecure, having his ways of sociability disintegrated (Castel 2005). In parallel, the classical structures of representativeness, such as unions, are immensely weakened. According to data from the ICJBrasil of 2017, only 29% of Brazilians trust unions.

The harshness of the labor market has as an immediate consequence the increase of psychological suffering of society. This suffering, however, is not perceived as collective and produced by contemporary capitalism; rather, it is perceived as individualized, giving rise to feelings of failure and guilt. Meritocracy takes the place of the politicization of suffering. Individualism is the prevailing logic. Individual and private dynamics prevail over collective and public dynamics. It is the time of the entrepreneur who thinks that the State is only a burden, of the citizen who wants a weapon at home to protect himself because the State is not able to protect him or her, and of the person who prefers to be informed by WhatsApp because he or she doesn't trust the big press. In this environment, the so-called "prosperity gospel" prospers in Christian churches, teaching that you can enter the Kingdom of God by working hard and contributing financially with the church. The rhetoric of the minimum state, the privatization of public services, and the logic of the self-made man appear as the only solutions to economic crises.

The political disenchantment of the most popular classes in Brazil who feel totally absent from state protection is enormous. Millions of Brazilians only count on family, neighborhood, or religious protection networks in a country of the Global South where, in 2018, the 10% of the poorest population held 0.8% of the income mass, while the 10% richest concentrated 43.1% (IBGE). Due to this situation, the Lavajatistic rhetoric of criminalization of politics and the State on the basis of anti-corruption discourses echoed with great force during recent years.

Operation Lava Jato (Car Wash Operation) conducted by its chief judge, the current Minister of Justice, Sergio Moro, imposes an anti-corruption strategy based on a moralistic, punitive, spectacle justice (Casara 2018), which places politics and the State as enemies. In the rhetoric of Moro and Bolsonaro, if the State is intrinsically corrupt, dishonest, ineffective, and spends too much money, the way out of the economic crisis, which is a political and moral crisis, is the replacement of the State by a private initiative and the replacement of public policies by entrepreneurial and individualistic dynamics and minimum state system. This is the context through which we can understand the justification for the anti-popular pensions reform initiative that will impoverish the poorest classes in Brazil even more, the privatization of important State companies such as Petrobras or Eletrobras (oil and energy companies), and the labor reform that decreases workers' rights enormously.

> We, the poor worker, can always change our life, of course. You'll hear "no" many times, but you can do it, just need to work hard in life. There are lots of poor people who do not want to work, they are lazy, they just want to depend on the State
>
> *Interview 23*

> The State is corrupt and ineffective, politicians just want their privileges. We should privatize everything, education, health, even the State itself! No politicians, just CEOs. Only private services, like companies. Public companies are total failure.
>
> *Interview 25*

Bolsonaro and the Political Crisis: Anti-system, Anti-partisanship, and Anti-petism

Like other politicians representing the extreme right, Bolsonaro builds himself electorally on the basis of scapegoat logic, transforming fear, insecurity, anger, frustration within the poor classes but also among the increasingly impoverished among middle classes, into political hatred. The logic of the enemy—defined as PT, cultural Marxism, teachers who indoctrinate students, feminists, LGBTs who want the end our Christian way of life, and black people of the periphery—these scapegoats are responsible for our suffering. The mystification of a more existentially secure past where the old social hierarchies ordered the world is part of this whole process. It is the politics of enmity (Mbeme 2017).

Anti-system, Anti-partisanship Rhetoric

One of the issues that most insistently appears in my interviews as justifying voting for Bolsonaro is that he represents "someone different": an outsider capable of facing a totally corrupted political logic. The word "hope" or "change" was linked to the figure of Bolsonaro appearing in all interviews. Bolsonaro is seen as honest and authentic, an anti-mainstream figure, capable of capturing the protest vote, channeling the frustration and anger against the political system. Traditional parties are perceived as equally dirty and concerned only with their own privileges. It is the binary conception of the old versus the new and the new is a category of enormous political impact. The old, traditional politics are rejected and the political novelty appears as a value in itself.

Corruption is at the heart of this argument. Not only would professional politicians be dirty and corrupt, but politically making itself. The State bureaucracy, even the representation system, awakens negative affections such as shame and rejection. Sergio Moro appears characterized in the interviews by concepts such as hero, savior, someone who "has a task," "is an envoy," and even more, "will clean Brazil" of corrupt politicians who, in a moralist and dualistic point of view, represent evil, the enemy to be exterminated, "a cancer." In the interviewees' speeches, the concept of "cleaning up" appears much more than the concept of "doing justice." A messianic, militant, and criminalizing justice increases the collective feeling that politics and political parties are despicable and heinous. Regardless of the many real cases of corruption involving the largest political parties in the country, what this chapter seeks to emphasize is that Operation Jet Lava was a key element in the rise of Bolsonarism. The way in which former judge Sergio Moro (current Minister of Justice and Public Security under Bolsonaro) conducted the anti-corruption operation, with a promiscuous relationship with the press, full of selective leaks, and very controversial spectacular maneuvers popularized the idea that political system as a whole was corrupt and that an outsider like Bolsonaro should be elected.

Paradoxically, the main victim of this anti-system rhetoric was not the PT, as Dilma Rousseff impeachment or the imprisonment of Lula might suggest. Rather, it is one of that party's traditional rivals, the PSDB (Party of Brazilian Social Democracy), which went from 34.8 million votes in the first round of the 2014 elections to five million in 2018.

> They're all the same. PT, PSDB. Power is power. They don't care about us. It's all corrupt, dirty, everything... I don't vote for left or right, I vote for the person. Left and right is all the same. Oh, I think Bolsonaro is different and can change all that. We believe in him. We have faith in him, hope, he is not the same.
>
> *Interview 15*

In the research I conducted with Pablo Ortellado and Lucia Nader during the pro-impeachment demonstrations throughout 2015, social pre-Bolsonarism was, in retrospect, already evident.[1] At the August 16, 2015 demonstration against PT on Paulista Avenue, 96% of those who demonstrated said they were not satisfied with the political system, 73% said they did not trust the political parties, and 70% did not trust politicians. Anti-partisanship and the rejection of the figure of the traditional politician appeared with great force. When we asked who inspired the most trust, Bolsonaro's name came first: 19.4% trusted him very much. In that same demonstration, only 11% said that they trusted the PSDB (party in which the majority of the people demonstrating voted in the 2014 election) and 1% trusted PMDB (the party of the Vice President Michel Temer that would occupy the Presidency of the Republic if the impeachment requested by the demonstrators were successful). Fifty-six percent agreed with the sentence "someone outside the political game would solve the crises," 64% said "an honest judge" would, and 88% an "honest politician." At that time, one could already detect the nascent creation of the figures of Bolsonaro and the judge Sergio Moro as the honest outsiders who could serve as saviors of the nation. The solution should come from outside the system. Faced with a scenario of perception of increased political corruption, values such as honesty and ethics appeared as indispensable in the prototype of the desirable politician.

Along with the disapproval of politics, collectivist solutions, and politicians generally, one sees a growing appeal for the logic of the private, of the intimate, and of personal relationships: personal effort, family, and religion reappear as the main circles of sociability and problem solving.

Anti-petism and Anti-leftism

Along with the denial of politics as a collective activity, anti-leftism was one of the elements most exploited by Bolsonaro's campaign. One of the most interesting facts at the symbolic level of the campaign was the resurgence of anti-communism in electoral propaganda. The anti-petism (anti-Workers' Party) rhetoric so prevalent during the pro-impeachment demonstrations of 2015 and 2016 could be easily converted into angry anti-left speeches during the 2018 elections.

Mara Telles and her research team studied this phenomenon at the pro-impeachment demonstration on March 12, 2015 in Belo Horizonte (Telles 2017). The demonstrators expressed their indignation with corruption (36%), but also their dissatisfaction with politics (18%). However, more than corruption, the theme that most connected the demonstrations was anti-petism. Ninety-one percent said that PT did great harm and 82% gave a score of 0 to PT government. The anti-petism can also be found in the judgment they made about their leaders: 81% considered Lula to be one of the country's main malefactors; 82% agreed that Rousseff was too. Professor Telles affirms that anti-petism is based on a powerful class factor and anti-egalitarianism.

Most of the demonstrators disagreed with PT government policies on social inclusion, such as Bolsa Família (77.8%), stating that people assisted by social programs can "become lazier." Already 37% of those who protested alleged that minorities, such as black people, women, and homosexuals, have too many rights in Brazil, and the racial quotas on university admissions are rejected by a majority of citizens: 70.1% declared that they should be eliminated. The presence of Cuban doctors in primary health-care programs in the poorest regions of the country, where many Brazilian doctors refuse to go, is also disapproved by 70.7%. A wide majority (75.6%) declared that the poor make poor political decisions.

Anti-petism, anti-leftism, anti-communism. In the first television electoral program of the second round of 2018 elections, Bolsonaro's propaganda exhibited supposed connections between PT and São Paulo Forum, which would be "a political group with left-wing communist ideology led by Lula and Fidel Castro" created in Latin America to spread communism. The electoral propaganda also exploited the PT's relationship with Venezuela and the Bolivarian countries and the danger of "Venezuelanism" in Brazil if PT won the elections. Only Bolsonaro, it was argued, could save Brazil of this imminent communist danger.

But the antagonism is not only built on the perceived danger of the PT. During the Bolsonaro campaign, the figure of the enemy is enlarged to include the entire progressive camp. The Bolsonarist conservatism built itself on religious values and romanticizing a better past, in which the traditional family, the heteronormative model, was of essential appeal, offering a binary, scapegoat logic of the good citizen versus the bandit, where the good citizen conforms to conservative and meritocratic standards, while the bandit, or the criminal, is anyone who opposes this figure: feminists who are too radical and anti-family, LGBTs who are too obscene, left-wing protesters who are "a bunch of vagabonds."

I am a good citizen who works, pays taxes, has a decent life and is unprotected. Where's the victim's human rights? Human rights end up being bad because it's for bandits, for criminals, for lefties, for feminists... what about us? The State does not protect us but Bolsonaro will change this situation PT created. He will protect good honest citizens.

Interview 1

For Bolsonaro voters, even the poorest, the crisis that is devastating Brazil is not the result of neoliberalism or a brutal unequal structure, a racist and colonial heritage; rather, it is fundamentally a crisis of values, where leftists, feminists, or gays are dangerous categories. It is the strategy of cultural wars (Hunter, 1991) of the moralization of politics and the demonization of opponents transforming them into enemies.

Bolsonaro and the Moral Crisis: Christianization and Militarization of Politics

Wendy Brown (2006) explains how in recent decades we have witnessed a new phenomenon that is the confluence of neoliberalism and neoconservatism. In order to rise as a regulatory force of subjectivities and collective life, neoliberalism needs a set of values and ethical configurations that reinterprets economic crises as moral crisis and the abandonment of traditional values. This is where the role of religion as the moral legitimizer of neoliberalism enters specifically in its meritocratic model of the theology of prosperity and the logic of sacrifice. This is also where, in front of the austerity policies, long-term unemployment, precariousness, impoverishment, and the traditional patriarchal and heteronormative family as the main social nucleus come into play. In this context, nationalism becomes attractive, as does the figure of the "good man" as a form of social cohesion against threats posed by "others." This further leads to the militarization of the political and public spaces to maintain the law and order necessary for the market to operate. Nancy Fraser (2017) interprets the advance of right-wing governments in the world as the end of what she called "progressive neoliberalism," an alliance between neoliberalism and certain emancipation ideas (feminism, anti-racism, LGBTQ rights). Thus, the Bolsonaro government represents this alliance between neoliberalism and neoconservatism, and resistance to the putative identity politics of the left is yoked to (at least token) resistance of economic globalization.

Current Bolsonaro's government composition is a perfect example of this combination between neoliberal and neoconservative politics. The Minister of Economy, Chicago Boy Paulo Guedes, an ultraliberal referent, who calls for a minimal state, can serve together in Bolsonaro's cabinet with a fundamentalist Christian pastor, the Minister of Family, Women and Human Rights, Damares Alves, for whom women should remain at home, and with Ernesto Araújo,

Minister of Foreign Affairs, for whom cultural Marxism is guilty of "globalism" and of forgetting God's role in History.

Identity movements are the main target of attack within this aspect of Bolsonarism. According to his voters, Bolsonaro is not misogynistic, racist, or homophobic; rather, he acts correctly in speaking shamelessly what he thinks, reacting against the dictatorship of political correctness. Identity movements are the guiltiest of the moral chaos of society. Still, for those who support Bolsonaro, the belief is that collective struggle does not guarantee the conquest of more rights; rather, personal effort and meritocracy do so.

> That homophobia thing didn't have it before. Now it's homophobia everywhere. Before there wasn't so much violence against gay people, but now it seems that they show off too much. Partially, they are guilty of the violence against them because they show themselves too much.
>
> *Interview 21*

> I'm against race quotas for public University. What about poor white people? There are rich black people. There is less and less racism now. There are many people who want to take advantage of being black. Slavery was a long time ago, you don't have to remember that all the time. There is racism on both sides.
>
> *Interview 2*

Bolsonaro often cites in his public appearances the Bible verse, John 8:32 "and you will know the truth and the truth will set you free." Although born Catholic, he was baptized on May 12, 2016 in the Jordan River by Pentecostal Pastor Everaldo, president of the Christian Social Party (PSC). The word God was one of the most repeated both in his campaign and in his inaugural speech on January 1, 2019 in Brasilia. A Datafolha survey of October 25, 2018 estimated the number of valid votes for Bolsonaro by religious segments: 29.9% Catholic, 21.7% evangelical Christian versus 28.7% Catholic, and 9.7% evangelical Christian of valid votes that went to Fernando Haddad. The evangelical Christian universe positioned itself with Bolsonaro by a wide margin after Bishop Edir Macedo, the powerful leader of the Universal Church of the Kingdom of God and an ally of PT until impeachment, and Bishop Silas Malafaia, the powerful leader of the Assembly of God Church, publicly supported him. Both leaders saw a great opportunity to increase their political influence under Bolsonaro's government in a moment where the relations of the big Christian Pentecostal and Neo-Pentecostal churches with PT were very weak and became even weaker when, during the campaign, PT candidate, Fernando Haddad, said to the press that Bishop Edir Macedo was a charlatan.

Politically, evangelical Christian neoconservatism is emerging strongly in Brazil, especially since 2002, with the idea that the traditional family is threatened and still recovering the anti-communist debate. The Evangelical Parliamentary Front (EPF) was created in 2003. Since then, and with PT governments, their influence and importance have grown. Valle (2018) explains that, although there were differences between PT and various evangelical groups, fundamentally Pentecostal and Neo-Pentecostal, the novelty already present in the 2014 presidential elections, which gains more strength in the municipal elections of 2016 and is consolidated in 2018, is the willingness of pastors to hold a speech of confrontation with the PT within the churches. In his research on the Assembly of God Ministry of Belem in Campo Limpo, São Paulo, Valle states that from 2014, the verbalization of anti-petism within the church starts to be vehement mainly using the debates on family related to LGBT policies happening with PT governments and corruption. Not only did he perceive this change among Christian leaders but also among the people attending those churches, including those who had voted for PT, among whom he observed a change in the political trajectory with a progressive disappointment with the Dilma government, fundamentally because of the economic deterioration, the centrality of the anti-corruption discourse, and the rhetoric of valuing the family and Christian ethics. On April 6, 2016, the EPF declared its support for the impeachment of Dilma Rousseff. Of the 81 congressmen who make up the EPF, also known as the Evangelical Bench, 75 voted in favor of the admissibility of impeachment. Knowing that PT would lose impeachment, evangelical leaders were preparing themselves and their bases for a new conservative government with more space for religious influence.

According to the information from the Interunion Parliamentary Advisory Department (Diap), based on data available on the website of the Supreme Electoral Court, in 2014, there were 75 federal deputies who followed the evangelical Christian doctrine, grouped into 18 parties. In 2018, 84 federal deputies were elected, identified with the evangelical Christian belief. The criminalization of abortion is one of the most representative bills of their agenda. They are strongly against the approval of bills such as PL 122/2006 (Anti-Homophobia Law), or PL 612/211 that allows the legal recognition of same-sex marriages.

> I vote for Bolsonaro because he defends our families; he's on the religious side. The PT wanted to make our kids gay, was going to release the prisoners, and children could choose in the birth certificate if they want to be boys or girls. PT would destroy families. They don't respect religion. They even had that gay bible thing. Good thing Bolsonaro won. All these people think about is sex, prostitution, orgies... Bolsonaro took an attitude, had courage...We are in a battle God against the demons. This time God won.
>
> *Interview 11*

Among Bolsonaro supporters, the role of religion as a regulator of social life is essential. One of the main causes for which we are in this crisis of values is the abandonment of religious ethical principles. The return of religiosity as a moral vector of society is fundamental, even the religious education in public schools is highly valued. Not only was the support of the evangelical leaders crucial for Bolsonaro election, but he also knew how to explore electorally religious narratives to deeply connect with evangelical Christian public. The main subtext of the moral content of Bolsonaro's campaign was that PT and the left were against religious values and only he would stand up for religion as the source of ethics that must guide private and public lives. This strategy of moralization and Christianization of politics matches very well with the Car Wash idea of a corrupted and "dirty" State:

> What we have today is a total crisis of values. Everything's backwards. It's all wrong. Television teaching you how to be gay. Kids don't have the values we had... You should have religious education in schools, yes, to learn ethics, to know what is right and what is wrong.
>
> *Interview 2*

In parallel to religion, the militaristic ground is also highly valued by Bolsonaro supporters. This ethical and moral chaos is also due to the lack of discipline, lack of authority, and lack of respect and hierarchy. Order is one of the most repeated words in my interviews. The left is responsible for this situation of disorder, chaos, and confusion, which can only be overcome by retaking military values as the foundation of social life.

> The kids don't care about anything now. We used to be raised with discipline at home and at school. It was "yes, sir," it was respect, it was authority. I am in favour of military school, yes, singing the anthem, the flag, because we have to teach children to have responsibility, discipline, if not is a mess.
>
> *Interview 16*

According to Datafolha, in 2018, seven out of ten Brazilians (68%) declared they had no confidence in political parties, 67% declared they had no confidence in the National Congress (the highest index in the historical series), and 64% in the Presidency of the Republic. In contrast, the Armed Forces were evaluated as the most reliable institution in Brazil for the majority of the population. Seventy-eight percent said that they trusted them.[2] In parallel to the anti-partisanship discourse and the rejection of the traditional way of doing politics, the Armed Forces gain credibility in the Brazilian public space.

Bolsonaro and his Vice President, General Hamilton Mourão, raise the presence of the military in public life in Brazil to historic highs during the democratic era. People for the Armed Forces have nine Ministries, some of them very important as the Government Secretary (General Carlos Alberto dos

Santos Cruz), General Presidency Secretary (General Floriano Peixoto Vieira), or Institutional Security Cabinet (General Augusto Heleno). In addition to this military presence in government, Bolsonaro's militaristic rhetoric has been present throughout the whole campaign. The only effective implementation of his electoral program on public security has been three changes: making it easier to carry weapons; reducing the age of criminal majority from 18 to 16 years; and changing the rules of engagement to be more tolerant of the use of lethal force by police.

While discussing the centrality of militarism to Bolsonaro's administration, we must remember the militarization of the National Congress. As discussed earlier, evangelical Christian politicians are organized in Brazil around the EPF, popularly known as the Bible Group. In public safety sector, we have the same format. Ex-military, police, and firefighters are part of the Parliamentary Front for Public Security, known as the Bullet Group with a punitive security ideology with the support of the arms industry, such as the company Taurus and the Brazilian Cartridge Company (CBC). According to the survey of the Congress in Focus, in 2019, this Bullet Group went from 36 national congressmen to 102, with 93 congressmen and 18 senators (had none in 2014) being most of them members of the Liberal Social Party, Bolsonaro's party.

Bolsonaro in Government: Where Is the Left?

In the first year of his Presidency, three sets of measures stood out in the new government: (1) those with a neoliberal profile, such as the reform of the social pensions system that attacks the most impoverished, the flexibility of labor laws, the end of legislation against labor in conditions analogous to slavery, the flexibility of controls against child labor; (2) the anti-environmental measures, with the release of 239 new pesticides, the attempt to abandon the Paris Agreement and the decree that gives the power of delimitation of indigenous lands to the Ministry of Agriculture dominated by the landowners; (3) direct attacks on public education, with a 30% budget reduction for federal universities and inquisitorial rhetoric and persecution of professors and activities critical to the government. In parallel, Bolsonaro follows the Trumpist model of government communication via Twitter by attacking the press repeatedly. In the same way, the rhetoric of the enemy and the warlike and reactionary tone against the opposition and progressive sectors remains the same as during the electoral campaign.

Until now, the difficulties the Bolsonaro government has faced in implementing its policy prescriptions are fundamentally due to the structure of Brasilia itself. Brazilian political architecture is based on coalition presidentialism. The president invariably needs to have a solid allied base in Congress. Dilma Rousseff lost it and ended up in impeachment. But the powerful machine of the Brazilian Congress is not for beginners. There are 513 deputies from 30 different parties, the largest number of parties since the Brazilian re-democratization. Instead of building his political base, Bolsonaro devoted himself to attack the old politics, trying to impose his agenda in an undiplomatic way and not respecting the Congress. He has thus earned many enemies. This political impotence has meant that the current control of Brasilia is much more in the hands of the President of the Chamber of Deputies, Rodrigo Maia, than in Bolsonaro's. Likewise, the new President accumulates negative editorials from even the country's most conservative newspapers, such as Estado de São Paulo and Veja magazine, which supported him during the electoral campaign and are widely known for their strong anti-PT positions. According to a survey published in early April 2019 by the Datafolha Institute, 30% of Brazilians consider their government bad, an increase of 8% over the previous survey published in February. This also represents the highest disapproval rating for any President after the first 100 days in office since re-democratization in 1985. For context, Lula had a disapproval rating of only 10% at this point in his Presidency.

As for the opposition in the streets, the situation is more ambiguous. The education sector has so far been the only one capable of staging huge anti-Bolsonarist demonstrations in defense of public, free and quality higher education. However, questions such as unemployment, the injustices of the pensions' reform, and the precariousness of work or unemployment do not succeed in mobilizing Brazilian citizens who feel defrauded by the unions. The political opposition doesn't have an easy life either. On the one hand, Fernando Haddad (PT) got 44.87% of the votes and with 56 deputies PT has the largest parliamentary group in Congress. In addition, PT continues to be hegemonic in the northeast, where, for example, in the first round, Rui Costa won the government of the very important State of Bahia. At the same time, however, the Workers' Party has also lost much of its capacity for mobilization and anti-petism continues to be very powerful, fundamentally among sectors of the traditional white middle class in the South and Southeast of Brazil. For these groups, anti-petism is based on a strong class feeling against PT public policies for the poorest. According to Datafolha statistics, Bolsonaro obtained up to 75% of the votes in Brazilian municipalities with medium and high incomes, but did not reach 25% in the poorest localities. Likewise, PT has also lost votes among the new middle classes, benefited by these same policies, but which now adopt the imaginary and subjectivity of the traditional middle class by adopting meritocratic and anti-petism discourses. But perhaps the major drama of PT is due to the loss of votes among the most popular sectors, in this case heavily influenced by the Pentecostal and Neo-Pentecostal churches, whose anti-petism is built on their conservative arguments for the protection of family and faith.

In order to address these problems, several sectors within PT affirm that the Workers' Party should go through a whole new foundation: returning to the poor peripheries abandoned when PT came to power, and renewing his program and his communication in a Brazil that is no longer the same as the one that led Lula to the Presidency in 2002. But how to build the post-Lulism when

Lula is imprisoned in Curitiba, presenting himself as a victim of a politicized judicial process and both the present and future of the PT?

What is certain is that, until now, the stronger political alternative to the Bolsonaro government is being built around the idea of some kind of center-right policy, with a totally neoliberal perspective, which is also presented as "new policy," "technical," "neither right nor left" but which, unlike Bolsonaro, is more sophisticated as both a political and ideological force. This movement is built by and around politicians with higher education and good international relations, who avoid the hard edges of moralism and cultural conservativism as well as reactionary rhetoric. João Doria, businessman and current governor of São Paulo for the PSDB (the traditional center-right party) and very likely candidate in the next elections in 2022, represents this possibility. In other words, the long-term continuity of neoliberal policies (the politics of no alternative seen around the world since especially the 1990s) does not seem to be at risk.

Conclusion

The victory of Jair Bolsonaro in 2018 is figured as an unparalleled event in Brazilian politics that was already going through very critical moments fundamentally since the impeachment process of President Dilma Rousseff and the arrest of former President Lula. His victory was a great perplexity for a large part of the political class, academia, and progressive social groups that refused to accept the categorical fact that Brazil had chosen as president a representative of the extreme right after 14 years of PT governments. This chapter is an attempt to overcome this perplexity and understand Bolsonarism as a phenomenon with profound implications for Brazilian social life, describing the elements that characterize Bolsonarism, some of them with deep and historical roots in Brazilian society such as religiosity and others more recent as anti-PT rhetoric.

This should also serve as a wake-up call so that, from the academic sectors, we have the sensitivity and intellectual perspicacity to study those dynamics or political personalities that represent the absolute opposition of liberal democratic ideals. Groups, leaders, and movements of the right and extreme right, especially when they show themselves as principled opponents of liberal democracy, must be well studied. We must move from our intellectual comfort zone to understand the profound dynamics that on various occasions place our democracy at risk.

Notes

1 Quantitative research with 571 demonstrators. Complete results, https://brasil.elpais.com/brasil/2015/04/14/politica/1429037495_877092.html Date of last consultation 27-08-2019
2 Complete data available at https://datafolha.folha.uol.com.br/opiniaopublica/2018/06/1971972-partidos-congresso-e-presidencia-sao-instituicoes-menos-confiaveis-do-pais.shtml Date of last consultation 01-12-2018

Bibliography

Almeida, Ronaldo. 2017. "A onda quebrada – evangélicos e conservadorismo." *Cadernos Pagu* 50: 15–38.

Azevedo, Reinaldo. 2008. *The Country of the Little Shrimps*. Rio de Janeiro: Record.

Brown, Wendy. 2006. "American Nightmare: Neoliberalism, Neoconservatism, and Democratization." *Political Theory* 34(6): 690–714.

Casara, Rubens. 2018. *Em tempos de pós-democracia*. Rio de Janeiro: Tirant Brasil.

Castel, Robert. 2005 *Social Insecurity: What Is to Be Protected?* Petrópolis: Voices.

Crouch, Colin. 2004. *Post-democracy*. London: Polity.

Fraser, Nany. 2017. "What Is Progressive Neoliberalism? A Debate." *Dissent* 64(2): 130–40.

Hunter, James. 1991. *Culture Wars: The Struggle to Control the Family, Art, Education, Law, and Politics in America*. New York, NY: Basic Books.

Laval, Chirtian, and Pierre Dardot. 2016. *The New Reason of the World. Essay on Neoliberal Society*. São Paulo: Boitempo.

Mbembe, Achille. 2014. *Critique of Dark Reason*. Lisbon: Antígona.

Mbembe, Achille. 2017. *Políticas da inimizade*. Lisbon: Antigona.

Pierucci, Antono Flavio. 2011. "Election 2010: Electoral Demoralisation of Religious Moralism." *New Studies CEBRAP* 89, 111–27.

Rabbit, Roberto. 2013. *By a Thread: The Suffering of the Worker in the Era of Flexible Capitalism*. Jundiaí: Paco Editorial.

Solano, Esther. 2019. "A bolsonarização do Brasil." In *Democracia em risco? 22 ensaios sobre o Brasil hoje*, edited by Sergio Abranches, et al., 307–22. São Paulo: Companhia das Letras.

Telles, Mara. 2017. "Corruption, Democratic Legitimacy and Protests: The Right's Boom in National Politics?" *National Interest* 30: 97–126.

Valle, Vinicius. 2018. Religion, Lulism and Vow: The Political Action of an Assembly of God and Its Faithful in São Paulo 2014–2016. Final thesis work, Federal University of São Paulo.

PART III

Epilogue

Persevering through a Crisis of Conviction

15

POPULISM AND DEMOCRACY

A Long View[1]

Craig Calhoun

Introduction

'Populism' is often a derogatory label for anti-democratic but popular leaders, and for popular voices raised in anger and resentment to condemn elites and politics as usual. But populism is not, in general, an attack on democracy.

First, populism expresses one core dimension of democracy, the will of the people. This can be positive, demanding attention to important issues and potentially expanding political inclusion. But populists purport to speak not just *for* but *as* 'the people,' unmediated and whole. Others may point out that the populists of the moment are not even a majority, let alone the whole of the people. The populist response is often just that the other people have not yet awakened to how they are threatened. Or, populists may say, those others are not part of the 'real' people. They are elites, or immigrants, or minorities, or deviants, or even enemies of the people. The claim to express a Rousseauian 'general will' is typically tendentious.

Second, populism predates democracy. It flourishes in non-democratic societies so long as there is some notion of popular political membership and the idea that political legitimacy might derive at least ultimately from the will or well-being of the people. It can be a demand for more democracy.

Third, claiming to speak directly for the people, populists challenge liberal and republican constitutional provisions. These are intended to achieve greater justice, e.g. by ensuring wide political representation and protecting minorities; to minimize corruption by promoting civic virtue and punishing self-dealing; and to stabilize democracy by ensuring that reflection has a chance to override transitory passions and that winners and losers work together after contentious elections. But the liberal and republican provisions produce a representative rather than direct democracy and a mixed government in which laws, courts, and legislative processes check and limit immediate expressions of popular (or executive) will. They give disproportionate influence to educated elites and professionals from lawyers and judges to journalists and scientists. On republican principles, these may govern or shape policy on behalf of the whole society. But they add to the frustration of populists when they feel that they are being ignored or even denigrated by elites.

Populism Has a Long History

Many ancient Greek political philosophers thought that all democracy tended toward populism. For this reason, they distrusted it. They thought it would be unstable, driven by resentment and other passions, and vulnerable to demagogues who could transform it into mob rule and then make that a short path to tyranny. Plato took it as exemplary that that the citizens of Athens compelled the death of Socrates precisely when they were organized as a democracy.

Greek thinkers typically saw all government as likely to cycle through phases of monarchy, aristocracy, and democracy—or worse, their degenerate forms of tyranny, oligarchy, and anarchy or mob rule. But democracy in their eyes was the least stable and most dangerous form of government.[2] Plato, especially, bequeathed this anxiety about democracy to the ensuring centuries of political thought.

While surely not an advocate for unalloyed democracy as practiced in his time, Aristotle saw a greater place for the expression of popular will, or at least recognition of popular grievances against elite monopolization of power and economic resources. He therefore recommended a form of political rule that came to be at the center of the republican tradition: mixed government. This is an attempt to stabilize politics by balancing elements from each of monarchy, aristocracy, and democracy in a virtuous polity. Jill Frank (2005) describes the result as a "democracy of distinction." Crucially, it is only partly democracy.

The Roman Republic gave proof that this project could work. It achieved considerable stability with a mixed constitution that gave all citizens the right to participate in electoral decisions, but unequally. Aristocrats had more votes and dominated the Senate and the actual work of government. A faction of Populares represented plebeians—commoners—including many farmers. A rational for this hierarchy was that plebeian citizens were thought less able to prioritize public over private interests and cultivate civic virtue. More complete exclusions affected non-citizens including women and slaves). But there were also 'tribunes of the people' to limit the power of the aristocratic Senate and magistrates. This arrangement did not resolve conflict between the different 'orders' of citizens, but for 400 years, it tamed it.

The Republic ended in the wake amid civil wars and intrigues. A populist leader, the victorious general Julius Caesar, attempted to seize power, becoming in effect the first Emperor. He was assassinated by rivals with a range of motives, but in the name of defending of the Republic, leaving posterity with an enduring moral drama. The Republic had become corrupt, chaotic, and disorganized. But writing in self-imposed exile, the aristocratic former consul and philosopher Cicero gave enduring articulation to republican ideals even as the Republic died.

Empire and monarchy (including the peculiar combination of imperial and monarchical elements in the Catholic Church) dominated Western European political structures through the middle ages. The republican tradition lived on only in urban enclaves. At larger scale, there was no attempt to organize public affairs through citizenship. Memories of local rather than distant kings and in some places 'tribal' notions of self-government were kept alive and later could inform Romantic nationalism as well as populist calls for voice and self-rule. But most people were simply subjects, with no voice in larger polities, with limited autonomy to self-organize at very local levels.

Feudal hierarchy was imposed with different degrees of severity. There was more freedom in Western Europe than the institutions of serfdom allowed in the East. Ethnic and regional solidarities underpinned opposition to consolidation of monarchical rule – as for example Anglo-Saxon England resented the 'Yoke' of Norman domination. Thus King Arthur mythically ruled with his Knights of the Round Table not simply over them. The Lords who got King John to sign the Magna Carta in 1215 secured protections and liberties for themselves and for the Chuch – and at least in principle greater rule of law - but nothing like a republican government. Outside cities, neither citizenship nor a notion of public was prominent.

Common people might attempt to avoid military service, resist specific impositions of power, or even on occasion rebel. They wanted to be treated in ways they considered right. But they did not claim inclusion in a political public because there was none. In that significant sense, they were not populiats. Not only rulers but people throughout the social hierarchy understood political authority to be a matter of divine right, legitimate inheritance, or sometimes conquest - not popular will or well-being. This changed in the early modern period.

As some Italian city-states grew wealthy from banking and trade, their elites renewed the old Roman struggle between central power and republican citizenship. The Florentine Republic, for example, was dominated by aristocratic families joined together by a strong ethos of mutual restraint and a normative order forbidding corruption—on pain of death!—and demanding that all officeholders be clearly committed to the public good over private interest. The Republic thrived on the basis of trade and banking and Florence grew into a major center of art, literature, and learning—the Italian Renaissance. However, the richest Florentine banking family, the Medicis, made their wealth the basis for enough political power to supplant the Republic (and indeed to engage in politics beyond the city, even eventually securing control of the papacy). This establishment of something close to monarchy was a defeat for republican ideals of government by citizens. But it should not be thought that the Florentine Republic was a democracy, since only some 3,000 of Florence's perhaps 50,000 residents were entitled to vote.

Corruption and inequality brought a populist sense of grievance among those who lived in the city but were not granted much say in its governance. Simultaneously, Florence was threatened by an invading army under Charles VII of France.

In this context of domestic and external threats, the Dominican Friar Girolamo Savonarola became perhaps the first modern populist leader. His followers expelled the Medicis and established a 'popular' republic. This relied on election to popular office with an expanded proportion of Florentines able to participate, notably, artisans, who had previously been excluded, were enfranchised. At the same time, Savonarola was always prepared to call his followers into the streets and bolstered by this extra-institutional pressure. He could be dictatorial and expect acclamation rather than debate from elections. Promising essentially to Make Florence Great Again —"richer, more powerful, more glorious than ever"—he launched a puritanical campaign against the decadence of both elite secular society and the Church (Weinstein 2011). Processions through the city culminated in "bonfires of the vanities" burning books, paintings, fashionable clothes, and even cosmetics. This brought down the wrath of the rich and of the Church. Savonarola was excommunicated and in due course executed. The Medicis regained power.

The travails of early modern Florence are especially prominent in political thought because they were the context and focus for the work of Niccolò Machiavelli, the first modern political theorist.[3] His enormously influential work is subject to numerous competing interpretations, not least because he explored both the potential to adapt and renew Roman Republicanism to make a virtuous polity and the best strategy for a leader whose concerns were with power not virtue—or, to follow Pocock (2016), with stabilizing rather than reforming the polity. Machiavelli served both the Florentine Republic and the Medicis, and wrote his most famous book, *The Prince*, hoping to gain a more prominent position with the Medicis. Neither a democrat nor a populist, he was nonetheless in agreement with much of Savonarola's program, including replacing hereditary government with elections, expanding political participation in the Republic, and trying to curb corruption. But he saw politics under the priest as rooted too much in passion and too little in reason. This made him dependent on crowds. He "was ruined with his new order of things immediately the multitude believed in him no longer" (Machiavelli 2015, Book VI). Crucially, Savonarola lacked the capacity to stabilize the polity and secure its defense from external threats, both of which were necessary to enjoying the benefits of a reformed republic.

In the background to the drama of Machiavelli's Florence was the disunity of fragmented Italy and its weakness before foreign invaders. Venice and Genoa were maritime powers, and trade linked the Renaissance city-states throughout the Mediterranean and on to Asia, the European North, and impressively much of the world. Contact with Arab civilization helped spark the intellectual Renaissance, both because they had preserved Greek thought that Europeans had lost and because of their own innovations. Trade helped the Italian city-states grow rich and this wealth supported art and architecture. For all the homages done to Greek and Roman antiquity, writing in Italian grew more prominent, not least in the work of Machiavelli himself. But there was no Italian state and little political coordination. The republican model worked at the level of cities not countries. The Church maintained a huge political role in Italy, even as its grip declined in Northern Europe. But the Pope was not able to defend himself, let alone Italy. Corruption in the Church made it less effective in worldly power struggles, ironically, even while the attention of many in the church hierarchy came to be more focused on material ends and less on God. Martin Luther's critique of corruption in the Church came a mere 20 years after Savonarola. He nailed his 95 theses to the door of Wittenburg castle church in 1517 (at least according to legend).

The ensuing Protestant Reformation and related wars of religion helped to make the modern European states and nations. Reading the Bible promoted literacy in vernacular languages. Citizen armies encouraged identification among 'the people' of countries in a way mercenary armies couldn't (as indeed Machiavelli himself noted in *The Prince*). Efforts to administer religion proceeded alongside administration of trade and taxation and the marshaling of resources for war. Northern Europe grew richer and the cultural life of its cities flourished ina. Continuation of the Renaissance. But countries remained kingdoms even as they also became far-flung empires. This combined trade and resource extraction with a new theater for competition among European states and missions to save souls. The story vastly exceeds our current scope, but two conclusions are crucial.

First, the scale of political and social integration was transformed. As the modern state was consolidated, the modern 'nation' appeared as the corresponding embodiment of 'the people.' States were not the whole story, of course, as economies and cultures were increasingly organized in national structures.

Second, the place of individual choice in social participation was transformed. From the spread of literacy and increasing education to wider social mobility to religious emphasis on personal salvation to the rise of entrepreneurship, on the one hand, and a consumer society, on the other hand, a much wider range of people claimed distinctive individual identities and the right to make choices based on them.

Which came first, nation or state, was and is a moot point. There was a prior history to what became modern national identities. An 'ascending' view of political authority had ancient roots in the 'folkmoot' and other pre-feudal assemblies and these had spokespeople to claim them (and eventually poets and composers to celebrate them).[4] This combination of history and myth was complemented by new cultural production shaping the European nations (as eventually others). But throughout Europe, political thinkers also laid claim to "the glory that was Greece and the grandeur that was Rome" and to the republican tradition of citizen government.[5] Modern democratic politics is shaped by both the solidarity of nations (and perceived threats to it) and formal constitutions and institutions with their rights and procedures. Ideally complementary, these are sometimes in tension. Partly because of its emphasis on individuals, liberalism is closely identified with formal institutions. Populism more often articulates the solidarity of nations.

In 17th-century England, the contest between monarchy and aristocracy was replayed in a Civil War. Religious struggles were part and parcel of politics and vice versa. Cromwell arguably played the part of Savonarola, though the analogy is imperfect. But Cromwell's New Model Army was in part a populist representation of The People. Arguably, the people were more often off-stage in the Civil War drama, with different more elite political figures either threatening to call them in or denouncing this possibility (see Morgan 1989). But in addition to the populist elements in mainstream Parliamentarianism, there were Levelers and Diggers and others who proclaimed the rights and needs of the people (Hill 1984). And there was what J.G.A. Pocock has called 'the Machiavellian moment' (Pocock 2016). This is the point at which promotion of a new and better republican constitution, including one open to more of 'the people,' confronts the need for institutional capacity to achieve stability and security. But this is also a moment of risk that capacity for leadership can bring a shift from democracy to dictatorship. Caesar's story informed the widespread notion that democracy would be but a waystation on the path to tyranny.

Democracy still remained a radical idea in the late 18th century, when the founders of the US enshrined democracy in its Constitution. Overall, the text is more indebted to republicanism, but it does begin with the very populist invocation of 'We the People.' Democratic demands from below had long been growing, but this was the first large-scale acceptance of democracy by an educated, propertied, elite.

Many among the founders were strong republicans and reluctant democrats. Some, like John Adams, were close readers of Machiavelli. Particularly in the South, desires for limits on direct popular action were strong. In an abundance of caution, the US founders restricted the vote to free men with property. Slaves, women, and most of the working classes were initially excluded. They protected the rule of law with a strong judiciary, including judges with lifetime appointments. They gave Senators longer terms than other congressional representatives seeking to establish a reflective elite more able to take a long-term view. Not least, they almost immediately amended the Constitution with a Bill of Rights protecting pluralism, minorities, and public action outside government control. In addition to stability, they sought security, both for property and in relation to external threats. Though much of this comes from the republican tradition rather than liberalism per se, it is more or less what is meant today by liberal democracy.

Still, even if anxious, the founders' embrace of democracy was remarkable. They called for much more popular participation in and guidance of government than any other country allowed at the time. They also set in motion an uneven but ongoing deepening of democracy that gradually reduced restrictions on popular participation. This didn't happen smoothly. It took waves of popular agitation and social movements, including not least recurrent populism. Indeed, some say that the US really became a democracy only with the Andrew Jackson's populist presidential election in 1828.[6] For the first time, a majority of white men had the chance to vote.[7] Jackson had enormous personal appeal, not least as a general victorious against both the British and the native Americans with whom the US shared the continent. He rode a wave of populism rooted in the greater inclusion of ordinary citizens as voters.[8] His famously rowdy presidential campaigns helped make politics a spectator sport. They were framed both as appeals to the common man and as criticisms of a corrupt aristocracy. He charged, in essence, both that there wasn't enough democracy and that existing democracy had degenerated.

Like many populists, Jackson played to one image of the people, implying that this was the only possible one. Famous for his war exploits against the Indian tribes of the interior South, once in office, Jackson signed the Indian Removal Act of 1830. And though he personally worried about the growing tensions over slavery, he presided over growing political polarization, especially over slavery. He remained active after leaving the presidency and supported bringing Texas into the Union as a slave state—a move that increased tensions. As often happens, agents of inclusion on one dimension are voices for exclusion on others.

The French Revolution followed the US one in short order and was significantly more radical in its embrace of the equality of citizens. But though it produced the powerful democratic slogan, *liberté, égalité, fraterité*, it did not prove stable. It contained its own drama of elite republican reformers pressed to play to the emergent political force of The People—sometimes with democracy and sometimes with violence.

Both liberal and conservative political traditions derive in part from observing that it did not adequately protect liberty. The conservative tradition also emphasizes the extent to which the French Revolution failed to protect fraternity, that is the solidarity of citizens, especially in families and communities. Radical and socialist traditions join conservatives in asserting the importance of solidarity and criticizing liberals for allowing versions of liberty to be corrosive of social cohesion. Of course, socialists and conservatives have different ideas about how to secure solidarity and especially how it relates to economic life. Socialists, conservatives, and liberals differ on the virtue of equality.

From both the mostly positive US example and the degeneration of the French Revolution into terror, the most successful builders of modern democracies drew the conclusion that democracy should be only part of a democratic constitution, not the whole. In any case, many argued, in a large-scale and complex society, government would necessarily be carried out by formal organizations led by an elite, not a matter for direct participation of all the people. The main democratic process was choosing the elite, not running the government. Democracy would be representative, not direct, and it would require stable institutions not constant mass mobilization. But it was also a democratic process to protest when elites failed to act in the interests of all citizens.

The Present Wave

The present wave of populism comes after 50 years in which ruling elites tolerated and often personally benefitted from economic transformations that did not reflect popular will or serve to benefit ordinary people: rising financialization, globalization organized largely to benefit corporations and capital, abrupt deindustrialization. Of course, these transformations also brought gains—not least a variety of new technologies. But they left individual lives, families, and communities devastated. It was salt in the wound that the elites called this progress and called those who resisted or complained backward.

The dominant political elites of this whole period were more or less liberal. There were conflicts between political parties, but policy differences were muted. Ostensibly socialist or social democratic parties stopped seeking deep economic transformation. Conservatives were not reactionary opponents of democracy or the liberal order. Indeed, one of the staples of the period was reference to 'post-ideological' politics (see Berkowitz in this volume for a further discussion of this issue). All major parties embraced the basic project of liberal democracy, including pluralism and rule of law. All embraced the basic marriage of liberal democracy to capitalism. They differed mainly on how much they wanted to extend liberal rights in a project of pluralist inclusion— of women, minorities (including immigrants), and alternative lifestyles or personal identities.

The 'mainstream' parties of Western democracies were more committed to economic growth than to equality. They supported finance-led globalization, embracing the project of competitiveness even when it meant curtailing social spending and trying to limit unions. Most were influenced by neoliberalism, an ideology that proclaimed liberty to be rooted in private property and insisted that government efforts to use tax revenues to improve social conditions were an illegitimate intrusion on these private rights.[9] They were more attentive to the progress of wealth, as measured, for example, by stock market indices, than to the welfare of those whose lives were disrupted by the path of growing wealth—for example, workers who lost both their jobs and their communities to deindustrialization. They embraced the growing power of finance, the idea of free markets, including free trade, and globalization.

There were differences among parties on specific issues, and sometimes sharp conflicts. In the UK, for example, Thatcherite Tories were committed to destroying unions and Labour was not, though Labour didn't do much to reverse the slide in union strength. Labour didn't pursue privatization as Tories had done, though it didn't undo it either or regulate finance as much as it might have. Labour did improve benefits for senior citizens. Austerity was a distinctively conservative imposition. In the US, Republicans undermined government agencies more (though government budgets still grew). They more actively denigrated the idea of public action to serve public interests, but even Democrats were also usually closer to Wall Street than unions. Perhaps the biggest difference was in judicial appointments with litmus tests for issues like abortion rights. In neither country did either leading party attempt serious reversal of growing inequality. Nor did those in most other developed capitalist countries—though as Thomas Piketty (2014) has shown, France did limit inequality more than most and for a longer time.

Populism is largely a complaint against the conduct of government by these liberal elites. It is not just a grievance against inequality and the existence of elites. It centers on the charge that liberal elites were poor stewards of the overall collective good. It complains bitterly that the conventional governing classes of all major parties lived well while others suffered and spoke of progress, while others bore the costs of change. And crucially, say the populists, those elites didn't care about us, listen to us, or even recognize fully that we existed and had a legitimate stake in the country. Populist charges against established elites are often unfair. They underestimate pressures and limits and indeed accomplishments. But they are not entirely false.

Populism is typically angry, resentful, reactionary, and illiberal. It can be a problem *for* democracy, but this is not because it is inherently undemocratic. It is because immediate representation of (ostensible) popular will is at odds with institutional arrangements that stabilize democracy and secure greater justice. Such institutional arrangements produce the hybrid political form commonly labeled liberal democracy (though in fact they derive at least as much from republicanism as liberalism). Populists are almost essentially illiberal; they refuse to prioritize the liberties and rights of individuals or smaller groups over popular will and what they understand to unite the people. Their anger at elites is often based on the view that those elites have put minorities ahead of the majority, and that they have managed public affairs to secure their own benefit more than that of the real 'people' of a country.

Populist anger has many sources, from economic grievances to a sense of cultural insult. Claiming and inflaming this anger is the stock-in-trade of populist demagogues from Donald Trump to Marine Le Pen to Victor Orban—or their more Leftist counterparts. Rightwing versions of populism are dominant in the present era, but Leftwing populism has been important in Spain and Greece. It is present among supporters of Brexit and of France's Yellow Vests.[10] Indeed, populism is more of a political style than it is a political ideology. In itself, it is neither Leftwing nor Rightwing. But it can be harnessed to Left-Right politics and co-opted by more conventional political parties and agendas.

When Hungary's Orban named his populist regime 'illiberal democracy,' he was playing rhetorical games, but he was not all wrong.[11] His regime did command widespread popular support. But it not only represented largely a non-metropolitan Hungary against more cosmopolitan Budapest, it was deeply engaged in manipulating public opinion. It offered only a very thin version of democracy, the chance to offer the regime popular acclaim and plebiscitarian approval. To shout 'Hurrah' or 'Lock them up' when opponents are mentioned, or to vote merely 'Yes' or 'No,' is not to participate seriously in government, policy-making, or organizing life together.

Populists have many targets, from professional elites to immigrants to foreigners exerting undue influence over their nations. Politicians may pander to pre-existing senses of grievance or they may seek to persuade populists to adopt targets of their own alongside those with deeper roots among ordinary people. Specific grievances and resentments differ among countries. Indeed, populism is always so embedded in the specifics of different national contexts, time periods, and relationships to mainstream politics that there are serious limits to trying—as I do here—to discuss populism in general. Nonetheless, there are also common themes and there is an inverse potential error in discussing each instance of populist mobilization only inside a particular national story and set of symbolic references. Throughout modernity, populism has been shaped by shared patterns in international political economy, demographic transitions like urbanization and immigration, and ever more intensive networks of communication.

Very commonly, liberalism itself is among populists' targets, as well as specific liberal elites. The rights liberals defend can seem like special treatment for minorities. In the decades since the 1970s, liberals focused more on cultural inclusion than on economic welfare. Many liberals defended a disempowering economic order on the grounds that it had roots in private property rights. Too many embraced globalization uncritically, as though it derived simply from legal equality and sheer modernity. They looked the other way as finance-led reorganization of global capitalism benefitted investors more than workers and eroded place-based communities and whole regions through deindustrialization. And when financial crisis struck, they spent billions of dollars rescuing banks and other companies but not helping people who lost homes, savings, or jobs in the crisis.

Liberals may not have been the primary drivers of these disasters, but they were among beneficiaries as well as blinded by the hegemonic ideology of the day. Not surprisingly, this encouraged populist resentment. This is often expressed in unfortunate ways, like protesting against public health measures in the coronavirus pandemic. But the distrust of liberal messages about what is best for the public good has reasons.

It is easy to talk about 'liberal elites' who mismanaged democratic government. We can imagine we mean others: elected representatives, people richer and more influential than us. Perhaps these do bear more responsibility and deserve more blame. But it is important to realize that most of 'us'—that is to say, educated, mainly middle-class participants in the political public sphere—have been complicit. We have allowed our societies to grow more hierarchical—with universities in the lead. We used what resources we had to fight for our own positions in the hierarchies, while many of our fellow citizens found their opportunities much more severely blocked. We have embraced the attractively 'cosmopolitan' side of globalization and paid less attention to the domination of financial capitalism. Indeed, we embraced a certain cosmopolitan style and attitude that made it harder for us even to see what was going on in the damaged communities of those whose style was not so sleek or educated or globally cultured or dignified.

As members of this privileged class, we were at ease talking about progress and feeling confident in it. This was reinforced when we saw things getting better in many ways. Partly, looking close to home, we saw an improvement in our living standards. We grew more likely to own houses; cars grew fancier; we enjoyed a rush of new consumer technologies (though sometimes we might be uncomfortable to realize how much all of this was based on debt). We lived mostly in places where we were not confronted directly by the downsides of either deindustrialization or globalization. But at least as basically, we focused on those gains that could be achieved without limiting economic growth or challenging the extent to which it was organized to advance wealth accumulation. Specifics, of course, varied with national context, but there were major and important gains in equality of opportunity on lines of gender, race, sexual orientation, differential ability, and other dimensions. These co-existed, however, with dramatic increases in overall inequality. We let returns on invested assets define national prosperity more than earned incomes and standards of living.

Educated professionals may not have been the cause of the inequality, damaged communities, and other downsides to the era of neoliberal globalization. Many of us were at least sympathetic to Left populist critiques such as that of the Occupy movements, if not active in pursuing structural change. So, we were shocked to find ourselves the face of the problem and focus of resentment for Rightwing populists. But when there is support for upper-class politicians who say "we have had enough of experts" who else is being targeted?

If experts really deserve their status and salary, critics suggest, they should have seen the mess their fellow citizens were in and fixed it. This is a disingenuous charge coming from someone like Michael Gove, an Oxford-educated

Conservative Minister and author, who declared during the Brexit campaign that "people in this country have had enough of experts."[12] But it is a charge that resonates with many less elite citizens who sense that the educated professional class looks down on the mostly non-metropolitan kinds of citizens drawn to populism.[13] Centrally, populists complain that elites—including experts—do not value and pay attention to the opinions of ordinary citizens—though this would be democratic.

Accelerating inequality is one of the causes of populism, though this does not mean that all populists see equality as the solution. While populists on the Left are commonly egalitarian, those more on the Right often see the issue not as inequality, but as who gets the good positions in an unequal system. They complain that liberals and experts have been behind distributing more of opportunities (like elite university admissions) and more of benefits (like good jobs) to minorities, immigrants, and women. It has been hard for liberals to realize that what they regard as successes like more equal opportunity seem like affronts to those who believe that they have a prior right to the relevant opportunities. But mainstream liberals have not been consistently egalitarian. Many accepted radically unequal access to educational and other institutions, seeking to ensure only that the inequality did not derive from certain protected categories like race or gender. They saw this as a matter of merit, not money or privilege (and ignored the possibility of creating less hierarchical institutions). The liberal focus has typically been on fairness in allocating unequal opportunities, not on how much inequality there should be. Implictly, they have accepted that so long as 'merit' determines access, scarcity in quality provision is acceptable. In somewhat different national packages, they have allowed education and health to be treated as private rather than public goods.

Critics of minorities and immigrants commonly stress the burden on welfare systems. But at least as important to populists are perceived blocks on upward mobility. Immigrant and minority success stories do not alleviate the concern but exacerbate it. As those Arlie Hochschild interviewed for *Strangers in their Own Land* put it, it's like these new claimants are cutting in line, but that's who liberals support.[14]

Populism is not inherently an ideology of Left or Right. It is a rhetoric of complaint against elites and self-assertion of 'the people' that can be drawn more in one way or the other. "We are the 99%" is as populist a slogan as "We are the Real Americans." The former is more centrally a critique of the power of wealth; the latter is obviously more explicitly national, and thus more easily linked to racism and hostility to immigrants. But both are claims to the importance and solidarity of The People. Populist movements are generally not composed of veteran politicians or policy wonks. They tend to be stronger on complaints than concrete policy proposals. They may develop more of these from within if they become well-organized enough and last long enough. The Farmers Alliance did in the late 19th-century US.[15] More commonly, political parties and ideologues with more resources try to harness populists to their causes. And a weakness of populist movements is the frequency with which they are claimed and mobilized, and manipulated by demagogues. Indeed, being motivated in part by the sense of being ignored or denigrated by one set of elites, populists are all too vulnerable to other elites who flatter them with attention—from Peron to Trump.

The Ambiguous People

Populism is not a precise analytic concept. It is a political term that is used as an accusation as often as it is claimed by ostensible populists. Sometimes, people say "I'm a populist. I speak for the people. I speak in the name of the people." But more often the label 'populist' is applied to those seen as violating the norms of conventional liberal democracy. It is applied to people held to be emotional rather than rational. It is a charge of having failed to appreciate complexity. The accusation of "populist" is likely to be made by those who believe in the knowledge of experts and seek a reasoned, rational debate on policy questions. These are hallmarks of liberal and republican thoughts added to democracy to improve it. But they do privilege some modes of participation in politics, and not the most popular.[16]

The moral standing of The People remains important. It is, however, more complicated than often acknowledged. Is there *a* singular people? Do we mean *some* people? *Most* of the people? What is the representation of the people that is involved? Often, appeals to The People are in truth appeals in the name of *all* the people against *some* of the people. But there are other moral claims. The native-born may claim to be the real people against immigrants. Youth may claim to be the morally significant people because they will live the future—and, say, face the potential devastations of climate change. The elites who are betraying the rest of the people, or those standing in the way of necessary action are seen to be legitimately excluded from the salient sense of The People.

In this reliance on 'we the people,' populism is often closely related to nationalism. Though populism and nationalism overlap, each appears in many forms and attached to many different ideologies. They overlap but are not identical. Nationalism shapes diplomatic relations and trade conflicts that are in no sense populist. Populist rhetoric informs local appeals against central states. Throughout the modern era, however, nationalism has been the primary rhetoric for appeals to citizen solidarity and rights at the scale of states—which are not surprisingly often described as nation-states. This can be as readily the basis for domestic projects, like providing early childhood or old-age benefits to a whole nation without discrimination, as for international rivalry or conflict. Demagogues too often find it easy to link nationalist and populist domestic solidarities to international enmities—mobilized against other countries or against immigrants. Nationalism is sometimes bellicose, and populist resentments can exacerbate this. Frustratingly, for those who would like good and bad dimensions of social life to remain more neatly separate, domestic solidarity may be enhanced by mobilization for war.

Populist politics are likewise rooted in an appeal not just to the people as a population but to the people as legitimate participants in a way of life.[17] The shared culture and social order makes a whole people rather than a series of individuals. It extends from families and local communities to the nation. It also reduces any potential sense of contradiction in excluding culturally or racially different fellow citizens from the category of the real people. There is a special pathos to this point today as many aggrieved citizens imagine the disappearance of people like them. From white nationalists to Evangelical Christians to True Finns, to Englishmen who fear the loss of Britain and those like the former Trump advisor Steve Bannon who see the eclipse of the West on the horizon, there is a widespread anxiety about the disappearance of ways of life—and populist identification of The People with these ways of life.

What populists seek to protect and advance cannot be reduced to either a particular set of people at one moment in time, or their material interests. Populists do have material grievances, of course, but populism is not merely a form of interest group politics. Indeed, populists typically reject interest group politics as little more than bargaining among elites. Its implicit logic of arithmetically counting the interests of individuals or responding only to organized power-groups downplays the politics of loyalties and values.

The oppositions of trade unions to business, urban to rural areas, young to old do have some predictive power in explaining who is more drawn to populist campaigns. Those organizing campaigns are realistic and know where to hold rallies and what symbols to invoke. But populist rhetoric tends to downplay these interest groupings. These imply legitimate divisions among the people, rather than populism's more typical distinction between the real people, as a whole, and others. They also imply a politics of compromises and diversity, which is not the populist style.

Contemporary populism is not just the national story of the US or France or Britain or Australia or Hungary or any other country. It is a shared story of this moment in globalization when there is a lot of pushback from people who feel that it is not working for them; when destabilizing socioeconomic change is causing fundamental problems. For both populists and nationalists, these problems put pressure on who 'we' are. They make 'us' ask: What is happening to our way of life? Will our children live in societies that are recognizably still the kind of societies that we know? Will they have opportunities and will they be prepared to seize them? When people think that maybe their children will be losing out, they tend to ask who is winning. In fact, a feature of populist politics is often a search for scapegoats or the people who are winning that should not be, or who are winning more than they should be. The scapegoat search is not a neutral analysis; it is largely constructed in first person terms. It is an effort to identify those who are getting ahead at 'my' expense or that of people like me. Material issues are entwined with cultural. It is misleading to ask whether the issues are mainly inequality or mainly the 'values' and 'identity' concerns of 'culture wars'. They are both at once, each exacerbating anxieties with roots in the other. It is not that poor people join populist campaigns because elites are rich. Many have been baffled by the enthusiasm for a billionaire like Donald Trump when people simultaneously complain about the injustice of inequality. For some this may be a cynical evaluation of what politician is most likely to address their issues. For many it is an expression of contempt for politics as usual. But it is also important to recognize that populists who do not like the professional classes may nonetheless respect rich people. They have something ordinary people want and perhaps can imagine having. It is harder to identify with those whose standing is based on education, professional attainment, and cultural polish.

Populists rhetorically appeal to The People—as though the referent is clear. But of course the mental image is culturally constructed, in processes that are not at all transparent. The People is never just a counting of votes, or an accurate representation of the various plural and differentiated groups in modern societies. The People becomes particularly important in contexts of polarization, where people live in somewhat different versions of the same country. There is a geography to it, as well as an element of social differentiation that makes it such that people do not just bump into people with different views. A common feature of the 2016 US Presidential election, the Brexit campaign, and others was the number of people who said: "I don't even know anyone who voted the other way." In the case of Brexit, there were a number of people in the North-East of Britain and certain generational and occupational groups who did not know anyone who was voting to stay in the European Union (EU). Conversely, there were a number of people in London who did not know anyone who was voting to leave the EU.

The same thing was true in the US, and it is important to reflect about why this happened. Thirty years ago, there was a viewership of a small number of television channels that would broadcast things like the evening news. People might have complained that it was all pretty much the same: ABC, NBC, and CBS showed the same news. The anchor person would have been different but equally centrist. What has happened over time is the decline of the audience for that kind of newscast and the rise of other kinds of much more differentiated channels so that different people could get different accounts of the news. This shapes what I have called "parallel media worlds." We live different versions of our countries, getting different news stories, even though we are still in the same nation. Geographical division has reinforced class, ethnic, political, and other views. The US has its blue and red states—and insulting terms like "flyover communities." In Britain, London became an even richer and more diverse global center, while much of the rest of the country—ex-industrial or ex-agricultural—declined. *La France profonde* is angry at Paris. Budapest is a cosmopolitan city resented by much of Hungary.

Steve Bannon, the former editor of the Rightwing website Breitbart and one-time senior advisor to President Trump, has been active in weaving an alternative narrative. This combines anxiety about the rise of China and America's declining global power with the notion of an end to Christian civilization and the argument that white people are threatened with 'substitution'. He says that the mainstream liberal press—the New York *Times* narrative of what it means to be an American—is deceitful. This is part of the Donald Trump story: "They are lying to you, here is the truth." The demagogues may pander to prejudices, instead of trying to give you a factual account, an account rooted in social science to possibly correct received opinions. They may play on them and build on them, promote a paranoid world view, or, what goes on most of the time, position real legitimate concerns and problems that people have in tendentious and not-so-realistic accounts of why they have those problems. In this context, populism is a sort of wake-up call, but it is not a program. One of the things we know in the case of Trump, Brexit, and other cases is that populists in power often do not have a full set of policies.

Populism is a politics of grievances, not of aspirations. It is about what has gone wrong, more than a program for what should go right. Yes, there is a program of America first, or Australia, or France… There may be a nationalist program in that sense. But not a detailed program. It is not a plan. To look for the plan that is going to lift people economically in populist politics is to misunderstand, to think that it is a set of policy proposals rather than this more emotional reflection of grievances. It is a defensive and often resentful response to the state of the world. Populist identity claims may have historical roots, but they also involve accentuating differences from denigrated others. Resentment is a problematic guide: it leads people to focus on what they do not have rather than what they do, or on past injustices and not ways forward.

Having a legitimate grievance does not necessarily give one a reasonable analysis or a sensible view of where to go. Donald Trump spoke to widespread anger about deindustrialization and job loss when he claimed to save an air conditioner factory in Indiana by talking to its owners and providing a federal subsidy. This was advertised as bringing jobs back from Mexico. But in fact the subsidy sustained the factory as it was automated. Machinery rather than globalization still put workers out of work. Transformation of labor markets in the world's richer economies did involve internationalization in search of lower-wage work, but also long, computer-managed supply chains not just the transplanting of individual factories. It was accompanied domestically by increased automation and a massive shift from industrial to service jobs. These were often less well-paid and less supported by unions. Crucially, they generally went to different people, not least women rather than men. In this transition, the interests of capital dominated over those of labor. There was too little retraining, too little support for stricken communities.

Manufacturing industry provided good jobs from the period of World War II to the 1970s when they began to erode, country after country. They were not all wonderful jobs, but relatively well paid, secure jobs. Deindustrialization could have been addressed as a high-priority problem in each country. Mitigating damages could have been at the top of policy agendas. The destruction of communities—and lives—could have been minimized, the coming of an opiate epidemic averted. Instead, elites focused more on the winners of the story: global investment bankers and traders and people with computer science degrees or shares in Google or Apple.

Populism reflects a collapse in trust— among ordinary people as well as in the government. Distrust among 'the people' is reflected in extremes of political polarization. But interpersonal trust has also declined. The coronavirus pandemic spurs gun-buying in the US because people do not trust their fellow-citizens.[18] And at the same time, trust in the government has fallen sharply in almost every advanced democracy. In the US, trust in government has fallen from approximately 60% to 20%, whereas in Norway, it has fallen from around 95% to 75% (Pew Research Center 2019). There are places where people trust the government more, but overall, there has been a widespread loss of trust (either due to corruption or lack of recognition). A key feature of this trend is the loss of trust and faith in conventional political parties. The political party system is in large part broken. It is not just that people think that one party is bad and the other is good; they don't think that any of them really speak to what they need and want. They think that the political parties are all full of people just seeking to benefit themselves or that they are representing other people, not them; or that they have made so many compromises that you cannot distinguish their stances. Multiparty parliamentary democracies work well when parties forge compromises, bring groups of people together, all of whom will get some of what they want and none of whom will get everything they want. In this way, they cooperate in order to achieve electoral majorities. This is becoming a less common feature of the party system. France offers an extreme example. Emmanuel Macron essentially ran as an independent against all parties. Whatever else his victory meant, it was very bad for the way French democracy had previously worked. Now, no established political party is responsible for working together to solve problems.

Conclusion

We, educated elites, spend too much of our time being angry at populists and not enough time being angry at the betrayal of the broad public interest by governing and economic elites in our societies. To address any of these issues would require us to rebuild social solidarity and to rebuild the cohesion of our societies. There is no addressing it by simply by making a new political announcement. It would take rebuilding the current political system from the ground up: having moral economies and (re-)introducing the idea that there can be moral and social values in the economy. There is no law of nature that says that the economy must be approached with no analytic metric besides profit and the accumulation of capital. Why can't it be approached by asking whether it creates jobs? Why can't it be approached by asking whether it creates good jobs for people? Why can't it be approached by asking whether the economy delivers on social and moral solidarity in society? Well, it can be; it just isn't most of the time or hasn't been approached this way in the past 40 years.

Though the scale and durability of modern democracy are new, the very word incorporates an old ambiguity. *Demos* is the Greek word for the people. But it can be used to refer to all the people—the way the framers of the US Constitution claimed to speak as 'We the People'—or it can be an elite reference to the lower classes, the ordinary people, the commoners who were not normally powerful and influential participants in government. Populism derives from the distance between the two usages. Populists seek to bridge the gap, to transform democracy run by elites into democracy run by all the people. In doing so, they often abandon the protections of pluralism, minorities, free expression, due process, and even rule of law that distinguish liberal democracy. But populists are not intrinsically anti-democratic. And waves of populism are commonly responses to genuine failures of the ruling elites to act with appropriate consideration for ordinary people, or indeed, to listen.

Notes

1 This text is based on the Thesis Eleven Lecture delivered by Craig Calhoun at La Trobe University, May 16, 2017. The lecture was transcribed by Simon Kastberg with revisions from Alonso Casanueva-Baptista and Raul Sanchez Urribarri. It has been revised to reflect the version which served as a keynote speech to the 25th International Congress of Europeanists, in Chicago, March 28, 2018.
2 See Ober (2008) for a wider view of democracy in Athens, showing limits to the views of the jaundiced philosophers. It needs to be stressed that even at its most democratic, Athens remained a slave society in which the large majority of residents—including women—were without political voice.
3 For this context, see Strathern (2016).
4 See Otto von Gierke's account of descending and ascending models of political authority in *Political Theories of the Middle Ages* (1987 [1900]).
5 Poe's poem that contain's the famous phrase, is itself testimony to the classicism that informed the cultural aspirations of 18th and 19th century Europe and North America.
6 For example, Samuel Huntington (1991) dates his account of the 'first wave' of modern democracy to Jackson's election in 1828.
7 Donald Trump has been vocal in his praise for Jackson. They are not similar in all ways, but it is noteworthy the extent to which Trump's base, like Jackson's, is animated by the idea that America should be white and traditional gender roles enforced. Jackson's brutality in displacing or killing Native Americans anticipated Trump's attempts to keep America white by blocking immigration and his use of a rhetoric of 'security' to support this.

8 The founding of the Democratic Party in 1828 was part of a shift from seeing parties as shifting factions and coalitions to seeing them more as enduring formal organizations. This reflected growing societal scale and complexity, and an early stage in the increasing professionalization and mediatization of politics that has continued into the present day. It did not stop shifts in party composition, appeal, and ideological orientation.

9 In the private sector, neoliberals insisted that projects of 'corporate social responsibility' were an illegitimate use of profits that should belong only to the owners of corporations. Other liberals argued for a broader recognition of legitimate stakeholders, including employees, suppliers and customers, and the communities in which businesses were located.

10 For a direct comparison of anti-system politics from both the left and the right across Western democracies, see Hopkin and Blyth in this volume.

11 Orban sometimes renders this "illiberal Christian democracy" (www.reuters. com/article/us-hungary-orban/hungarian-pm-sees-shift-to-illiberal-christian-democracy-in-2019-european-vote-idUSKBN1KI0BK). See Atanassow, Krastev, and Plattner in this volume for further elaboration of this issue.

12 H.Mance, "Britain has had enough of experts, says Gove," Financial Times, June 3, 2016. https://www.ft.com/content/3be49734-29cb-11e6-83e4-abc22d5d108c

13 This is a prominent observation of sympathetic studies; see Hochschild (2018).

14 Ibid.

15 See Lawrence Goodwyn (1976), a valuable corrective to many common views of populism.

16 See the Introduction to this volume for a further discussion of the term populism and infelicities surrounding its use in recent debates.

17 Here, there is an echo of Tocqueville's point that democracy is not simply a political system but a way of life (Tocqueville 2003 [1835/1840]). See Atanassow in this volume for a fuller articulation of a Tocquevillian response to recent illiberal movements.

18 This process did not start with the recent wave of populism, nor with the financial crisis, nor indeed with the 9/11 attacks. It reflects longer-term transformations in citizen experience and public communication (see Meyers 2008).

Bibliography

Frank, Jill. 2005. *A Democracy of Distinction: Aristotle and the Work of Politics*. Chicago, IL: University of Chicago Press.

Gierke, Otto von. 1987 [1900]. *Political Theories of the Middle Ages*. Cambridge: Cambridge University Press.

Goodwyn, Lawrence. 1976. *Democratic Promise: The Populist Movement in America*. Oxford: Oxford University Press.

Hill, Christopher. 1984. *The World Turned Upside Down*. London: Penguin.

Hochschild, Arlie. 2018. *Strangers in Their Own Land*. New York, NY: The New Press.

Huntington, Samuel. 1991. *The Third Wave: Democratization in the late 20th Century*. Norman: University of Oklahoma Press.

Machiavelli, Niccolò. 2015 [1532]. *The Prince*. London: Penguin.

Meyers, Peter A. 2008. *Civic War and the Corruption of the Citizen*. Chicago: University of Chicago Press.

Morgan, Edmund S. 1989. *Inventing the People: The Rise of Popular Sovereignty in England and America*. New York, NY: Norton.

Ober, Josiah. 2008. *Democracy and Knowledge*. Princeton, NJ: Princeton University Press.

Pew Research Center. 2019. "Public Trust in Government." Pew Research Center. www.people-press.org/2019/04/11/public-trust-in-government-1958-2019/.

Piketty, Thomas. 2014. *Capital in the 21st Century*. Cambridge, MA: Harvard University Press.

Pocock, John Greville Agard. 2016 [1975]. *The Machiavellian Moment*. Princeton, NJ: Princeton University Press.

Strathern, Paul. 2016. *Death in Florence: The Medici, Savonarola, and the Battle for the Soul of a Renaissance City*. New York, NY: Pegasus Books.

Tocqueville, Alexis de. 2003 [1835/1840]. *Democracy in America*. London: Penguin.

Weinstein, Donald. 2011. *Savonarola: The Rise and Fall of a Renaissance Prophet*. New Haven, CT: Yale University Press.

CONTRIBUTORS

Ewa Atanassow is Junior Professor of Political Thought at Bard College Berlin. She is the co-editor of *Tocqueville and the Frontiers of Democracy* (2013) and *Liberal Moments: Reading Liberal Texts* (2017). Her current book project, *Liberal Dilemmas: Tocqueville on the Crisis of Democracy in the 21st Century*, reexamines democracy and liberalism through the lens of Tocqueville.

Roger Berkowitz is Founder and Academic Director of the Hannah Arendt Center for Politics and Humanities and Professor of Politics, Human Rights, and Philosophy at Bard College. His research interests range from Greek and German philosophy to legal history and from the history of science to politics and constitutional democracy. He is the author of *The Gift of Science: Leibniz and the Modern Legal Tradition* (2010).

Mark Blyth is the William R. Rhodes '57 Professor of International Economics at Brown University. His research focuses upon how uncertainty and randomness impact complex systems, particularly economic systems. He is the author of *Great Transformations: Economic Ideas and Institutional Change in the Twentieth Century* (2002) and *Austerity: The History of a Dangerous Idea* (2013).

Craig Calhoun is University Professor of Social Sciences at Arizona State University and Centennial Professor of Sociology at LSE. His publications address politics, economics, the impact of technology, and cultural and social change, and include *Nations Matter: Citizenship, Solidarity and the Cosmopolitan Dream* (Routledge, 2007), *The Roots of Radicalism* (2012), and *Does Capitalism Have a Future?* (2013).

Gülçin Balamir Coşkun is Einstein Fellow at the Institut für Sozialwissenschaften, Humboldt-Universität zu Berlin. Her work focuses on authoritarianism, theories of democracy, media, and refugee movement. She has lately published with Aslı Yılmaz Uçar on local responses to the Syrian refugee movement in *Movements - Journal for Critical Migration and Border Regime Studies*.

Jonathan Hopkin is Associate Professor of Comparative Politics in the Department of Government at the London School of Economics. He has published widely on European politics and political economy, with a particular focus on political parties, finance and politics, corruption, and inequality, especially in the UK, Spain, and Italy. His most recent book is *Anti-System Politics: The Crisis of Market Liberalism in Rich Democracies* (2020).

Aysuda Kölemen is a research fellow at Bard College Berlin. Her current research interests include autocratization and discourses on gender and family policies in Turkey. She has previously worked on the differences in public discourses on the welfare state in Europe and the USA and the political dimensions of new religiosities in Turkey.

Ivan Krastev is the chairman of the Centre for Liberal Strategies in Sofia and permanent fellow at the Institute for Human Sciences, IWM Vienna. A founding board member of the European Council on Foreign Relations and a contributing opinion writer for the New York Times, he was awarded the 2020 Jean Améry Prize for European Essay Writing. His most recent book *The Light that Failed* (Allen Lane, 2019; with Stephen Holmes) won the Lionel Gelber Prize.

Christian Lammert is Professor of Political Systems in North America at Freie Universität Berlin. He has published widely on nationalism and regionalism, social policy in comparative perspective, and the politics of health care reform in the United States. His most recent publication is *Democracy in Crisis: The Neoliberal Roots of Popular Unrest* (2019, with Boris Vormann).

Brian Milstein teaches international political theory at Goethe-Universität Frankfurt. His research focuses on questions related to crisis theory and the concept of crisis in social and political thought. His work has appeared in the *European Journal of Philosophy*, *European Journal of Political Theory*, and *Philosophy & Social Criticism*. He is author of *Commercium: Critical Theory from a Cosmopolitan Point of View* (2015).

Marc F. Plattner is the founding co-editor of the *Journal of Democracy* and the co-chair of the Research Council of the National Endowment for Democracy's International Forum for Democratic Studies. His books include *Democracy Without Borders? Global Challenges to Liberal Democracy* (2008).

Sir Roger Scruton was a writer and philosopher who has published more than forty books in philosophy, aesthetics, and politics, translated in multiple languages. A fellow of the British Academy, of the Royal Society of Literature, and a Senior Fellow at the Ethics and Public Policy Center, Washington D.C., he taught in both England and America, lastly in Philosophy for the University of Buckingham.

Esther Solano is Professor of Social Science at Federal University of São Paulo and teaches in the Master program on Latin America and the European Union at University of Alcalá (Spain). Among other publications she has recently edited: *Is there a way out? Critical essays on Brazil* (2017); *Hate as politics* (2018); and *Brazil in collapse* (2019).

Nandini Sundar is Professor of Sociology at the Delhi School of Economics, Delhi University. Her recent publications include *The Burning Forest: India's War in Bastar* (2019); *Civil Wars in South Asia: State, Sovereignty, Development* (co-edited with Aparna Sundar, 2014); and Inequality and Social Mobility in Post-Reform India, Special Issue of *Contemporary South Asia* (co-edited, 2016).

Kristin Surak is an Associate Professor of Japanese Politics at SOAS, University of London whose research on international migration, nationalism, and political sociology has been translated into a half-dozen languages. She is the author of *Making Tea, Making Japan: Cultural Nationalism in Practice* (2013), which received the Book of the Year Award from the American Sociological Association's Asian Section.

Boris Vormann is Professor of Politics and Director of the Politics Section at Bard College Berlin. His research focuses on the role of the state in globalization and urbanization processes; nations and nationalism; and the crisis of democracy. His most recent books are *Democracy in Crisis: The Neoliberal Roots of Popular Unrest* (with Christian Lammert, 2019), and *Contours of the Illiberal State* (2019).

Michael D. Weinman is Professor of Philosophy at Bard College Berlin. He is the author of three books, most recently, *The Parthenon and Liberal Education* (2018, co-authored with Geoff Lehman), and the editor (with Shai Biderman) of *Plato and the Moving Image* (2019). His research focuses on Greek philosophy, political philosophy, and their intersection.

Claudia Wiesner is Professor for Political Science and Jean Monnet Chair at Fulda University of Applied Sciences and Adjunct Professor in Political Science at Jyväskylä University. Her main research interests lie in the comparative study of democracy, political culture, and political sociology in the EU multilevel system. Her most recent monograph is *Inventing the EU as a democratic polity: Concepts, Actors and Controversies* (2018).

INDEX

Cordero, Rodrigo 28, 32
corporocracy 211
corruption 3, 20, 39, 104, 159, 176, 192, 195, 196, 213–15, 227, 229, 230, 231, 243
cosmopolitanism 16, 22, 94–5, 116
Costa, Rui 221
Costa Rica, 2018 elections 44
creditor–debtor relationships 114
The Crises of the Republic (Arendt) 96
crisis consciousness, crisis of 27–40
crisis of democracy ix, 3, 15, 16, 27, 29, 31, 40, 86–9, 124–138
Cromwell's New Model Army 232
crony capitalism 195
Crouch, Colin 27, 37
Cruz, Carlos Alberto dos Santos 219–20
Çukurova Holding 173
culture war 130
Czech Republic, illiberal revolution in 158, 159

Dahl, Robert A. 11, 64
debt crisis 14, 114, 116, 163
decommodification 5, 14, 17, 36, 114, 118
deliberative democracy 142
Demir, Ali 180
Demirtaş, Selahattin 171
democracy: constitutional 45; crisis of ix, 3, 15, 16, 27, 29, 31, 40, 86–9, 124–138; definition of 189; deliberative 142; enemies of 7; equality of conditions 93–4; free 64; guardianship 64; illiberal ix, 11, 16, 43–56, 58–68, 158, 164, 166–183, 189–191, 236; liberal viii, 3–6, 8, 10, 11, 15–17, 21–23, 27, 29, 31, 40, 43–46, 48–56, 60, 62, 68, 85–97, 110, 157, 158, 163, 164, 166, 167, 222, 233–235, 239, 244; *vs.* liberalism 61–2; post-democracy 27, 38, 211; representative 88, 89, 92, 94, 96, 97, 136, 141; revising 18–19; social equality *vs.* popular rule 62–4; sovereign 11, 59; Western 8, 9, 19, 22, 46–8, 76, 91, 101–20, 234, 245n10
Democracy in America (Tocqueville) 66
democratic deficits 58, 94; economic origins of 112–14; in EU 140–53, 166; demos-building via politicization 149–53; new perspective on 143–7; possible solutions, approaching 147–9; short summary of 142–3; problem fields 141, 143–7
democratic freedom 63, 65, 66, 68, 93, 96

Democratic Party 135
democratic procedure 124, 167
democratic recession 189, 196
democratic sovereignty 58, 65
democratization 21, 61, 62, 66; Brazilian re-democratization 220–1; de-democratization 6, 144; of EU 149–52; political 170; third-wave of 46, 166; waves of 8, 157
demos 4, 5, 13, 15–19, 20, 21, 141, 142, 244; building via politicization 149–53
Deneen, Patrick 53–4
Denmark 161; income inequality in 128
DeVos, Betsy 132
Diamond, Larry 189
differentiated integration 145–6, 148–50
digital revolution 86
Dodd-Frank Act of 2010 136
Doğan, Aydın 173
Doğan Group 173
Doğuş Media 173
Doria, João 222
Dubai, cosmopolitan elites in 88
Dündar, Can 177
dystopian ideology 88

Earned Income Tax Credit (EITC) 127
Eastern Europe 12, 19; fraternity 160–2; geopolitics 162–4; illiberal revolution in 157–64; liberty 160–2; normality 160–2; people power 158–60
ECB *see* European Central Bank
economic liberalism viii, ix, 7–9, 11, 13–16, 21, 89, 137, 140, 146
economic nationalism 104
EC *see* European Council
Ecuador 48
EDRI *see* European Digital Rights Initiative
Egypt 177
EITC *see* Earned Income Tax Credit
electoral autocracy 166–83
Eletrobras 212
elite failures 86–9
elite prejudices 92–6; collectivist nationalism 94–5; cosmopolitanism 94–5; individualism 94–5; individual rights 93–4; moralization of political opposition 95; security over freedom, prioritizing 95–6
Emanuel, Rahm 90
embedded liberalism 110
Endangered Species Act 136